Gender and the Modern
Sherlock Holmes

ALSO EDITED BY NADINE FARGHALY

Unraveling Resident Evil*: Essays on the Complex Universe of the Games and Films* (McFarland, 2014)

EDITED BY NADINE FARGHALY AND EDEN LEONE

The Sexy Science of The Big Bang Theory*: Essays on Gender in the Series* (McFarland, 2015)

Gender and the Modern Sherlock Holmes

Essays on Film and Television Adaptations Since 2009

Edited by
Nadine Farghaly

McFarland & Company, Inc., Publishers
Jefferson, North Carolina

LIBRARY OF CONGRESS CATALOGUING-IN-PUBLICATION DATA

Gender and the modern Sherlock Holmes : essays on film and television adaptations since 2009 / edited by Nadine Farghaly.
      p.   cm
   Includes bibliographical references and index.

   ISBN 978-0-7864-9459-0 (softcover : acid free paper) ∞
   ISBN 978-1-4766-2281-1 (ebook)

   1. Sherlock Holmes films—History and criticism.
   2. Sherlock Holmes television programs—History and criticism.
   3. Doyle [sic], Arthur Conan, 1859–1930—Characters—Sherlock Holmes.   4. Doyle [sic], Arthur Conan, 1859–1930—Film adaptations.   5. Doyle [sic], Arthur Conan, 1859–1930—Television adaptations.   6. Detective and mystery stories, English—History and criticism.   7. Sex role in motion pictures.   8. Sex role on television.   9. Holmes, Sherlock.   I. Farghaly, Nadine, 1981– editor.

   PN1995.9.S5G46 2015
   791.43'651—dc23   2015030584

BRITISH LIBRARY CATALOGUING DATA ARE AVAILABLE

© 2015 Nadine Farghaly. All rights reserved

No part of this book may be reproduced or transmitted in any form or by any means, electronic or mechanical, including photocopying or recording, or by any information storage and retrieval system, without permission in writing from the publisher.

Front cover: Rachel McAdams as Irene Adler (Warner Bros./Photofest)

Printed in the United States of America

McFarland & Company, Inc., Publishers
  Box 611, Jefferson, North Carolina 28640
    www.mcfarlandpub.com

For the families we choose ourselves

Acknowledgments

So many people were involved in this project, both helping with the actual work and providing whatever support I needed. I want to thank all the people who were not only wonderful peer-review readers, but also dear friends who supported me throughout this endeavor and never stopped believing that it would be a success, especially Eden. All my love to my mother and my sisters for their incredible support and belief in me. Cheers and my love to all my friends who let me rant and wail to my heart's content before they tried to help me fix whatever crisis I had (whether imagined or real). Thank you all so much.

Table of Contents

Acknowledgments	vi
Introduction NADINE FARGHALY	1
The Evolution of Sherlock Holmes: An Examination of a Timeless Figure Amid Changing Times GREG FREEMAN	7
There's a Name Everyone Says: Irene Adler and Jim Moriarty in *Sherlock* BENEDICK TURNER	21
Return of "the woman": Irene Adler in Contemporary Adaptations RHONDA LYNETTE HARRIS TAYLOR	40
"Of dubious and questionable memory": The Collision of Gender and Canon in Creating *Sherlock*'s Postfeminist Femme Fatale MARIA ALBERTO	66
"Feeling Exposed?" Irene Adler and the Self-Reflective Disguise KATHARINE MCCAIN	85
I Am Sherlocked: Adapting Victorian Gender and Sexuality in "A Scandal in Belgravia" LINDSAY KATZIR	98
The Woman and the Napoleon of Crime: Moriarty, Adler, *Elementary* JOSEPH S. WALKER	118
Joan for John: An Elementary Choice ELIZABETH WELCH	133
Joan Watson: Mascot, Companion and Investigator LUCY BAKER	146
Conflations of "Queerness" in 21st Century Adaptations AYAAN AGANE	160

A Questionable Bromance: Queer Subtext, Fan Service and the
  Dangers of Queerbaiting in Guy Ritchie's *Sherlock Holmes*
  and *A Game of Shadows*
    HANNAH MUELLER   174
Sherlocked: Homosociality and (A)Sexuality
    KARMA WALTONEN   192
The Veneration of Violation in *Sherlock*
    ZEA MILLER   208
"Now, Watson, the fair sex is your department": The BBC's
  Sherlock and Interpersonal Relationships
    KATHRYN E. LANE   223

About the Contributors   245
Index   249

Introduction

Nadine Farghaly

"I've found it! I've found it" are the first words spoken by Sherlock Holmes in *A Study in Scarlet* (Conan Doyle). These words not only embody the formidable personality of Sherlock Holmes, but also set the stage for the journey readers undertake when picking up the memoirs of his companion, Dr. John Watson. This curious, driven, and arrogant detective, a creation of Sir Arthur Conan Doyle, has captured readers' imaginations for 187 years and gone beyond Conan Doyle's printed words to encompass numerous adaptations that include board, console and computer games, graphic novels, cookbooks, novels, plays, music, and movies. Television series such as *Elementary* and *Sherlock* have taken the Holmes and Watson characters to a whole new level in their portrayal of the enigmatic detective and his trusted friend.

More than seventy actors have played the part of Sherlock Holmes in more than two hundred movies (Fox). Among the actors who have assumed the mantel of Sherlock are Sir Ian McKellen, Charlton Heston, Jeremy Brett, Christopher Lee, Roger Moore, Basil Rathbone, and Frank Langella. While the duo have never really been forgotten, Sherlock Holmes and Dr. Watson have never garnered as much attention as they do now.

Conan Doyle's character has been Japanese, French, Russian, Finnish and many other nationalities, but this volume focuses on director Guy Ritchie's adaptations *Sherlock Holmes* (2009) and *Sherlock Holmes: A Game of Shadows* (2011); CBS's *Elementary* (2012–present); and the BBC's *Sherlock* (2010–present).

While Ritchie's movies place Holmes and Watson in their original Victorian setting, both *Elementary* and *Sherlock* place the duo in *contemporary* times; *Elementary* in New York and *Sherlock* in London. And although there are some similarities between these two television adaptations, the ways in which they differ are more prominent. *Elementary* showcases a sexually active, recovering drug addict who recuperates in one of his father's brownstone properties. Here he works with a sober companion, Joan Watson, paid by his father. Although this is not the first time that the gender of one of these characters has been changed, it is the first time that one of them has been successfully received as a woman, actress Lucy Liu playing Dr. Watson. While critics may have had their doubts in the beginning, Dr. Joan Watson has transformed the role of Holmes' sidekick to equal partner. For example, Watson functioned as an advisor to the New York Police Department when Sherlock relocated for six months to the UK. Although the creators are playing with the chemistry of Joan and Sherlock, they have yet to take their relationship from a friendly, professional, and platonic one into a romantic one. A fact that in no way diminishes the show's success, on the contrary, Liu's portrayal of Watson as a professional partner and companion is a nice change from the idea that men and women cannot work together without having romantic feelings as is so often the case.

Across the pond, the BBC's *Sherlock* has attracted attention because of its sexual undertones. The relationship between John and Sherlock has never been as blatantly homosexual as it is here, as shown by the frequent comments from Mrs. Hudson regarding Holmes and Watson's living arrangements. Martin Freeman, the actor who plays John Watson in *Sherlock*, has commented,

> [It's about the relationship] and how it develops and how it changes and the things that wind each other up, the things that they genuinely sort of love about each other as well. It's the gayest story in the history of television.... People certainly run with that which I'm quite happy with! But we all saw it as a love story. Not just a love story, but those two people who do love each other—a slightly dysfunctional relationship sometimes, but a relationship that works. They get results [Wightman].

Although never really proven in the show itself, the relationship is more than just subtext; it has become canon for *Sherlock*. The deep affection between these two characters is genuine and palpable. It is no surprise that fans everywhere happily jumped on the bandwagon and started shipping like never before in the Sherlock Holmes universe.

The 21st century popularity of Sherlock Holmes is something Arthur Conan Doyle may not have envisioned. Conan Doyle created a character that still entices his audience even though he was conceptualized during the Victorian era. Sherlock Holmes is a brilliant, if flawed, detective who appears in four novels and 56 short stories, of which he narrates two. The popularity of this sleuth and his partner in crime, Dr. John H. Watson, has never been more interesting than it is now. However, the different incarnations of his characters and locations challenge fans to contemplate new ideas, such as the role of gender. Although there are a few books and various essays that discuss this theme, this collection focuses on the gender of these characters and poses questions such as *What is the importance of a female Dr. Watson? In what ways was Irene Adler updated for modern viewers? Does the romantic subtext in many adaptations play a role or is it just there to attract viewers?* The following essays endeavor to answer these questions and more.

Greg Freeman kicks off this collection with his essay "The Evolution of Sherlock Holmes: An Examination of a Timeless Figure Amid Changing Times." Here, Freeman discusses the various changes Sherlock and John had to undergo and how these changes were influenced by the needs and wants of society. He skillfully leads his readers on a journey through the most recent Sherlock Holmes adaptations, all the while analyzing their importance.

In "There's a Name Everyone Says: Irene Adler and Jim Moriarty in *Sherlock*," Benedick Turner takes a close look at Sherlock's most famous adversary, Moriarty. Turner shows how the original Moriarty is never quite on a par with the skilled sleuth and argues that Conan Doyle's Irene Adler is really more deserving of being called Holmes's nemesis. He reveals how the BBC's *Sherlock* changes this by appropriating Irene Adler's essential capacity and grafting it onto Moriarty to create a masterful villain.

Rhonda Lynette Harris Taylor continues the focus on Miss Adler in "Return of 'the woman': Irene Adler in Contemporary Adaptations." Here she explores the various representations of Irene Adler as well as her relationship to Sherlock Holmes and her importance in the fandom. Furthermore, Taylor takes her readers back to Adler's origins and the women who inspired the character.

In "'Of dubious and questionable memory': The Collision of Gender and Canon in Creating *Sherlock*'s Postfeminist Femme Fatale," Maria Alberto discusses Irene Adler and Mary Morstan, in particular their importance in the original stories as well as in the adaptations. She highlights the differences between these characters and how their changed roles are important to viewers nowadays.

Katharine McCain scrutinizes the idea of disguise in "'Feeling Exposed?' Irene Adler and the Self-Reflective Disguise." McCain analyzes both the original Irene Adler and the version of the character created by the BBC's *Sherlock* with a focus on their very different ideas about disguise.

In "I Am Sherlocked: Adapting Victorian Gender and Sexuality in 'A Scandal in Belgravia'" Lindsay Katzir examines themes such as sexuality and gender performance within Conan Doyle's "A Scandal in Bohemia" and the BBC's *Sherlock*. Arguing that Conan Doyle's original Adler is much harder to define than Moffatt's, she highlights the changes in performance and the consequences that arise from this.

In "The Woman and the Napoleon of Crime: Moriarty, Adler, *Elementary*," Joseph S. Walker examines the repercussions of conflating the only woman Sherlock Holmes ever loved and the only criminal worthy of his genius, arguing that *Elementary*'s decision to merge Irene Adler and James Moriarty into one character has far reaching implications. Walker explores these consequences as well as the manner in which this change was carried out.

Elizabeth Welch, in "Joan for John: An Elementary Choice," discusses the criticisms laid upon the show's choice to change John to Joan and how, regardless of the original literary writings, this decision both displays and represents the steady progression in effectively equalizing the representation of women in the media. She highlights how patriarchal structures are still all too present in the media and how *Elementary* tries to undermine patriarchal power.

"Joan Watson: Mascot, Companion and Investigator" by Lucy Baker examines the aspects of Joan Watson's characterization that are in reaction to the absences and imbalances of the original and Archontic iterations, and how this intersects with the feminine homosocial relationship exhibited with Moriarty. Baker argues that although the relationship between these two female characters can be read as feminine competition for masculine attention, it really is a homosocial relationship between the pair that is mediated through Sherlock.

In "Conflations of 'Queerness' in 21st-Century Adaptations," Ayaan Agane writes about the gender politics of the BBC's *Sherlock* and the Warner Bros.' *Sherlock Holmes* film franchise alongside differing definitions of "queerness" in the twenty-first century.

In "A Questionable Bromance: Queer Subtext, Fan Service and the Dangers of Queerbaiting in Guy Ritchie's *Sherlock Holmes* and *A Game of Shadows*," Hannah Mueller discusses the three-way influences between the fictional texts, the creative aspect, and the fans. She states that *A Game of Shadows* directly responds to fan reactions to the first movie by both encouraging and containing resistant interpretations of Holmes and Watson's relationship.

Karma Waltonen, in "Sherlocked: Homosociality and (A)Sexuality," writes about the relationship between John and Sherlock in the BBC's *Sherlock* and how *every* relationship, with men or women, family or strangers, friends or foes, strengthens the link between these heroes. Here she explains how the show counters Eve Sedgwick's traditional notion of homosociality.

In "The Veneration of Violation in *Sherlock*," Zea Miller writes about the complications of unexamined fandom in the BBC series. He examines the ways in which the central male characters of the series have interacted with women in their adventures, the ultimate result of which calls into question the hero worship, or at the least the reflexive admiration, the series cultivates.

In the final essay, "'Now, Watson, the fair sex is your department': The BBC's *Sherlock* and Interpersonal Relationships," Kathryn E. Lane writes about the relationship between John and Sherlock. She contends that the series writers are intentionally calling attention to the romantic of the legendary partnership. She argues that in today's society in which almost nothing is private, the full scope of their relationship is. She examines the interpersonal and power dynamics of Holmes and Watson.

While there are many more issues that need to be addressed when discussing such an old, respected, and highly popular franchise, this collection offers starting point for those interested in gender studies as well as the *Sherlock Holmes* adventures. I hope this franchise will continue to inspire audiences for generations to come.

Works Cited

Conan Doyle, Arthur, and Owen Dudley Edwards. *A Study in Scarlet*. Oxford: Oxford University Press, 1993. Print.
Fox, Chloe. "Sherlock Holmes: Pipe Dreams." *The Telegraph*. Telegraph Media Group, 15 Dec. 2009. Web. 15 Jan. 2015.
Wightman, Catriona. "Martin Freeman: 'Sherlock Is Gayest Story Ever.'" *Digital Spy*. N.p., 23 May 2011. Web. 15 Jan. 2015.

The Evolution of Sherlock Holmes
An Examination of a Timeless Figure Amid Changing Times

Greg Freeman

Sir Arthur Conan Doyle's celebrated Sherlock Holmes remains an extraordinary character more than a century following his debut on the literary scene. A most clever and insightful detective and master of disguise, the fictional Holmes is credited for his pioneering methods and groundbreaking discoveries in the fields of forensics and crime scene investigations. Conan Doyle's mentor, Dr. Joseph Bell, as related in the documentary film *How Sherlock Changed the World* (2013), inspired the creation of Holmes and the methodology employed by the meticulous sleuth and his real-life investigative contemporaries today. Holmes, the film asserts, was "120 years ahead of his time." The prodigious detective not only remains relevant in the twenty-first century because of his deductive insights eras ago, but his popularity has continued to soar as the film, television and literary worlds recreate his role in modern-day adaptations of Conan Doyle's Victorian era stories as well as newly written ones set firmly outside late 1800s/early 1900s England. Reflecting shifting social values, exploring sexuality, occasionally challenging gender roles and often taking on sexier identities, Sherlock Holmes, his devoted companion Dr. Watson and their fellow cast of characters have come a long way since Holmes' earliest arrival within the pages of *Beeton's Christmas Annual* in 1887 and subsequent issues of *The Strand Magazine*.

If the Sherlock Holmes of Conan Doyle's earliest short stories represented a mere semblance of his inspiration, Dr. Bell, indeed the contemporary Holmes/Watson duos portrayed in the Guy Ritchie-directed films, *Sherlock Holmes* (2009) and *Sherlock Holmes: A Game of Shadows* (2011), and the two popular television series *Sherlock* (BBC) and *Elementary* (CBS), stand in stark contrast to their counterparts played by Jeremy Brett and David Burke/Edward Hardwicke in the ensemble of preceding Granada Television series *The Adventures of Sherlock Holmes* (1984–1985), *The Return of Sherlock Holmes* (1986–1988), *The Casebook of Sherlock Holmes* (1991–1993) and *The Memoirs of Sherlock Holmes* (1994), as well as the British company's made-for-television movies such as *The Sign of Four* (1987) and *The Hound of the Baskervilles* (1988). Granada's shows and films were painstakingly produced as to accurately depict the people, places, culture and events of Conan Doyle's short stories, unlike more recent television shows and movies portraying Holmes in which *licentia poetica* is liberally employed and the detective, in one instance (arguably two), is transformed into a mobile phone-toting metrosexual with an affinity for sending witty and often seemingly psychic text messages.

Regardless, a quick keyword search at one of the most visited international pen pal websites stands as a testament to the widespread, global phenomenon of Sherlock Holmes, revealing that a plethora of individuals of diverse ages, residing in locales as varied as London, Rome, Istanbul, Melbourne, Thessaloniki, Tokyo, Boston and Casablanca, are avid devotees of both the new and old Holmes. Fans—from all walks of life, residing on different continents and representing myriad values and ideals—collectively enjoy the most recent adaptations/derivations of Conan Doyle's works and appear receptive to the central figures' modern manifestations. To better comprehend the transformation of Holmes and company, it is beneficial to review some of the characters and stories of Conan Doyle's original canon and discover how their counterparts have evolved through the years, finding themselves well-adapted to the twenty-first century's mainstream culture.

"You know my methods, Watson"

Perhaps no other character in Conan Doyle's stories, besides Holmes himself, proves quite as integral or intriguing as Dr. Watson. For someone as astute as Holmes, it seems curious that the detective would need Watson at all, but we find time after time that Holmes has relied on the assistance of Watson, sending telegrams (and, more recently, text messages) with the memorable petition: "Come at once if convenient, if inconvenient come anyway." Reflecting on Holmes' dependence on Watson, Sandra Kromm has aptly noted:

Although Sherlock is fond of Watson, pleased by his obvious admiration, his readiness to drop everything and dash off at Sherlock's summons, his physical assistance, his readiness with revolver, his usefulness as witness to events, and his willingness to serve as sounding-board for Sherlock's theories, one wonders, in light of Sherlock's resistance to other companions, if his primary function is not to record the master's phenomenal success from the position of passionate admirer even at the cost of looking a trifle dim [Kromm 272].

Throughout Conan Doyle's works, Watson remains Holmes' nearly constant companion, although he is "frequently used to demonstrate Sherlock's one-upmanship" (Kromm 272). Respected within the realm of academia, particularly the medical community, Watson never quite measures up to Holmes' genius, but his well-established reputation among intellectuals ensures that his written accounts of adventures shared with Holmes secure the masterful detective a notable place for posterity's sake. After being together for so long, Holmes and Watson become quite comfortable with their relationship. Vincent Starrett elaborates: "About his own share in the partnership Watson had no illusions; but he was not servile. Thousands of his readers, as he must have known, would happily have traded places with him" (Starrett 56).

While Conan Doyle's short stories avoid depicting Watson as Holmes' equal, they certainly never present him as nearly constrained by incompetence as he has been made to appear through the decades in print or on screen. The Twentieth Century–Fox/Universal Studios 1939–1946 film series—in which one of Conan Doyle's stories, *His Last Bow* (1917), was audaciously adapted to the World War II era and involved the pursuit of a Nazi agent—starred Basil Rathbone/Tom Conway (Holmes) and Nigel Bruce (Watson). The films played their role in perpetuating Sherlock Holmes' popularity, but have prompted much criticism. Film producer, director and screenwriter Nicholas Meyer has asked, "Who can for a moment believe that Bruce's dim-witted buffoon is the chronicler whose voice we hear when we read the case histories? Why does a genius hang out with an idiot? Why have the 'Rathbone' Holmes stories been removed from their proper time and place? In short, why are they so dumb?" (Meyer 3). Others have been equally critical of Bruce's performance, but one noted writer/editor has asserted that the Rathbone/Bruce team noticeably elevated Watson's significance and "after Bruce, it would be a near-unthinkable heresy to show Holmes without him" (Barnes 256).

Fast forward to the Granada Television series produced during the last two decades of the twentieth century, and Dr. Watson is transformed into the articulate, intelligent and honorable gentleman more akin to the figure Conan Doyle had conceived in Watson. Though Holmes is quick to say, "You know my methods, Watson," the doctor often finds himself teetering on the edge of clarity, but lacking Holmes' superior skills of deduction, which prompts him to acknowledge: "When I hear you give your reasons ... the thing always appears to me to be so ridiculously simple that I could easily do it" ("A Scandal in Bohemia"). Nonetheless, he fails to do so.

Still, the Watson portrayed by David Burke, and later Edward Hardwicke, for Granada Television remains true to the character's role in demonstrating elements of humanity of which Holmes is hopelessly devoid, thus making him the ideal Watson—the complementary figure Conan Doyle, no doubt, originally envisioned. Diligent, compassionate, discreet, up to date on the latest medical science and brilliant in his own right, Watson is juxtaposed to capably assist Holmes whether the client is the target of a master blackmailer, the next most likely murder victim of an Italian mafioso or an old suitor of a missing member of the aristocracy. And, when duty demands it, he is poised with revolver in hand to serve as defender. In "The Disappearance of Lady Frances Carfax," Henry Peters (unscrupulously posing as a wheelchair-bound, Christian missionary, Dr. Schlessinger) suggests to Watson in an encounter that he surely would not dare shoot a man in his condition, to which, without hesitation, Watson replies, "I was a soldier in India, sir. I've shot nobler creatures than you" ("The Disappearance of Lady Frances Carfax").

Like an Old Married Couple

Throughout the Granada episodes, one observes two colleagues, two bachelors, two close friends, carrying on with their daily lives in mutuality in some respects like a settled married couple, but their relationship remains non-romantic and visibly asexual throughout. Though they are far from being perceived as misbehaving playboys or crass, rugged brutes, their masculinity or sexuality is never called into question. Starrett acknowledges:

> It is clear, at any rate, that the occasional social exercises of the pair were largely cultural. When they went forth from Baker Street, it was upon a trail of evil import or to a place of decent entertainment. Occasionally, to a Turkish bath; and very likely—one suspects—now and again to Madame Tussauds. On the whole, however, they preferred to stay at home. Away from it, the detective's temper was always uncertain, Watson tells us: "Without his scrapbooks, his chemicals, and his homely untidiness, he was an uncomfortable man" [Starrett 50].

While Burke and Hardwicke arguably came the closest to playing Conan Doyle's version of Watson, there is much to be said of their twenty-first century contemporaries Jude Law, Martin Freeman, and Lucy Liu, who embolden the character's role with freshness and acceptable relevance, counterbalancing Holmes' eccentricities, social inadequacies and personality shortcomings. Remaining true to the Victorian era, the Guy Ritchie movies, *Sherlock Holmes* and *Sherlock Holmes: A Game of Shadows*, feature a younger, sexier Holmes/Watson duo, Robert Downey, Jr., and Jude Law, while *Sherlock* (BBC) presents Holmes/Watson in a modern London milieu and *Elementary* (CBS) acquaints us with a female Holmes cohort, Dr. *Joan* Watson.

In the Ritchie films, Downey Jr. and Law provide an unprecedented take on the masculinity and romantic interests (or lack thereof) of Holmes and Watson, all the while delighting their scores of fans—male and female, of varying sexual persuasions—who admire the pair's striking good looks, entertaining banter/interplay and enduring friendship. In *Sherlock Holmes: A Game of Shadows*, Watson has plans of marrying and supposedly abandoning detective work for the domestic life, although Holmes is quick to point out that he has not acquired a ring, hinting that he is subconsciously putting off nuptials or perhaps avoiding marriage altogether. Like an old married couple, the two engage in one of their succinct and witty conversations—common parlance between the two, it appears—as they make dinner plans, and for once Watson appears to have the last word:

WATSON: You're free this evening?
HOLMES: Absolutely.
WATSON: Dinner?
HOLMES: Wonderful.
WATSON: The Royale?
HOLMES: My favorite.
WATSON: Mary's coming.
HOLMES: Not available.
WATSON: You're meeting her, Holmes.
HOLMES: Have you proposed yet?
WATSON: No, I haven't found the right ring.
HOLMES: Then it's not official.
WATSON: It's happening whether you like it or not [*A Game of Shadows*].

While Holmes seems reluctant to fully relinquish Watson to his fiancée and appears to consider the courtship a detestable distraction, at first suggesting to the casual observer an ulterior motive of a homosexual nature, he ultimately becomes supportive of Watson's need for the love and affections of a member of the opposite sex. Nonetheless, the case at hand threatens to thwart a lifetime of wedded bliss for Dr. and Mrs. Watson, as Holmes' archenemy Professor Moriarty, keenly aware of Holmes' devotion to Watson, vows to target the couple. Even Mary Watson plays an integral role in crippling Moriarty's empire. At the conclusion of the film, which is strongly reminiscent of Conan Doyle's "The Final Problem," Watson and Mary, having presumed that Holmes and Moriarty perished at Reichenbach Falls, attempt to move on with their lives. Watson resumes rhapsodizing in his memoirs, undoubtedly employing hyperbole, sentimentality and romanticism as he thinks of his dear Holmes and their memorable adventures, but he soon discovers a clue via a delivered parcel that Holmes is indeed alive and well. Though enjoying the intimacies of a loving relationship with his wife, Watson exhibits a sense of renewed hope, an obvious relief, at the thought of his beloved comrade lurking around the next corner. Little does he realize how near his friend really is!

A Fine Bromance ... or Is There More to It?

Actor Jude Law, though quite comfortable appearing nude as evidenced by his uninhibited roles in other movies, is not called upon to reveal his bare physique or engage in a steamy love scene in either Ritchie film (both of which are rated PG-13), but he transports the role of Watson to a realm of sexiness and virility not observed before in film or on television for the affable character. Exuding charm, confidence and sophistication, Law manages to attract with his dashing good looks, smart, period dress and clever personality, prompting A.O. Scott of the *New York Times* to recognize the actor "is looser and more mischievous than he's allowed himself to be in quite some time," adding, "the mustache suits him" (Scott). The quintessential Victorian gentleman, Law's character comports himself in no untoward way, particularly when in the company of ladies, especially his fiancé, Mary, but he is not without his vices. Possessing a penchant for betting and embarrassingly accruing gambling debts, Watson, in one scene, is particularly pleased that Holmes managed to win back his money. Indicative of the depth of their friendship, Holmes fails to divulge to Watson that he actually procured the money by beating an unsavory opponent significantly larger than he in a brutal, bare-knuckle fight, but only after Holmes—in masochistic fashion—had endured the savage's repeated blows amid the jeering screams of betting onlookers. Meanwhile, Holmes, seeking neither credit nor subordination from Watson, seems sufficiently gratified that he was able to aid his unlucky gambling companion.

With the advent of the Downey Jr./Law portrayals, Holmes and Watson display physical prowess and machismo unparalleled by their predecessors, and their relationship embodies what is frequently referred to in twenty-first century popular culture as a bromance, a *portmanteau* of "brother" and "romance" describing an intense friendship between two or more males. Eric Ditzian likens their relationship to being "far closer to the bro-fest in *I Love You, Man* than it is to the sexual liaisons in *Brokeback Mountain*" (Ditzian). In a 2009 interview, director Guy Ritchie relates to Ditzian:

> As a heterosexual couple that at moments could seem gay, they play it off very well.... These guys are sort of in love with each other. It's real mateship. It's trying to keep that balance. You have to endear yourself to them, and at times you skate on thin ice, because it's such a relationship about two men.

The BBC's *Sherlock*, premiering in 2010, presents a twenty-first century John Watson—a post-traumatic stress disorder-suffering veteran of the conflict in Afghanistan—who relishes adrenaline-inducing activity and is no stranger to animalistic violence. The doctor, reminiscent of his memoir-penning Victorian counterpart, writes about his life in a weblog, but he has abandoned blogging of late, resulting in a rebuke from his therapist, who happens to be a woman. Seemingly clumsy in speech around attractive women, namely Mycroft Holmes' sexy employee in "A Study in Pink," Watson, played by Martin Freeman (winner of the 2014 Primetime Emmy Award for Outstanding Supporting Actor in a Miniseries or a Movie for his role in *Sherlock*), comes on the scene appearing depressed, financially strapped, wounded, washed up and in desperate need of a boost to his male ego. His introduction to Sherlock Holmes (played by 2014 Emmy winner Benedict Cumberbatch) and their decision to share a flat (after Watson's initial trepidation) begins a remarkable journey, one in which the two become yet another unique version of the Holmes/Watson team inspired by Conan Doyle's original characters. Asked to tag along with his "consulting detective" flatmate, Watson is soon thrilled by the action, forgetting about his psychosomatic limp and replacing his self-pity with renewed manly confidence.

Meanwhile, it seems that everyone, who encounters Holmes with Watson, assumes the two are homosexual partners. Holmes' endearing landlady, Mrs. Hudson, announces to Dr. Watson that a separate bedroom is available should he require it, to which Watson says, "Of course we'll be needing two." Garnering no response from Holmes to the insinuation, Mrs. Hudson reassures, "Oh, don't worry; there's all sorts round here. Mrs. Turner next door's got married ones" ("A Study in Pink"). After conducting their first crime scene investigation together, Holmes and Watson venture to a small restaurant where Holmes is greeted with enthusiasm at the door. After the two are seated, Angelo, presumably the restaurateur, approaches their window-side booth to graciously welcome Holmes and his companion. "Anything on the menu, whatever you want, free," he insists. "On the house, for you *and* for your date." Watson's repeated retort—"I'm not his date!"—seems to fall on deaf ears. An awkward conversation ensues, one in which Watson inquires about Holmes' personal life. "You don't have a girlfriend, then?" "Girlfriend? No, not really my area," Holmes answers. For a few moments, the two make assumptions about each other's sexuality, and Watson says, "Right. Okay. You're unattached. Like me. Fine." After a moment of contemplation, Holmes speaks, "John, um ... I think you should know that I consider myself married to my work, and while I'm flattered by your interest, I'm really not looking for any...." "No. No, I'm not asking. No," Watson insists. "I'm just saying, it's *all* fine" (*Sherlock* "A Study in Pink").

Watson's open mind regarding Holmes' sexual orientation (whatever it might be) in *Sherlock* contrasts vividly with the viewpoints expressed by the Victorian characters in Conan Doyle's stories and the fact that by 1885 private homosexual acts in Great Britain had been legislated against, resulting in the 1886 incarceration of playwright Oscar Wilde. One might recall Conan Doyle's "The Adventure of Charles Augustus Milverton" in which Milverton—an art dealer and ruthless blackmailer, armed with discreetly obtained, incriminating letters—targets an array of titled aristocrats, socialites and high-ranking soldiers. One of his prey, Colonel Dorking, is engaged to marry, but the colonel's clandestine obsession with a back-stabbing drag queen becomes one of Milverton's latest exploits. Unable or unwilling to pay Milverton's "absurd sum of twelve hundred pounds" to "[settle] the question," Dorking is spurned by the Honorable Miss Miles, prompting a societal scandal and his ultimate decision to commit suicide. Indeed, marked differences exist between the original Sherlock Holmes stories and their most recent contemporaries as well as the divergent England of Victorian days and the twenty-first century (at which time members of the House of Windsor are friends with openly gay figures like Sir Elton John).

Sexual orientation aside, Cumberbatch and Freeman's characters develop an undeniable bond, *à la* Downey Jr. and Law's Holmes/Watson, trusting each other with their very lives. In pursuit of justice, the pair, remaining consistent with Conan Doyle's storyline, assist the police and find themselves facing the recurring villain, Professor Moriarty. *Sherlock*'s Watson, having been warned by Scotland Yard's Sergeant Donovan that Holmes "doesn't *have* friends," accepts the detective in spite of his idiosyncrasies and peculiarities, and the two remain steadfastly committed to one another as the adventures continue.

Dr. Joan *Watson?*

If the complexities of a platonic Holmes/Watson bromance, like those observed in the Ritchie films and even *Sherlock*, seem difficult enough for some to comprehend, the introduction of a female Watson in CBS' *Elementary*, which debuted in September 2012, takes the relational challenges to a whole new dimension, leaving viewers to speculate whether dating and sexual trysts between Holmes and Watson are eminent. The series' Dr. Joan Watson, played by Lucy Liu opposite Jonny Lee Miller (Holmes), has introduced skeptical Sherlockians to yet another dynamic couple. "Liu's Watson," CBS' Jessica Derschowitz writes, "is stoic and pragmatic but still vulnerable, making her a formidable foil" (Derschowitz). Michael Starr describes the chemistry between Holmes and Joan Watson as "palpable." Employed by Holmes' father to make sure Holmes, a British-born recovering drug addict now residing in Brooklyn, New York, avoids a relapse, Watson presents herself as his "sober companion." A valuable consultant to the New York Police Department, Holmes soon discovers that Watson, a former surgeon with a dark past of her own, displays an aptitude for assisting him in his investigations. Of Liu's role, Starr says Watson "is no shrinking violet, softening Sherlock's verbal blows with an 'are you kidding me?' stance while, in her own sly way, getting all up into her partner's grill—while respecting his ethereal brilliance" (Starr and Stewart).

Elementary's creator Robert Doherty is resilient in his quest to keep Holmes and Watson clearly defined as friends and colleagues, quelling any predictions the show's fan base has made regarding the future of the series' principal characters. In an interview with *TV Guide*, Lucy Liu explained:

> It's like going to a nude beach: It's all there, there's nothing to see, it's done. But when you go to an actual beach and people have bikinis on, there's something more sexual. So this is a much more interesting dynamic than actually having intercourse and a post-coital scene. This is much more energized. There are some things that have to be sacred, and right now, where we are is where we need to be [Fretts].

Doherty has indicated that a love affair between the two protagonists might always appear to loom in the forecast, but he rather enjoys the challenge of exploring their complicated coexistence outside the confines of romance, while permitting just the right amount of underlying tension to make the couple's interactions suspenseful. Season three of *Elementary* finds Watson seeking romance with Andrew Mittal (Raza Jaffrey) and Holmes welcoming the arrival of Kitty (Ophelia Lovibond), his new protégé, thus contributing further to the complexity of their relationship.

Is Holmes Evasive? Or Is Love Elusive?

As if the diverse assortment of Dr. Watsons is not enough to stir curiosity or sustain interest, the recent depictions of Sherlock Holmes and his responses to the delightfully seductive Irene Adler or long-held rivalry with his nemesis Moriarty have captured the avid devotion of fans, old and new alike.

While playwright William Gillette, with permission from Conan Doyle, crafted *Sherlock Holmes*, a play in which Holmes marries Miss Alice Faulkner, Holmes' love life is non-existent in Conan Doyle's stories and dubious, at best, in most everything that has been introduced since. Gillette's production debuted on November 6, 1899, at New York's Garrick Theatre, enjoying a run of over 200 performances before making the transatlantic journey to Sir Henry Irving's Lyceum Theatre in London. However, the Holmes of literature, film and television has managed to thrill his vast constituency—not as an open book highlighting a heartwarming tête-à-tête between lovers or soliloquy about the finer points of marital ecstasy, but as an eligible *and* disinterested bachelor, unyielding to the charms of the opposite sex. Starrett reminds us: "There is a line of text in Watson from which we learn that all emotions, but particularly that of love, were abhorrent to the 'cold, precise but admirably balanced mind' of Mr. Sherlock Holmes" (Starrett 115).

The product of a patriarchal society, Conan Doyle's Holmes functioned in an era in England during which women, unable to vote or own property, adhered to the strictest of laws and customs. "It is not to be wondered at then, that so many distressed Victorian women, feeling compelled to seek male advice, should knock at 221B," Kromm writes. "The man they found there was not just the *compleat* detective, but the *compleat* Victorian gentleman" (Kromm 278).

"You'll miss me, Sherlock"

Observe the detective in Ritchie's *Sherlock Holmes*, and one gets the distinct impression that Holmes has loved and even experienced sexual intimacy, but he recoils—perhaps due to a past negative experience or a tug of war between personal life and career. If the latter is the case, career is declared the obvious victor. In a conversation with his old friend, the gorgeous, but dangerous Irene Adler, Holmes inquires of her latest criminal pursuits and most recent failed marriage, to which she declares, "I'm Irene Adler again" (*Sherlock Holmes*). Desiring his assistance in locating someone, Adler, employing her alluring qualities, conspicuously reaches inside her brassiere to retrieve something. Holmes reacts, not with wandering eyes, but with an outstretched arm, at once ready to defend himself should she produce a weapon. "Why are you so suspicious?" she asks. With his trademark wit, Holmes replies, "Shall I answer chronologically or alphabetically?" Handing an envelope to Holmes containing the necessary clue, Adler refuses to divulge for whom she is working. As she takes her coat and prepares to exit, Holmes examines the envelope, noting the origin of the stationery, "The Grand Hotel, Piccadilly, London." Just then, Adler asks, "Do you remember The Grand? They gave me our old room."

Contrasting with Conan Doyle's written interactions between Holmes and Adler, Ritchie's films suggest the existence of history *and* chemistry between the two, but one's decision to do good and the other's choice to serve evil interests naturally deem the couple incompatible. Regarding Conan Doyle's portrayal of Adler, Kromm writes:

> Irene Adler was not simply a retired adventuress/opera singer who impresses that fastidious connoisseur, John Watson, but singular in outwitting the arch-sleuth himself. While Watson admires her beauty, Sherlock is enamored of her brains [Kromm 276].

And yet a different take on Holmes and Adler is presented in the BBC's series, *Sherlock*. Adler, a dominatrix whose relationship with her camera phone is likened by Cumberbatch's character to that of a mother and child, proves as surprising (but welcomed, nonetheless) to viewers as Holmes, a metrosexual who—far from effeminate, but hardly hyper-masculine—fails to clearly project his sexual orientation. While Holmes' modern-day exchanges with Adler and other women present him in different lights, Kromm's suggestion—"the idealization of reason, associated with Sherlock, is not one that feminists either past or present tend to challenge" (Kromm 276)—still rings true today, for the most part.

"Give me problems, give me work"

Frequently, Holmes' egocentricities, outright arrogance and innate desire to solve a challenging mystery affect his relationships with men just as thoroughly as with women, often bringing out the rude, bloodless side of him that few find tolerable. Of *Elementary*'s Holmes actor, Jonny Lee Miller, Michael Starr writes that Miller "imbues Holmes—arrogant and condescending—with just the slightest bit of vulnerability, making us like and admire him in spite of ourselves while Miller fires off his elaborate, florid dialogue effortlessly (or seemingly so)" (Starr and Stewart).

When he is not easily irked or engaged intently in his deductive work, Holmes exhibits a propensity for going from one extreme to another. Of the Victorian Holmes, Starrett states:

> It is, of course, notorious—we have Watson's word for it—that Sherlock Holmes "loathed every form of society with his whole Bohemian soul." The word *society* has other connotations today. What Watson intended to convey was that *social life* offended the Bohemian soul of his companion; in consequence of which emotion Holmes preferred to spend his time in Baker Street when others might have gone to teas and parties; "buried among his old books," as Watson says, "and alternating from week to week between cocaine and ambition—the drowsiness of the drug and the fierce energy of his own keen nature" [Starrett 51].

Easily bored and repulsed by the *status quo*, Holmes is not content to spend all his time solving trivial cases or living in leisure. The moody sleuth in Ritchie's film *Sherlock Holmes* echoes the sentiments expressed originally in Conan Doyle's "The Sign of Four": "My mind rebels at stagnation. Give me problems. Give me work." When a coveted case of consequence presents itself, Holmes responds eagerly, like a famished vulture feeding upon a fresh carcass. Often, it is Scotland Yard, not Watson or Mrs. Hudson, that endures the brunt of his whims, verbal jabs or unvarnished honesty. In Conan Doyle's short stories, Holmes is sometimes viewed as one who interferes with police business, but generally he remains respected by Inspectors Gregson, Hopkins, Lestrade, and Bradstreet. Upon playing the pivotal role in solving a case, Holmes exhibits a faint (arguably feigned) sense of modesty, permitting the Yard to take credit in the press. In the back of his mind, of course, he is aware of Watson's diligence in chronicling their work, and it is Watson who will portray him most flatteringly for future generations. And, on occasion, Holmes "is not averse to allowing his own sense of justice to supersede that of British law when he feels it is appropriate" (Hecox 191). The Yard's reliance on his assistance undoubtedly contributes to Holmes' enlarged ego, elevating him in terms of intellect and even his sense of masculinity, as he often one-ups the police and its array of daunting male figures. The one-upmanship is less prevalent in *Sherlock* and *Elementary*, because Holmes is viewed as a consulting detective to the police rather than a competitor in the quest for justice.

Holmes on film and television has journeyed light years from the days when Nicholas Meyer asked, "Why is it that watching Holmes on film feels like getting kissed over the telephone?" (Meyer 5). Indeed, Holmes and Watson are more action-oriented than ever, catering to younger audiences who might otherwise turn to reality television or other cinema fare. Case in point: Downey Jr., physically fit and noted for his sex appeal, readily assumes an action-craving persona in the fight scene in *Sherlock Holmes: A Game of Shadows* in which he wins back Watson's money. It is indeed laughable to imagine previous Holmes actors, Basil Rathbone or Jeremy Brett, participating in such violent portrayals, much less appearing naked to the waist. As Scott concedes, "Holmes has never been much for physical violence, and the chief innovation of this new, franchise-ready incarnation, directed by Guy Ritchie and played by Robert Downey, Jr., is that he is, in addition to everything else, a brawling, head-butting, fist-in-the-gut, knee-in-the-groin action hero" (Scott).

"You need me, or you're nothing. Because we're alike, you and I"

Mysteries abound throughout the various Sherlock Holmes portrayals of the twenty-first century. In the case of Guy Ritchie's movies, the history between Holmes and Adler comes to mind. And what of Moriarty, Holmes' staunch admirer and enemy? One gets the sense that Moriarty—whose behavior in the *Sherlock* series arguably suggests he could be bisexual—is attracted to Holmes, intellectually *and* physically. Describing Holmes as 'the virgin,' Moriarty attempts to taunt his archenemy with remarks like "I gave you my number. I thought you might call. Is that a British Army Browning L9A1 in your pocket, or are you just pleased to see me?" Such sexually-charged remarks lend to the thought that Moriarty knows something the viewer doesn't, adding to the show's intrigue and the viewer's speculation.

Ever-Changing Social Mores, An Ever-Changing Holmes?

What does the future hold for Sherlock Holmes and his fellow characters? Given that the 7th U.S. Circuit Court of Appeals in Chicago declared in June 2014 that U.S. copyright law did not apply to some fifty Sherlock Holmes works published before 1923, the possibilities are limitless. Writing for the three-judge panel, Circuit Judge Richard Posner stated, "When a story falls into the public domain, story elements—including characters covered by the expired copyright—become fair game for follow-on authors." Among the story elements resting firmly in the public domain are "references to Holmes, his sidekick Dr. Watson, his archenemy Professor Moriarty, 221B Baker Street, and even Holmes's cocaine use" (Stempel). That said, writers, directors and even fans (in the form of fan fiction) are bound to continue producing a steady repertoire of ever-evolving Sherlock Holmes–themed works, reflecting the ever-changing social responses to gender roles and sexuality, thus contributing to the mastermind's timelessness in the midst of changing times.

Works Cited

Barnes, Alan. *Sherlock Holmes on Screen: The Complete Screen History*. London: Titan Books, 2011. Print.
Derschowitz, Jessica. "'Elementary' brings a new Sherlock Holmes and Dr. Watson to TV viewers." CBSNews.com. *CBS News*. 28 September 2012. Web. 23 August 2014.
"The Disappearance of Lady Frances Carfax." *The Case-Book of Sherlock Holmes*. ITV. SCETV, Columbia. 6 July 2013. Television.
Ditzian, Eric. "Guy Ritchie Explains the Tender Bromance in 'Sherlock Holmes.'" MTV.com. *MTV News*. 4 August 2009. Web. 23 August 2014.
Fretts, Bruce. "*Elementary*'s Jonny Lee Miller and Lucy Liu Answer Readers' Burning Questions." TVGuide.com. *TV Guide*. 8 October 2013. Web. 25 August 2014.
Hecox, Steve. "The Holmesian World of John Le Carré: Another View of George Smiley." *Sherlock Holmes: Victorian Sleuth to Modern Hero*. Eds. Charles R. Putney, Joseph A. Cutshall King, and Sally Sugarman. Lanham, MD: Scarecrow Press, 1996. Print.
Kromm, Sandra. "A Feminist Appraisal of Intellectual One-Upmanship in the Sherlock Holmes Stories." *Sherlock Holmes: Victorian Sleuth to Modern Hero*. Eds. Charles R. Putney, Joseph A. Cutshall King, and Sally Sugarman. Lanham, MD: Scarecrow Press, 1996. Print.
Meyer, Nicholas. "Sherlock Holmes on Film: A Personal View." *Sherlock Holmes: Victorian Sleuth to Modern Hero*. Eds. Charles R. Putney, Joseph A. Cutshall King, and Sally Sugarman. Lanham, MD: Scarecrow Press, 1996. Print.
"A Scandal in Bohemia." *The Adventures of Sherlock Holmes*. ITV. SCETV, Columbia. 12 November 2011. Television.
Scott, A. O. "The Brawling Supersleuth of 221B Baker Street Socks It to 'Em." *New York Times*. 24 December 2009. Web. 23 August 2014.
Sherlock Holmes. Dir. Guy Ritchie. Perf. Robert Downey, Jr., Jude Law, Rachel McAdams, Mark Strong and Eddie Marsan. Warner Home Video, 2010. DVD.
Sherlock Holmes: A Game of Shadows. Dir. Guy Ritchie. Perf. Robert Downey, Jr., Jude Law, Naomi Rapace, Jared Harris and Stephen Fry. Warner Home Video, 2012. DVD.
Starr, Michael, and Sara Stewart. "'Elementary' vs. 'Sherlock': Who's the better Holmes?" *New York Post*. 16 January 2014. Web. 23 August 2014.
Starrett, Vincent. *The Private Life of Sherlock Holmes*. Chicago: University of Chicago Press, 1960. Print.
Stempel, Jonathan. "Sherlock Holmes belongs to the public, U.S. court rules." Reuters.com. *Reuters*. 16 June 2014. Web. 24 August 2014.
"A Study in Pink." *Sherlock*. Dir. Paul McGuigan. Perf. Benedict Cumberbatch, Martin Freeman, Una Stubbs, Rupert Graves, Louise Brealey. BBC Home Entertainment, 2010. DVD.

There's a Name Everyone Says
Irene Adler and Jim Moriarty in Sherlock

BENEDICK TURNER

During the climactic sequence of "A Study in Pink" (2010), the first episode of the BBC television series *Sherlock*, the taxi-driver who has just claimed responsibility for the murders being investigated reveals to Sherlock[1] that the latter has a "fan," someone who is watching him. Naturally, Sherlock wants more information, but the killer tells him "that's all you're going to know—in this lifetime."[2] Despite the apparent finality of this statement, the killer mentions Sherlock's "fan" twice more in the next few minutes, as if he is incapable of staying silent on the matter; his assertion that "there's a name no-one says, and I'm not going to say it either" thus hardly seems believable. To his credit, the killer does not actually reveal the name until he has been shot and Sherlock is pressing down on the wound with his foot: Sherlock's desperation to know the identity of his admirer is such that he uncharacteristically resorts to physical brutality. The name—Moriarty—bursts into the series not as a spoken word, but as a dying man's howl of pain, his final utterance. In the episode's closing moments, John asks Sherlock to explain his enigmatic smile: when Sherlock responds with "Moriarty," John quite reasonably follows up with "What's Moriarty?" John's question requires a better answer than Sherlock's "I have no idea," and this need to discover more about Moriarty—not just who he is, but what he is—keeps the audience on tenterhooks for the rest of the first two seasons.

In what follows, I will argue that *Sherlock* takes Arthur Conan Doyle's poorly developed Moriarty and turns him into a complex character who represents a worthy adversary for the famous detective—a character who deserves to be the subject of fascination, for the audience and for other characters. First, I will show how the Moriarty that appears in Conan Doyle's stories never lives up to Holmes's description of him as a genius and that ultimately the character is little more than a flimsy plot device. Next, I will contend that in Conan Doyle's stories Irene Adler is more impressive as a nemesis for the famous detective. Finally, I will argue that *Sherlock* appropriates Irene Adler's defining talent and grafts it onto Moriarty to help create a true supervillain.

In developing my argument, I consider the various identities of the Adler and Moriarty characters (as they appear both in Conan Doyle's stories and in adaptations and pastiches, especially *Sherlock*) in relation to the work of two gender theorists, one focused on the masculinities of Victorian men, and the other on the masculinities of 20th-century women. In *Dandies and Desert Saints* (1995), James Eli Adams argues that the varied masculinities of Victorian males (and indeed masculinities in general) are all fundamentally theatrical in the way they "inevitably ... appeal to an audience, real or imagined" (11). In *Female Masculinity* (1998), Judith Halberstam also finds male masculinity to be performative, but avers that it can never be theatrically entertaining since it is endlessly repetitive; Halberstam argues that only masculine women can entertain their audiences with original performances of masculinity.[3] Although my analysis of Conan Doyle's Irene Adler owes much to Halberstam's thinking, I argue that this character adds her own twist to the female performance of masculinity by the way she integrates multiple masculinities with conventional femininity; further, my analysis of *Sherlock's* Jim Moriarty shows that, even if male masculinity is typically an endless series of repetitions, this character is entertaining in his presentation of multiple masculinities, sometimes with one layered on top of another.

The Unimpressive Origins of Moriarty

Moriarty is one of the most well-known characters in the Sherlock Holmes universe—perhaps as well known as any of the characters besides Watson and of course Holmes himself. But he is not mentioned in any of Conan Doyle's stories until "The Final Problem" (1892), the story the author originally intended to be the last in the Sherlock Holmes series. And since it is immediately made clear that Moriarty is dead at the time Watson is writing (Watson notes that he is responding to letters written in defense of Moriarty's memory), readers never get to think of Moriarty as a character who is still "alive" in the world of Conan Doyle's texts (737; vol. 1).[4] At the start of "The Final Problem," Holmes claims that he has sensed some "deep organizing power" behind London's crimes for years, yet Watson has never heard of him;

Conan Doyle (through Holmes) explains that the "genius" of Moriarty is that he can "pervade" London without anyone hearing of him—an explanation that is itself ingenious in the way it explains why the *reader* has never heard of Moriarty (739; vol. 1). But the character nevertheless seems like a hastily prepared device to kill off Holmes and bring an end to the series—and even this purpose is lost when Conan Doyle brings Holmes back to life in "The Adventure of the Empty House" (1903). And the fact that Professor Moriarty and his brother Colonel Moriarty are both given the first name James (the arch-villain is so identified by Holmes in "The Adventure of the Empty House" (777; vol. 1); his brother by Watson in "The Final Problem" (737; vol. 1) even suggests a careless disregard for this character on the author's part. Although Holmes describes Moriarty as "my intellectual equal" and explains that "my horror at his crimes was lost in my admiration of his skill" (740; vol. 1), Moriarty's actions as they are described in "The Final Problem" are more those of an enraged child than those of a worthy adversary for the cerebral Holmes. The first—and only—glance that Watson gets of Moriarty is of a man "pushing his way furiously through the crowd and waving his hand as if he desired to have the train stopped" (746; vol. 1). And once Moriarty finally catches up with Holmes at the Reichenbach Falls, he attempts to defeat the detective with muscle rather than with wit by wrestling him over the edge of the falls, as Holmes recounts to Watson when he finally resurfaces—this is hardly behavior worthy of a genius. Moriarty's heavy handed-approach seems all the more ridiculous in comparison to Holmes's subtlety in this story: the latter's disguise as an elderly priest is so effective that he is able to share a train compartment with Watson for several minutes without his friend recognizing him. Although Conan Doyle (through Holmes) promises the reader an intellectual equal for the great detective, what he ultimately delivers is a bumbling ruffian.

Conan Doyle's Irene Adler: A Worthy Adversary for Holmes

If Holmes ever comes across a true intellectual equal in the Conan Doyle stories, it is in the person of Irene Adler. The Adler who appears in "A Scandal in Bohemia" (1891) wins the admiration of Holmes, of Watson, of her former lover the King of Bohemia, and probably of most who read the story. After all, she outwits Holmes. At the climax of the adventure, Holmes pays an early-morning visit to her home, his rather crude plan being that since she will not yet have risen from bed, he and his companions will be left alone in her sitting room, giving them the opportunity to steal the photograph with which she has threatened to blackmail the King. But when they arrive at Adler's address, they learn she has discovered Holmes's plan and fled the country with the photograph in her possession. The manner by which she comes to know that Holmes is closing in on her shows that, in addition to being his equal (or superior) intellectually, Adler also shares the detective's well-established talent for—and love of—disguise. In this story, Holmes employs not one but two disguises: first, he turns himself into a groom so that he can infiltrate the mews by Adler's house and thereby gather information about her; later, he becomes a sympathetic clergyman in order to penetrate her home and discover where the photograph is hidden. Watson's reaction to seeing his friend in this second disguise is significant: he notes that Holmes adopts a "character," not just an appearance, and declares that "[t]he stage lost a fine actor, even as science lost an acute reasoner, when he became a specialist in crime" (254–55; vol. 1). Watson's choice of words connects Holmes to his adversary in this story, for Adler is a retired opera singer who graced such stages as La Scala and that of the Imperial Opera of Warsaw (246; vol. 1). And it is by employing what she learned on the stage that Adler is able to spy on Holmes and discover his plan to steal the photograph: dressed as a man, she waits by the entrance to 221B Baker Street and eavesdrops as Holmes explains his intentions to Watson. Adler's written account of the eavesdropping shows that she was quite consciously mirroring Holmes's strategies, and also reveals that this is by no means the only time she has cross-dressed: "You really did it very well. You took me in completely.... But you know, I have been trained as an actress myself. Male costume is nothing new to me—I often take advantage of the freedom which it gives" (261; vol. 1). Later in the letter, Adler notes that after she left Holmes she went to meet her husband—although it is not stated, the implication is that she stayed in her "male costume" somewhat longer than was necessary, enjoying its freedom during a night out with her spouse.

Adler's fondness for wearing men's clothing reflects other traits usually understood as masculine. The King first describes her as "the famous adventuress, Irene Adler" (246; vol. 1); later, he explains how "[s]he has a soul of steel ... and the mind of the most resolute of men" (247–48; vol. 1). And at the end, when Holmes is dumbfounded by Adler's escape, the King reminds Holmes how he had told him that Adler was "quick and resolute" (262; vol. 1). But the King might not be so ready to praise Adler's supposedly masculine virtues if he recognized that his own masculinity seems rather fragile in comparison. Although the King is massively built, the "barbaric opulence" of his attire strikes Watson as being in bad taste and does not accord with middle-class late Victorian standards of male apparel, which were mostly very conservative (244; vol. 1). Further, his clumsy attempt to pose as an underling suggest both stupidity and cowardice. And of course, the King's failed attempts to recover the photograph himself force him to beg for help from another man, who is himself quickly outmaneuvered by Adler. Indeed, by the end of the story, Adler seems in various ways to be more manly (according to the prevalent Victorian definition of that term[5]) than both her former lover and the detective hired by him.

But part of what makes Adler such a complex character is that her supposedly masculine virtues are paired with conventionally feminine beauty.[6] The King praises her as possessing "the face of the most beautiful of women" (247; vol. 1), while the grooms employed at the nearby mews all agree that she is "the daintiest thing under a bonnet on this planet" (249; vol. 1). Watson is "seized with compunction" when he realizes what a "beautiful creature" he is conspiring against (257; vol. 1). Even Holmes, who according to Watson is immune to love, remarks that Adler is "a lovely woman, with a face that a man might die for" (although this last remark shows how the detective connects female beauty with peril: 239, 252; vol. 1).

Conan Doyle's Adler thus surpasses Halberstam's standards for female masculinity: she comes across as more manly than her former lover, and she uses her experience of theatrical cross-dressing to outwit the most intelligent of men; but she does all this while possessing a feminine beauty that dumbfounds her male pursues, making her performance all the more entertaining. This combination of supposedly masculine character traits and feminine beauty has been treated variously in adaptations and pastiches of the story. The 1984 Granada Television adaptation celebrates the conjunction: Adler's role is acted by former fashion model Gayle Hunnicutt, and flashbacks show the character was already reveling in masculine attire and masculine behavior during her days with the King (then Crown Prince) of Bohemia. As the King recounts the time he spent with Adler, the viewer is presented with scenes of Adler shooting with the King (and drawing his applause with her accuracy), riding with the King (no sidesaddle for her—she jumps her horse just as well as her male companion), and accompanying the King to a burlesque while dressed in top hat and tails. In contrast, Michael Harrison's written pastiche "Sherlock Holmes and '*The* Woman'" (1999) manifests Adler's masculinity in her physique as well as her character, and Harrison's Watson cannot reconcile himself to the mixing. After conceding the beauty of her hair and eyes, Watson describes the qualities of Adler (here referred to by her "real" name, "Lillie Langtree") that discomfort him:

> I found myself startled by the inescapable conclusion that ... there was, if not more masculine than feminine in her composition, then there was surely too much of the masculine that she might lay claim to a complete femininity. Her shoulders, too wide for femininity; hands which were large and (one felt) strong; a jaw too firm for female beauty—and with all these physical paradoxes, an assurance stopping only this side [of] arrogance [121–22].

Harrison's Watson apparently understands masculinity and femininity as ultimately mutually exclusive: having too much masculinity makes it impossible to be completely (adequately, he seems to imply) feminine. The Granada adaptation, and indeed Conan Doyle's story, allows more flexibility: Adler can be quite masculine without sacrificing any femininity.

Sherlock's *Irene Adler: From Dominatrix to Damsel in Distress*

In contrast to all of these, the BBC's *Sherlock* strips Adler of her masculinities. More than that, it makes her femininity her defining characteristic. When, in Conan Doyle's story, Holmes refers to Adler as "*the* woman," he does so to express his opinion of her as one who "eclipses and predominates the whole of her sex" (239; vol. 1). But in the *Sherlock* episode "A Scandal in Belgravia" (2012), "The Woman" is the title by which Adler refers to herself on the website advertising her professional services as a dominatrix. The word *dominatrix* refers to one who dominates, of course, but it also is a word used exclusively to refer to women; its origin is the feminine form of the Latin word *dominator*. This feminine appellation reflects the degree to which Adler's femininity—and in particular her conventionally feminine beauty—shapes her character. The first shot of Adler is of her hand with its long, red fingernails and dainty ring. As the camera pulls back, the viewer sees Adler's slender yet shapely lower body; eschewing the dominatrix's usual apparel—the leather, latex, or PVC corset that protects its wearer from cuts and penetration—Adler is instead dressed in sheer, easily-torn lingerie. Only then, after her femininity and sex-appeal have been firmly established, is Adler's name divulged.

The reimagined Adler's strict adherence to conventional femininity can be understood as part of the character's more general unwillingness—even inability—to assume different identities. She chooses to be nude when she meets Sherlock; since she does so because she correctly surmises that this will deny him the opportunity to analyze her clothing for clues to her personality, this might be considered a form of disguise. But she is not really naked; rather, she is wearing lipstick, mascara, high heels, and a conventionally feminine coiffure—even unclothed, she is draped in the accouterments typical of her gender. And in contrast to Conan Doyle's character, who enjoys putting disguise to good use, this Adler abhors the very idea: as she tells Sherlock in this scene, "the big problem with a disguise ... [is that] ... however hard you try, it's always a self-portrait" ("A Scandal in Belgravia"). At that moment, Adler seems to have a strong argument—she makes this statement after "defrocking" Sherlock by pulling off the white dog collar that was the whole of his attempt to disguise himself as a clergyman. (A sharp contrast with Holmes's performance as a clergyman in Conan Doyle's story, which is so virtuoso that it fools even a similarly accomplished actor, this slap-dash affair, like most of Sherlock's other attempts at disguise in the series so far, only betrays his disdain for other people's perceptive abilities.) And at the end of this meeting, Adler clearly has the upper hand over Sherlock: after injecting him with a sedative, she hurls her catch-phrase in his face—"Know when you are beaten"—and snatches back the smart phone he had taken from her. Adler also shows some fighting skills in this scene; although it is not clear whether fighting can still be gendered masculine in an age when female mixed martial arts champions are made into sex symbols, it nonetheless denotes strength.[7]

But over the course of the episode Adler's gets weaker and more dependent on men for help, and as she is forced into hiding, her aversion to disguise begins to work against her. Adler's situation at this point somewhat resembles that of Holmes after he kills Professor Moriarty, as described to Watson in Conan Doyle's "The Adventure of the Empty House" (767–68; vol. 1). Like the original Holmes, *Sherlock*'s Adler lets it be thought that she has been killed; indeed, faking her death by supplying a body-double corpse with a smashed-in face is as close as this Adler gets to assuming a disguise—a kind of inversion where she presents somebody else as herself rather than presenting herself as somebody else. Yet whereas Conan Doyle's detective can use his talent for disguise to spend the next three years traveling the world incognito, patiently eliminating his enemies, *Sherlock*'s Adler is unable to keep her own identity hidden for more than a fraction of that time. Although the way she lures John to a secret meeting by employing Mycroft's usual approach—sending a beautiful woman to pick up John in a black Jaguar—could be considered something like a disguise (indeed, John momentarily believes he is being taken to meet Mycroft), when Adler deliberately reveals herself to John, she inadvertently reveals herself to Sherlock (who has followed John to the rendezvous), thereby blowing her cover.

Adler cannot even disguise her feelings—later in the episode, she pretends that her earlier flirtations with Sherlock were merely her way of manipulating him; but Sherlock, recalling the elevated pulse and dilated pupils that accompanied those gestures, knows that Adler's attraction to him is real, and at this instant he realizes that the access code to her smartphone consists of the first four letters of his own name. Sherlock somewhat viciously takes this opportunity to remind Adler of the disdainful attitude towards disguise she expressed when they first met: with her phone unlocked, Adler has no leverage with which to guarantee her safety, and Sherlock tells Mycroft that if he's feeling kind he should incarcerate Adler, because out in the world she will never be able to hide from her enemies. Adler seems to agree, and with teary eyes she begs for help. Indeed, the notion of a successfully disguised Adler is here made so absurd that Mycroft is later unable to maintain the cover story that she assumed a new identity in an American witness-protection program. The episode's penultimate scene shows what really happened—Adler is on her knees, evidently about to be executed by one of the factions who suffered when the material on her phone was accessed. Even in this moment, apparently her last, her identity cannot be disguised: although her hair is veiled, her face is more visible than that of any of the other characters in the scene. Her fate seems sealed, but then the camera pans up to show that the masked executioner is actually Sherlock, who has tracked her down and—more significantly—donned a disguise in order to save her life.

Whereas Conan Doyle's Adler outwits Holmes through the use of a disguise, this version of the character, opposed to disguise on principle, is soundly defeated by Sherlock, and owes her life to *his* use of a disguise (indeed, his only convincing disguise in the series so far). Whereas Conan Doyle's Adler presumably performed a variety of roles at La Scala, *Sherlock*'s Adler is apparently only capable of performing a single role—that of a conventionally feminine dominatrix. But this transformation of Adler's character does not occur in isolation: *Sherlock* takes Adler's talent for disguise away from her and bestows it upon another character, the one who in this version of the Sherlock Holmes universe is truly the detective's nemesis, Jim Moriarty. Indeed, even when Adler appears to be triumphing over Sherlock and Mycroft—in the moment just before Sherlock cracks the code to her smartphone—she admits that her success depended on Moriarty's help.

Sherlock's *Moriarty: A Master Performer*

As I will argue, when Moriarty first appears in *Sherlock* he is wearing not one but two disguises. Later, he pretends to be the actor Rich Brook and convinces the British press that the Jim Moriarty persona is itself a creation. And even when Moriarty is not disguised, he assumes a variety of identities, ranging from businessman to tourist to king, identifying himself first as Sherlock's counterpart, later as his opposite, and finally identifying Sherlock and himself as one and the same person.

But before Moriarty even enters the narrative, *Sherlock* tricks its audience into believing they are encountering him when in actuality they are being introduced to another character entirely. Barely thirty minutes into the first episode of the series, "A Study in Pink," John Watson is coerced into meeting with a shadowy but obviously powerful figure. This character initially demonstrates his influence by making several payphones ring as John walks past them; when John finally answers one of the phones, the somewhat threatening male voice on the line directs his attention to four nearby security cameras, each of which immediately turns to focus on John. John is so intimidated by this demonstration of control over communication and security networks that he does not hesitate to follow the voice's instruction to get into the car that has just pulled up. When they come face to face in an empty warehouse, John's abductor explains that the location and the manner in which John was delivered there were necessitated by his wish to avoid Sherlock Holmes's attention; he then identifies himself as Sherlock's enemy ("in his mind, certainly")—these remarks suggest an antagonistic relationship between this character and Sherlock, especially when taken with his offer to pay John for information about Sherlock's activities. When John refuses the offer, the mystery man attempts to intimidate him by referring to details from the confidential notes made by John's therapist—clearly, his ability to gather information is even more exceptional than previously demonstrated. When John demands to know the identity of his abductor, the latter only tells him that "it's time to choose a side," strengthening the impression that he and Sherlock are locked in some kind of struggle. When John describes this meeting, Sherlock later does nothing to disabuse him (or the audience) of this notion, and even describes this individual as "the most dangerous man you've ever met."

If they are familiar with Conan Doyle's stories, first-time viewers are likely to assume that this mysterious character is none other than Moriarty. That he has spies all over London (many of them electronic) recalls Conan Doyle's description of Moriarty as a spider at the center of a web ("The Final

Problem," 740; vol. 1); both he and Sherlock have made remarks suggesting that an antagonistic relationship exists between them; and in accord with the description of Conan Doyle's Moriarty, this man is tall and possesses a domed forehead (741; vol. 1). It is not until the end of the episode, some forty minutes later, that the truth comes out, but just before it does, the viewer is further encouraged to associate this character with Moriarty. His reappearance comes just moments after the killer identifies Moriarty as the name of his sponsor, and when they meet he asks Sherlock, "Did it never occur to you that you and I belong on the same side?" and asserts that the two of them "have more in common than you like to believe. This petty feud between us is simply childish" ("A Study in Pink"). These references to being on opposite sides of a feud reinforce the notion that this man is Sherlock's nemesis, and the mention of them having things in common recalls Conan Doyle's attempt to present Professor Moriarty as not just Holmes's equal, but in many ways his reflection.

When this character is finally identified by Sherlock as his brother, Mycroft, John's shock is doubtless shared by many viewers. Those more familiar with Sherlock Holmes adaptations and pastiches—which generally amplify the role of Moriarty, but not of Mycroft—than with Conan Doyle's stories are even more likely to be taken in by the misdirection. So powerful is the association between Mycroft and Moriarty that Mycroft can be understood as the first of Moriarty's many identities; somewhat like the body-double corpse Irene Adler uses to fake her death in "A Scandal in Belgravia," until Sherlock identifies him, the Mycroft character functions as a sort of inverse disguise for Moriarty—rather than Moriarty appearing on screen made-up to seem like another character, another character appears on screen and is made to seem like Moriarty. More generally, this association of *Sherlock*'s Mycroft with the original Moriarty serves to amplify the sense of Moriarty's influence in the series.

Moriarty himself first appears, in disguise, about eighteen minutes into the third episode, "The Great Game" (2010); and towards the end, he appears in his own persona to claim responsibility for the crimes Sherlock has been investigating. However, for much of this episode, viewers are encouraged to associate these crimes with Irene Adler. This episode references several of Conan Doyle's stories, but none more so than "A Scandal in Bohemia": at the beginning of the episode Sherlock identifies the envelope used by the bomber as "Bohemian—from the Czech Republic" (Sherlock's clarification is necessary because the term *Bohemian* is rarely used in this way today, making it even more conspicuous as a reference to Conan Doyle's story) and remarks that the handwriting is clearly a woman's; later, Sherlock and John grapple with a killer named Golem ("after a Prague legend," Sherlock notes); and later still they interrogate an art curator named Wenceslas (a reference to the Bohemian ruler celebrated in the St. Stephen's Day carol "Good King Wenceslas"), at which point Sherlock comments that "this whole case has a Czech feeling about it." By this point, any viewer at all familiar with Conan Doyle's stories must be thinking of "A Scandal in Bohemia," a story that features one letter written on Bohemian stationary and another written by a woman, and especially of Irene Adler.

But Adler is never identified as the envelope's sender, nor is there definite evidence of her playing any role in the crimes investigated in this episode: the only reason to believe she is involved at all is that the next episode suggests she is in Moriarty's employ. So whether or not Adler is at work in this case, Moriarty is the one pulling the strings; the fact that he has in a sense taken this "Bohemian" episode away from Adler is but one of many ways in which this series takes aspects of Conan Doyle's Adler and uses them to develop the Moriarty character. Moriarty even seems to have taken over the original Adler's fondness for crossing gender lines: When Sherlock and Moriarty first talk, Moriarty—who has yet to reveal himself—is speaking through a woman's voice, the voice of his first potential bombing victim: he types from some remote location, his words appear on a pager held by the victim, and she reads those words to Sherlock over the phone. Moriarty continues to speak to Sherlock through the voices of his later victims: a man, a much older woman, and a child—this variety suggests how much Moriarty likes playing different roles.

When his first conversation with Moriarty ends, Sherlock mutters "the curtain rises," immediately acknowledging the theatrical nature of their initial interaction, and suggesting that he expects Moriarty to provide him with the entertainment he has been craving: an interesting case. And Moriarty delivers exactly this: two of the most dramatic—that is to say, drama-filled—scenes from later in this episode are also dramatic in the sense that they take place in locations resembling theatres: Sherlock is attacked by Moriarty's hit-man Golem (whose monstrosity recalls horror films) in a planetarium, and the showdown between Sherlock and Moriarty himself takes place in a swimming arena. The new Moriarty may not be a former actor and opera singer like Conan Doyle's Adler, but he certainly knows how to put on a show.

Indeed, the confrontation in the swimming arena is a masterpiece of theatre. The last person to be kidnapped and wired with explosives is John Watson, but whereas the previous victims were positioned in secret locations around England, Watson is put directly in Sherlock's way, at the pool where the victim of Sherlock's first case was murdered. Sherlock (and the audience) is momentarily led to believe that John is in fact the bomber himself: before he opens his coat to reveal the bomb strapped to his torso, John recites the words Moriarty speaks to him through a earpiece, and his first lines—"This is a turn-up, isn't it? ... Bet you never saw this coming" ("The Great Game")— suggest that Sherlock has come face-to-face with his adversary. This is yet another instance of inverse disguise: Moriarty is presenting another character—this time, John Watson—as himself.

Although it does not immediately seem to be very significant, Moriarty's first appearance on screen, earlier in this episode, is just as theatrical, for Moriarty is playing not one but two dramatic roles: for his audience at large he is playing Jim from I.T., Molly Hooper's boyfriend; but for Sherlock in particular he is playing Jim the closeted homosexual, Sherlock's secret admirer who is only using Molly to get close to the real object of his desire. Whereas Conan Doyle's Adler uses disguise to cross gender lines, Jim Moriarty uses it to assume a different sexuality. This double-layer costume is the perfect deception to use against Sherlock: the detective's penetrating gaze allows him to see through most disguises, but he is not used to finding one disguise beneath another. When Sherlock looks at Molly's boyfriend and performs his usual analysis of the visible clues, he sees a gay man and believes that he has gotten to the bottom of things; it is not part of his routine to investigate whether the revealing details—in this case hair product, dyed eyebrows, and visible designer underwear—are actually deceiving rather than revealing.

Moriarty has only just appeared, but already he has fooled Sherlock in a way that Conan Doyle's Moriarty never fools Holmes. But to what end? This meeting does not seem to serve any rational purpose for Moriarty. Perhaps its only goal is the joy it brings him to successfully play a role (or rather two). Indeed, when he appears at the end of the episode in his own (or what we must assume is his own) persona, he elicits his audience's appreciation: as he confronts Sherlock in the swimming arena, Moriarty calls attention to his earlier performance, explaining that he has "loved this little game of ours: playing Jim from I.T.; playing gay—Did you like the little touch with the underwear?" ("The Great Game"). In this respect, he again has more in common with Conan Doyle's Adler than with Conan Doyle's Moriarty. As can be seen when she writes to Holmes explaining how she used her "male costume" to spy on him, Conan Doyle's Adler likes to take credit for her performance and be appreciated by its intended audience. (And indeed Holmes is duly impressed.) Conan Doyle's Moriarty maintains his anonymity for as long as possible and only confronts Holmes when he feels it absolutely necessary;

in contrast, *Sherlock*'s Moriarty, like Conan Doyle's Adler, chooses to take a bow.

In the second season's final episode, "The Reichenbach Fall" (2012), Moriarty launches himself onto a much bigger stage and expands his repertoire. Moriarty first appears in the guise of a tourist visiting the Tower of London. Although he is again wearing a v-neck t-shirt, his outfit does little to recall his role as gay Jim: instead of homosexuality, it suggests a different otherness—that of the foreigner. By far the most eye-catching part of this otherwise drab outfit is his hat: with "London" written in large letters and bold colors across both front and back, and the Union Flag spread across the peak, it is the type sold at airports to international travelers as a memento of their visit to Britain's capital. This supposed costume might be understood as to some extent an expression of Moriarty's true self: in the montage of newspaper headlines that follows Moriarty's arrest, one of the articles refers to the mastermind as "Irish-born Moriarty."

But even if Moriarty is 'just being himself' in this scene, he is nevertheless still very much performing. As he sends the orders to open Pentonville Prison and the Bank of London vault while he breaks into the case holding the Crown Jewels, Moriarty (and the audience) is listening to the overture to Rossini's *The Thieving Magpie*. Magpies are traditionally believed to have a penchant for stealing shiny objects, including jewels, but the choice of music is significant for another reason: the operetta débuted at La Scala, where, in Conan Doyle's story, Irene Adler had been a regular performer. Moriarty even performs a few ballet steps in his approach to the jewel case. And as Conan Doyle's Adler might have done many times at La Scala, Moriarty executes a rapid costume change, removing his hat and jacket to don the crown, mantle, and scepter—in mere moments he goes from foreign visitor to ruler of the nation. That he writes "Get Sherlock" on the jewel case just before smashing it shows he is aware he has an audience watching him through the security cameras as he puts on royal apparel. Moreover, he makes no attempt to flee the scene—indeed, he is still posing on the throne when the police arrive—indicating that he wants to be caught so that he can be photographed and filmed being arrested, thereby assuring himself of the largest possible audience.

But Moriarty's most brilliant performance perhaps comes when he pretends that there *is* no Moriarty, that he is an actor named Rich Brook, and Moriarty is a just a role Sherlock paid him to act so that Sherlock could be seen defeating a nemesis. The physical disguise is fairly rudimentary—Rich Brook looks a lot like a shabbily dressed, poorly groomed version of Jim from I.T. What makes this performance so convincing is that it has records to back it up: Moriarty shows John clippings of Rich Brook's career as a television actor. For a moment it seems that John might be convinced. Indeed, the viewer might start to doubt Sherlock if it were not for the fact that the words "make believe" appear on the wall of the flat where this encounter takes place, suggesting this whole encounter is a ruse. But this too is ambiguous—does "make believe" mean that Rich Brook is an invention or that Moriarty is (and thus that Sherlock is a fraud)?[8]

Even on the occasions when Moriarty interacts with Sherlock without pretending to be Jim from I.T., Rich Brook, or anybody else, he is still performing—not performing a disguise, but performing an identity so as to define himself in relation to his main audience, Sherlock himself. At the first such meeting, at the swimming arena, he tells Sherlock, "I'm a specialist—like you," and Sherlock finishes the thought by calling Moriarty a consulting criminal—the counterpart to his own role as a consulting detective ("The Great Game"). Moriarty is dressed accordingly: consisting of a dark Westwood suit over a white shirt, a dark tie with a small tie-pin positioned low-down where it is just barely visible, and only the suggestion of a handkerchief poking out of the breast pocket, his attire in this scene expresses his determination to claim his place as Sherlock's professional counterpart. His style is not dissimilar from Sherlock's in that they both wear dark, modern-cut suits. Moriarty's ensemble is a little more formal, but the markers of that formality—tie, tiepin, and handkerchief—are all quite subtle.

In contrast, in the first half of the "The Reichenbach Fall" Moriarty's presentation of himself emphasizes the differences as well as the similarities between him and Sherlock. After his trial ends with acquittal, Moriarty visits Sherlock at his flat and tells him that "we're just alike, you and me ... except you're boring—you're on the side of the angels." This episode began with a sequence of scenes in which Sherlock expressed his distaste for certain men's fashion accessories—one grateful client gave him a tie-pin, and Sherlock muttered, "I don't wear ties"; another gave him a pair of cufflinks, to which he responded, "All my shirts have buttons." These remarks drew attention to Sherlock's fashion sense in such a way that Moriarty's can now be recognized as its opposite. The suit Moriarty wears to court looks like it might be another Westwood, but his appearance is quite different from what it was when he confronted Sherlock in the swimming arena: this time the suit is a light beige (in contrast to the black Sherlock always wears); the tie is an even brighter shade, and his handkerchief is much more visible (Sherlock never wears ties and keeps his handkerchief out of sight); most importantly, his tie-pin is large, shiny, and positioned up-high near the knot, where it is impossible to miss. And as becomes evident at the exact moment following the trial when Moriarty notes the crucial difference between himself and Sherlock (Sherlock is boring—he's on the side of the angels), Moriarty is wearing cufflinks. He is flaunting every single one of the men's fashion accessories that Sherlock spurns, highlighting the difference between them even more.

And Moriarty's clothing is not the only part of his self-presentation that he manipulates to present himself as the anti–Sherlock at his trial. As his flashy clothing contrasts with Sherlock's somber apparel, so too does his silence contrast with Sherlock's loquaciousness. On the way to the courthouse, John tells Sherlock to keep his testimony "simple and brief"; when Sherlock responds with "I'll just be myself," John's exasperation expresses his realization that limiting his speech is quite outside Sherlock's repertoire. Sure enough, Sherlock's inability to stick to answering questions is such that he is soon jailed for contempt. In contrast, Moriarty, who took so much pleasure in describing his exploits at the end of "The Great Game," is remarkably silent: he does not say a word in his own defense; nor does he allow his lawyer to argue on his behalf or call any witnesses to do so.

At their final meeting near the end of "The Reichenbach Fall," Moriarty has changed his appearance once more, but this time, rather than a conscious attempt to express what he believes to be the difference between himself and Sherlock, his attire anticipates his realization of their likeness. At the start of their conversation on the roof of Bart's Hospital, Moriarty expresses his disappointment with Sherlock. By this point, Moriarty has discredited Sherlock and found the process entirely too easy for his liking: rather than the worthy adversary Moriarty thought he was, Sherlock has turned out to be "ordinary," just like everyone else—everyone except for Moriarty himself, of course. But before long, Sherlock has convinced him otherwise—Sherlock may be on the side of the angels, but he is not one of them. Moriarty sees the truth of this so clearly that he twice exclaims, "You're me!" Although this is a contradiction of what Moriarty stated at the beginning of the scene, it is the sentiment that he has been expressing with his wardrobe the entire time. The light suit and tie from the trial are gone, as are all the flashy accessories. Instead, Moriarty is dressed in the dark colors he wore at his first meeting with Sherlock, the same dark colors Sherlock himself prefers. But one feature in particular distinguishes what he is wearing now from what he wore at the swimming pool—in an apparent homage to Sherlock's signature look, Moriarty's jacket has what appears to be a permanently turned-up collar.

Moriarty's performances never cease to entertain: while playing Molly's boyfriend Jim, he is simultaneously playing gay; while playing a foreign tourist, he dresses up as the King of England; and while playing Rich Brook, he convinces the press that Moriarty is a fiction and Sherlock is a fraud. Even when he is "just being himself," he constantly varies his attire, sometimes drawing attention to his male fashion accessories, sometimes hiding them, and sometimes eschewing them entirely, all depending on how he relates to his audience—Sherlock—in that particular scene. He thus defies Halberstam's definition of male masculinity as endlessly repetitive; of course, as I have argued, his ability to do so springs from the fact that he has been imbued with a female character's talent for self-transformation.

Moriarty is finally defeated by Sherlock, or at least that seems to be the case: at the end of their meeting atop Bart's, Moriarty is shown shooting himself, and the closing scene of the episode shows that Sherlock survived his leap off the roof; moreover, in the first episode of the following season, "The Empty Hearse" (2014), Sherlock suggests that he and Mycroft were one step ahead of Moriarty all the time and had worked out a number of contingency plans for the final showdown. On the other hand, Sherlock is explaining all of this to Anderson, and as Anderson himself points out, he is the last person to whom Sherlock would reveal the truth; furthermore, the third season closes with Moriarty appearing to have made a return from the dead. Charles Augustus Magnussen, the villain in the finale of the third season ("His Last Vow," 2014), is perhaps even more formidable—Sherlock has to resort to physical violence to defeat Magnussen, much as Conan Doyle's Moriarty does when he attempts to defeat Holmes. But whether or not Moriarty was ever close to defeating Sherlock or is even the most dangerous villain in the series is not the point; rather, his success as a character comes down to the fact that every time he appears he presents a new aspect of himself to his audiences (Sherlock; the viewer)—a stark contrast to Conan Doyle's Moriarty, who never lives up to Holmes's description of him.

Conclusion

So what are we to make of all this? How does it ultimately matter that *Sherlock* takes Conan Doyle's underdeveloped Moriarty and turns him into a complex character and a true nemesis for Sherlock? Moriarty's own explanation of this is that "[e]very fairy-tale needs a good old-fashioned villain" ("The Reichenbach Fall"); but despite all the other fairy-tale references worked into this episode (the copy of *Grimm's Fairy Tales* at the scene of the kidnapping, the gingerbread man Moriarty sends to Sherlock, to name but two), the series as a whole does not seem much like a fairy tale: although not all viewers may find it realistic, it at least seems to aim for believability. A more common response is to liken *Sherlock* to DC Comics, specifically the Batman series: see, for example, James Butlin in his Huffington Post blog posting "*Sherlock* Is Good, But Haven't We Seen This All in *Batman*?" (2012). There is a lot to recommend this idea: "DC" stands for "Detective Comics"; Batman was in part inspired by Sherlock Holmes; and many people have likened *Sherlock*'s Moriarty to Batman's nemesis, The Joker (see, for example, Sherlockology.tumblr.com).[9] But while *Sherlock* gives the impression that the title character is in some ways superhuman, more so even than Conan Doyle's Holmes (the on-screen graphics representing Sherlock's thoughts suggest superhuman memory and mental-processing speed), this version of the character does not always seem heroic, yet alone super-heroic. Sherlock even tells John, "Don't make people into heroes ... heroes don't exist, and even if they did, I wouldn't be one of them" ("The Great Game"), and Francesca M. Marinaro and Kayley Thomas argue convincingly that Sherlock's heroism is more potential than actual and is still waiting to be coaxed out through John's guidance (2012). So if Sherlock is not a superhero, it is still unclear why he would need a nemesis.

Nevertheless, it is undeniable both that *Sherlock* greatly amplifies the Moriarty character from Conan Doyle's original and that, although it drains Irene Adler of the talent that makes her so formidable in Conan Doyle's story, it nevertheless gives her star billing in one episode (whereas most of the many characters in Conan Doyle's stories will probably never be mentioned in the series). In both these respects, *Sherlock* resembles the other two popular screen adaptations of the Sherlock Holmes series to appear recently: the two Sherlock Holmes feature films directed by Guy Ritchie (*Sherlock Holmes* 2009 and *Sherlock Holmes: A Game of Shadows* 2011), and CBS's series *Elementary* (2013–). Furthermore, all three adaptations create some kind of close relationship between the two characters (*Elementary* even makes them one and the same), whereas Conan Doyle made them quite independent of each other. What can we conclude from this? Perhaps that audiences today require (or at least are thought to require) both an impressive villain and a female lead, and in particular, that the female lead should be at least somewhat villainous herself. Conan Doyle's Adler is not a criminal—her threat to destroy the King of Bohemia's marriage plans seems to be the reaction of a lover whom he had "cruelly wronged" and is abandoned once she has sanctified her union to "a better man than he" (261; vol. 1). But the Adlers in Ritchie's films, *Elementary*, and *Sherlock* are all either criminals in their own right or working with criminals. And in the end they are all defeated (and in Ritchie's second film, killed), whereas Conan Doyle's Adler seems to have a life of happiness ahead of her at the end of "A Scandal in Bohemia."[10] Alarmingly, each of these recent, very popular adaptations takes perhaps the most well-known female character from Conan Doyle's Sherlock Holmes canon, one who provides the detective with the challenge he and the reader both crave for him, and first turns her into a threat—to society in general and to Holmes in particular—before rendering her powerless.

Notes

1. I refer to the detective and his doctor friend from *Sherlock* as "Sherlock" and "John," respectively; I refer to Conan Doyle's characters as "Holmes" and "Watson."
2. Quotations from the television episodes were made with reference to the transcripts at http://arianedevere.livejournal.com/.
3. Before both Adams and Halberstam, Judith Butler argued for an understanding of gender as performative in her 1990 book *Gender Trouble*.
4. The only exception to this is the (probably rare) reader who encounters *The Valley of Fear* (1914) before any of the short stories in which Moriarty is mentioned: although that novella was written later, it is set "at the end of the [18]80's," several years prior to the events described in "The Final Problem" (170; vol. 2). (This creates a continuity error since Watson claims he has never heard of Moriarty in "The Final Problem," but Holmes describes him to Watson at the beginning of *The Valley of Fear* and mentions him again at the end.) Moriarty's role in arranging a murder in this novella perhaps gives weight to the claims Holmes makes in "The Final Problem" about Moriarty's influence, but Moriarty's character is only developed to the degree that an official police detective describes him as fatherly and as having the appearance of a minister; what Holmes notes about his lack of any legal culpability could be assumed from the detective's remarks about his anonymity in "The Final Problem." Furthermore, Moriarty never appears in the narrative, and since twelve chapters go by without him being mentioned, the reader may have forgotten his involvement by the time he is credited with the murder at the end of the story.
5. In late–Victorian England, the prevalent characteristics of middle-class manliness included independence, determination, energy, restraint, and forthrightness. Adler surpasses both Holmes and the King in the first four, but since all three employ some kind of disguise, none can be said to be especially forthright.
6. This combination of masculine and feminine virtues makes Adler interesting, but not unique in late Victorian literature. In Alfred Tennyson's 1886 poem "Locksley Hall—Sixty Years After," the speaker praises a female character as "she with all the charm of woman, she with all the breadth of man" (l. 48).
7. In a Google search for "female mixed martial arts champion" on November 22, 2013, a site listing "The 12 Hottest Women in MMA" was the ninth hit.
8. Evidently, the Rich Brook ruse convinced so many people that it led to an official investigation: in the first episode of the third season, "The Empty Hearse," Anderson and Greg Lestrade watch as a news reporter is filmed explaining that the police eventually determined Brook to be Moriarty's invention and that Sherlock's reputation was cleared in court.
9. My thanks to my students at St. Joseph's College, Lindsay Hysler and Chelsea Medina, for bringing this to my attention.
10. The third season of *Sherlock* develops John Watson's fiancée (and later wife), Mary Morstan, into a more major character than she ever is in Conan Doyle's stories, but she too fits

this pattern: she has a dangerous, possibly criminal past and is still very formidable with a gun in her hand, but she is reduced to a rather pitiful situation, waiting for months to see if John will accept this past after Sherlock exposes it. Like Adler, she momentarily appears to get the better of Sherlock, only to be humiliated by him, and like Adler, this humiliation hinges upon her love for a man (albeit John rather than Sherlock).

Works Cited

Adams, James Eli. *Dandies and Desert Saints: Styles of Victorian Masculinity*. Ithaca: Cornell University Press, 1995. Print.
Butler, Judith. *Gender Trouble: Feminism and the Subversion of Identity*, 10th anniv. ed. New York: Routledge, 1999. Print.
Butlin, James. "*Sherlock* Is Good, but Haven't We Seen This All in *Batman*?" *Huffington Post UK*. 16 Jan. 2012. Web. 9 Jan. 2014.
Conan Doyle, Arthur. *Sherlock Holmes: The Complete Novels and Stories*. Edited with an introduction by Loren D. Estleman. 2 vols. New York: Bantam Classic, 2003. Print.
"The Empty Hearse." *Sherlock: Season Three*. Writ. Mark Gatiss. BBC Worldwide, 2014. DVD.
"The Great Game." *Sherlock: Season One*. Writ. Mark Gatiss. BBC Worldwide, 2010. DVD.
Halberstam, Judith. *Female Masculinity*. Durham: Duke University Press, 1998. Print.
Harrison, Michael. "Sherlock Holmes and '*The* Woman.'" *The New Adventures of Sherlock Holmes*. Ed. Martin H. Greenberg, Carol-Lynn Rössel Waugh, and John L. Lellenberg. London: Robinson, 1999. Print.
"His Last Vow." *Sherlock: Season Three*. Writ. Steven Moffat. BBC Worldwide, 2014. DVD.
Marinaro, Francesca M., and Kayley Thomas. "'Don't Make People into Heroes, John': (De/Re)Constructing the Detective as Hero." *Sherlock Holmes for the 21st Century: Essays on New Adaptations*. Ed. Lynnette Porter. Jefferson, NC: McFarland, 2012. 65–80. Print.
"The Reichenbach Fall." *Sherlock: Season Two*. Writ. Steve Thompson. BBC Worldwide, 2012. DVD.
"A Scandal in Belgravia." *Sherlock: Season Two*. Writ. Steven Moffat. BBC Worldwide, 2012. DVD.
"A Scandal in Bohemia." *The Adventures of Sherlock Holmes: Boxed Set Collection*. Granada Television. MPI Home Video, 2002. DVD.
"Sherlock Begins—Steven Moffat's Batman." Sherlockology.tumblr.com. Web. 9 Jan. 2014.
Sherlock Holmes. Dir. Guy Ritchie. Warner Home Video, 2010. DVD.
Sherlock Holmes: A Game of Shadows. Dir. Guy Ritchie. Warner Home Video, 2012. DVD.
"A Study in Pink." *Sherlock: Season One*. Writ. Steven Moffat. BBC Worldwide, 2010. DVD.
Tennyson, Alfred. "Locksley Hall—Sixty Years After." *Ballads and Other Poems*, Vol. VI of *The Works of Tennyson*. Ed. Hallam Tennyson. London: Macmillan, 1908. Print.
"The Woman." *Elementary*. CBS. WCBS, New York. 16 May 2013. Television.

Return of "the woman"
Irene Adler in Contemporary Adaptations
RHONDA LYNETTE HARRIS TAYLOR

The Singular Miss Adler

In Sir Arthur Conan Doyle's fifty-six short stories and four novels about Sherlock Holmes, Irene Adler appeared in only one story, "A Scandal in Bohemia" (1891). However, she has become one of the canon's *de rigueur* characters for the superfluity of print and media pastiches, parodies, and so on created over the 125 years since Holmes's first appearance in print. How iconic she has become, even for the most commonplace of Holmesian resurrections, is exemplified by the choice of characters included in the 2009 *Sherlock Holmes Paper Dolls* (Tierney). Besides those personages who appeared repeatedly in the canon (Holmes, Watson, Mrs. Hudson, and Moriarty) there is Adler. She is an intriguing choice for a children's paper doll since the "A Scandal" terms her a "well-known adventuress" (Conan Doyle 165), a designation used by the King of Bohemia who is her former lover. One would assume that her solitary appearance in the canon, coupled with the sexuality implicit in Watson's description of her "dubious and questionable memory" ("A Scandal in Bohemia" 162), would preclude her inclusion in a children's product. The canon does offer other female characters who would not need to be sanitized, as is common when "A Scandal" is included in children's anthologies.[1] However, modifying Adler in fundamental ways to fit perceived audience preferences is long-standing practice in adaptations.

The Cases of the "Real" Irene Adler

Adler, as portrayed in the canonical "A Scandal in Bohemia," has been deemed "a proto-feminist: a strong female character who was just as smart as the smartest man" (Rocha and Rocha 154). Various analyses (e.g., Redmond 52; Baring-Gould, *The Annotated Sherlock Holmes* 354) have identified the inspiration for Adler's character as one or more infamous women of the Victorian era. They include Lillie Langtry and Lola Montez, women who would have been termed, as Adler was, "adventuresses." And yet, despite their notorious (sexual) reputations in their nineteenth-century society, the legacy of their influential celebrity status has netted them entries in the *Oxford Dictionary of National Biography*.

A potential model for Adler was Emilie Charlotte Le Breton, also known as Lillie Langtry and The Jersey Lily, because of her birth in 1853 on the island of Jersey off the coast of Normandy, France. Langtry was beautiful and intelligent. During her lifetime, she was the subject of artworks, an advertising model for Pears soap, a stage actress who was in a film, the owner of a winery and of race horses, the mistress of Albert Edward, Prince of Wales (during her first marriage), and others, the wife of a baronet (her second marriage), the author of her own biography, and eventually, an American citizen (Brough "Langtry").

Another suggestion for the potential inspiration for Adler was Eliza Rosanna Gilbert, born in Ireland in 1821. Gilbert was noted for her beauty and her temper. She became famous as a "Spanish" dancer under the name Lola Montez. She married three times and once was prosecuted for bigamy. Montez had affairs with Franz Liszt and others and was mistress to King Ludwig I (Anton Walbrook) of Bavaria, a relationship that resulted in the title of Countess of Landsfeld. As an actress, dancer, and lecturer, she toured Canada, Ireland, and the United States, and she authored an autobiography ("Lola").

The shared attributes of these fascinating historical women are also present in Conan Doyle's description of Adler, as articulated by the main characters of "A Scandal" (Conan Doyle). Of "*the* woman" herself, Holmes notes such dry facts as Adler is an opera star, born in New Jersey (165), but then he is quite enthusiastic in his description of her physical attributes, declaring that she is "the daintiest thing under a bonnet on this planet. So say the Serpentine-mews" (168) and "a lovely woman, with a face that a man might die for" (169). It is her former lover, the King of Bohemia, who pays tribute not only to Adler's beauty but to her exceptional intelligence: "she has a soul of steel. She has the face of the most beautiful of women, and the mind of the most resolute of men" (166). In describing herself and her actions in the plot of the story, Adler asserts that "I love and am loved by a better man" (175) than the King, that she retains a compromising photograph only for self-protection from the King (175), and that one reason that she has been able to outwit Holmes, The Master Detective, is because "I have been trained as an actress myself. Male costume is nothing new to me" (174–5). Thus the "real" Adler is bright, quick-thinking, utilizes her stage experience in disguise for service to her personal agenda, plots out her own path to personal happiness, and leads a life that many of the time period would deem scandalous because of her willingness to use the coin of her beauty and her sexuality. She has also integrated her emotions with her cerebral advantages and maintains an effective balance of the two. She justifiably feels emotionally wronged and physically threatened by the King, but she devises a practical strategy to keep him in check. She loves the lawyer, Norton, and uses that affection to guide the clever plans that will guarantee them a shared future. Within the canon, Adler is viewed as notorious and she is certainly unconventional, but she is not a criminal, although she is frequently so portrayed in adaptations.

Most importantly, the canonical Adler is not a romantic interest for Holmes, per Watson's testimony that while "to Sherlock Holmes she is always *the* woman.... It was not that he felt any emotion akin to love for Irene Adler.... And yet there was but one woman to him, and that woman was the late Irene Adler, of dubious and questionable memory" (Conan Doyle, "A Scandal" 161). The lack of romantic involvement between the canonical Adler and Holmes has been repeatedly ignored in non-canonical presentations. Thus, the historical models for Adler and her canonical incarnation could arguably be said to be presentations of modern women, while their successors of modern fictional Adlers have actually been diminished in power.

The "Problem" of the Adventuress

In British, American, and Canadian book, film, and theatre adaptations (by notable authors and with major stars and directors and garnishing important recognitions) since the original publication of "A Scandal," Adler has frequently been recast into a role best described in a 1967 article by Dickensheet: "Irene Adler is considered primarily in the context of her amatory relations, or lack of them, with Sherlock Holmes" (qtd. in Redmond 57). More than thirty-five years after Dickensheet's assessment, Carole Nelson Douglas, who created a mystery series about Adler, also addressed this oft-repeated simplification of that character, asking, "Why Can't They Get Irene Adler Right?" (2013). She notes receipt of "e-mails that decry 'always sexualizing and criminalizing' Irene Adler," and summarizes her own description of the original Adler as "the gutsy, emphatic, and clever woman whom Holmes respected" (26). Similarly, a query about the incongruity between the original and new Adlers was raised in a 2012 PBS broadcast of a question and answer session in New York with fans and a panel of *Sherlock*'s star Benedict Cumberbatch, co-creator Steven Moffat, and producer Sue Vertue (*Sherlock* 2). An audience member asked, "Could you respond to critiques that say your version of Irene Adler is weaker because she is rescued versus the original story in which she gets away ... scot-free." In his response, Moffat is dismissive of the canonical Adler, saying, "Her triumph in the original story is to move house with her husband," and noting that as a young reader, his response to her portrayal was "I thought, 'Sherlock, why are you so keen on her?'" He does not directly address whether the *Sherlock* version is "weaker," but his assessment of the canonical Adler contrasts with Douglas' description of a "gutsy, emphatic, and clever woman" (26).

One of the reasons for Holmes's respect for Adler might be traced to a fundamental attribute of her character, which is that besides her willingness to transgress societal norms regarding sexuality, she also pushes the boundaries of legality. However, she has her own clear sense of ethics to guide that behavior. So, while Adler possesses property (the picture) to which the King feels entitled and, while, according to him, she has threatened to publicize their relationship, she has done so to protect herself. Indeed, regarding criminal behavior, it is the King who has paid for five attempted thefts of the picture. The King himself pays tribute to Adler's principles. After reading Adler's statement that she will retain the picture "to preserve a weapon which will always secure me" ("A Scandal" 175), he declares, "I know that her word is inviolate. The photograph is now as safe as if it were in the fire" (175).

While they begin as antagonists in "A Scandal," the canon demonstrates that Adler and Holmes are actually quite similar in their views of the boundaries of the law as it applies to themselves. Like Adler, Holmes is outspoken about devising his own path, which includes his independence from legalities in deciding what actions to take as he relies on his personal sense of justice. In "A Scandal," he plans subterfuge to retrieve the photograph from Adler's home and solicits Watson's help by asking, "You don't mind breaking the law?" (169). In "The Five Orange Pips," Holmes declares that in seeking revenge for his murdered client, "I shall be my own police" (Conan Doyle 228). In "The Boscombe Valley Mystery," Holmes keeps secret the confession of a murderer because of the man's terminal illness and because Holmes considers the homicide justifiable, since "there, but for the grace of God, goes Sherlock Holmes" (217). In "The Adventure of the Blue Carbuncle," he does not reveal the identity of a thief to authorities because, he asserts, "I am not retained by the police to supply their deficiencies. If Horner [the innocent man accused] were in danger, it would be another thing; but this fellow will not appear against him, and the case must collapse" (257). One might wonder if the arrested Horner would appreciate the delay in his release. Holmes's own guidelines for justice seem quixotic, if not high-handed. In comparison, Adler's boundaries look more balanced.

In too many non-canonical presentations, the complexity of the original depiction of Adler has repeatedly been reduced to the simplicity of a love interest for Holmes, serving to reinforce both the representation of his heterosexual masculinity and his deductive superiority over Adler, who no longer bests Holmes at the end of the stories. Simultaneously, Adler is presented as an actual danger to Holmes's life and/or career, which was certainly not the canonical depiction: Holmes was quite casual in "The Five Orange Pips" about having "been beaten four times—three times by men, and once by a woman" (Conan Doyle 219). The consequences of Holmes's involvement with the later incarnations of Adler, whether he does or does not ally with her romantically, results in the loss of his career, leaves him damaged psychosocially, and/or allows him to defeat her in a way that allows him to walk away triumphant.

Transforming the canonical Adler into a romantic interest for Holmes provides affirmation of his heterosexuality, which seems to be important to a wide audience. Holmes's sexuality, if any, and its orientation, has long been debated in critique (e.g., Atkinson 47–49; Payne; Redmond; Rosenberg). And, the question of "Is he, or isn't he?" is a persistent theme in contemporary non-canonical works. In the canon, Watson's narration and Holmes's conversations offer seemingly conflicting hints. Watson is unequivocal in the assertion that "all emotions, and that one [love] particularly, were abhorrent to his [Holmes's] cold, precise but admirably balanced mind.... Grit in a sensitive instrument, or a crack in one of his own high-power lenses, would not be more disturbing than a strong emotion in a nature such as his" ("A Scandal" 161). But Holmes is not as dogmatic as Watson, and his own references to love center on heterosexuality rather than asexuality, which is hardly surprising in a nineteenth-century context. In the denouement of "The Adventure of the Devil's Foot," he comments, "I have never loved, Watson, but if I did and if the woman I loved had met such an end, I might act even as our lawless lion-hunter has done" (Conan Doyle 970). In "The Adventure of the Lion's Mane," he says of the young woman who is at the center of a presumed murder that "women have seldom [note the choice of "seldom"] been an attraction for me, for my brain has always governed my heart, but I could not look upon her perfect clear-cut face, ... without realizing that no young man would cross her path unscathed" (Conan Doyle 1088). And, in "The Valley of Fear," he ruminates, "Should I ever marry, Watson, I should hope to inspire my wife with some feeling which would prevent her from being walked off by a housekeeper when my corpse was lying within a few yards of her" (Conan Doyle 801). Holmes also has no problem extending his disguise as a workman to include a formal engagement with Charles Augustus Milverton's housemaid because he "wanted information" (Conan Doyle, "The Adventure of Charles" 576).

Some contemporary writers have focused on the close friendship between Watson and Holmes as fodder for speculation about Holmes's sexual orientation. However, "nineteenth-century English culture exalted male friendship particularly and ... allowed it a language of intimacy and range of emotion we now think 'proper' only for relationships between heterosexual or homosexual lovers" (Payne 92). The closest current model of such male friendship would be the non-romantic bromance, a term that originated in the twenty-first century ("Bromance").

Holmes's frequent use of disguise has also facilitated questions about his orientation; he does not restrict his costume to male characters. In "The Adventure of the Mazarin Stone," Holmes is so well disguised as an "old woman" that he fools Billy, the pageboy for the Baker house (Conan Doyle 1012–3). The cross-dressing theme in the Holmes canon is subject to multiple interpretations. Regarding "A Scandal," Fernald (2008) notes that "in the highly masculine world of Sherlock Holmes, both characters in the story cross-dress: while Holmes disguises himself as a clergyman (a profession in which men regularly wear long, dress-like robes), Adler dresses as a man" (835). Fernald also suggests that one interpretation is that "this mutual cross-dressing hints at a more playful inter-penetration of spheres, a flirtation perhaps" (835). Another possibility is that "the powerful combination of ... male-female elements render Adler even more complex and incomprehensible to Holmes" (Krumm 195). Cross-dressing should serve the same primary purpose for Holmes, which is to become "that which is mistaken, misread, overlooked" (Garber 187) as he goes about his investigations.

Contributing to the seemingly conflicted gender role representation in the canon is the fact that "Conan Doyle indisputably aligns Holmes with manliness by linking his character to science, practical application, exact knowledge, logic and system, all elements gendered masculine in the nineteenth century" (Kestner 29). If masculinity is so defined, then femininity must be the opposite, allied to endeavors identified with Adler: the arts, including the theatre and music. However, this distinction would seem to be blurry, since Holmes's own serious interest in the arts, specifically music, manifests itself in his "remarkable" playing of the violin (Conan Doyle, "A Study in Scarlet" 22) and his appreciation of professional performances of the violin (Conan Doyle, "The Red-Headed League" 184) and of the music of Wagner (Conan Doyle, "The Adventure of the Red Circle" 901). But the ideas of Fernal and Kestner can be merged, if one considers the masculinity/science and femininity/arts characteristics are a more figurative way for Holmes and Adler to be cross-dressed.

One explanation for the gender role flexibility that often accompanies Adler's appearance in contemporary adaptations can be found in Atkinson's assessment that Holmes must maintain a sexual purity (abstinence) to retain power, which has a long tradition in male norms (49). Thus, the tension of simultaneously maintaining a heterosexual identity for Holmes (who crossdresses in his practice), acknowledging Holmes's appreciation of the heterosexual appeal of "*the* woman" who is equal to men (and assumes their guise), accepting the closeness of Holmes's long-term relationship with a male partner who is the heterosexual "middle-class British Victorian male professional" (Erisman 177), and sustaining Holmes's power through purity leads to seemingly mixed signals in a nineteenth-century setting as well as in contemporary circumstances. However, one reconciliation of the conflicted signals is found in Payne's assertion that Holmes can be presented as celibate but he cannot be "sexless," because "that implies impotence or the flaccid malevolence of the eunuch" (114). Celibacy, as opposed to asexuality, allows him total focus on his very serious calling (114).

Adler in the Cases of Three Adaptations

The presentation of Adler as Holmes's "amatory" interest who reinforces his heterosexuality and his cognitive superiority while simultaneously posing a threat to Holmes's very identity are overt in three contemporary, very popular, and critically acclaimed cinema and television adaptations. These include the two Guy Ritchie directed movies set in Victorian England (*Sherlock Holmes* in 2009 and *Sherlock Holmes: A Game of Shadows* in 2011); the second and third seasons, which aired in Britain in 2012 and 2014, of the BBC's *Sherlock* television series (with a contemporary young Sherlock Holmes); and CBS's *Elementary* series, which began in fall 2012 (with Holmes relocated to contemporary New York). All three productions' popularity has spurred either their continuation or interest in continuation. There have been hints of a third *Sherlock Holmes* movie to be directed by Ritchie ("Jude"), shooting is scheduled in 2015 for a fourth series of the BBC *Sherlock*, and *Elementary* returned for a third year of broadcast in 2014.

All three productions have long lists of impressive recognitions.[2] Such acclaim emphasizes the breadth of critical and popular acceptance of these present-day accounts, presumably encompassing their characterizations, including that of Adler.

Before the Three Cases: The Many Returns of Irene Adler

These three highly successful productions continue a decades-long pattern of constructing Adler's primary role as a love interest for Holmes. An exception is Carole Nelson Douglas' late twentieth/early twenty-first century mystery book series about Adler, who is a detective in her own right. The series was well-received and continues to be reprinted. The first book, *Good Night Mr. Holmes* (1990), received a *Romantic Times* Award for Best Historical Mystery and appeared on the 1991 *New York Times* Notable Book list. In Douglas' series, Adler is perhaps most notable for not being Holmes's romantic focus. Instead, this Adler is married to Godfrey Norton (*Good Night*), the lawyer whom she wed in the Conan Doyle story. But this canonical adherence is not the norm for Adler's reappearances.

One variation of Adler's inclusion in non-canonical storylines is that of Adler surrogates thinly disguised with the veneer of other identities, who become romantic interests for Holmes. However, even camouflaged, these pseudo–Adlers are easily recognizable because of their shared features hearkening back to the original Adler. They are at the very least "non-traditional" women if not actual "adventuresses," will have connection with acting, on or off the stage, and will ignore legalities. This type of reincarnation occurred even in nineteenth-century endeavors such as William Gillette and Conan Doyle's 1899 play, *Sherlock Holmes* (Cullen). The production was popular enough that Gillette, who played Holmes, appeared in multiple revivals of it for thirty-five years (Cullen 16). In the play, Adler's character is recast as Alice Faulkner, held captive by blackmailers who use force and starvation to elicit from her the combination of a safe holding the evidence that would embarrass the cad who misused her sister, now deceased. Faulkner has retained the items because she wants "to get even" (Conan Doyle and Gillette) with the nobleman, and she remains resolved to do so through most of the play. Moriarty becomes involved in the case, and by the play's end, when Faulkner rushes into his trap to warn Holmes, she is bound and gagged by the villains. Holmes then saves her. Later, Holmes agitatedly confesses to Watson about his feelings for Faulkner and tells Watson that this will be his last case. Romantic entanglement with "*the* woman" is ending his career. The play ends with Faulkner and Holmes in an embrace. Frequently quoted is Conan Doyle's reaction to Gillette's proposal to incorporate this non-canonical romance in the play: "You may marry him, murder him, or do anything you like to him" (Sir). While Conan Doyle's flippancy might be attributed to his primary interest in the project being economic (Sir), the conjunction of marriage/romance and murder/death/ending has been a persistent thread in adaptations of the Adler character.

There are numerous other, more recent examples of the disguised Adler's casting as the focus of Holmes's affections in print and productions. One is the 1970 movie *The Private Life of Sherlock Holmes*, which was nominated for a 1971 Edgar Award for Best Picture from the Mystery Writers of America and for a 1971 Writers Guild of America award for Best Comedy Written Directly for the Screen. In it Holmes is initially bested by a beautiful client, Gabrielle Valladon, who is eventually discovered to be a German spy in search of military secrets. In addition to her alias, Valladon uses her physical presentation as an amnesiac woman to disguise her identity. Thus Holmes makes deductions from her clothing, her shoes, and her wedding ring. Valladon provides Holmes with further clues in her guise as a nude sleepwalker who mistakes him for her husband. He uses her answers to his questions as well as transferred ink on her palm to follow the clues. Her body is an important part of her disguise, a device that will be used in later adaptations.

It has been suggested that the film is an exploration of romantic attraction between Holmes and Watson (Morgan; Professorfangirl; Sherlock Holmes Society) and presents what has been described as a "wonderfully ambiguous Holmes" (Gunn 99). For instance, Watson has begun to wonder about Holmes' orientation, but Holmes avoids answering Watson's questions about the topic. Also, Holmes has no qualms about suggesting that he and Watson are a couple, in order to avoid the awkwardness of a proposition from a Russian ballerina. However, the Holmes/Valladon relationship apparently serves to emphasize that Holmes is not gay. Holmes's heterosexuality is emphasized when he reveals to Valladon that he was engaged (but his fiancée died) and also by his obvious emotional investment in Valladon's future. Ultimately Holmes deduces the intricacies of the plot, including Valladon's duplicity, but he still arranges for her to be returned home. At the movie's conclusion, he is very disturbed when he learns that her resumption of espionage results in her death. Upon hearing of Valladon's execution in Japan, he returns to his use of cocaine. In this movie, as in other productions, both the life and the death of "*the* woman" are chaotic intrusions in the career of The Great Detective. This was certainly not the case with his canonical encounter with Adler.

The plotline in *The Private Life of Sherlock Holmes* that requires a surrogate Adler to be a romantic diversion for the cerebral Holmes is also found in the 1976 movie *The Seven Percent Solution*. It was based on the 1974 book pastiche of the same title by Nicolas Meyer, who penned the script, and it received two Oscar nominations and was recognized by the National Board of Review as one of the top ten films of 1976. The movie provided Holmes with a romantic interest, Lola Devereaux, who is a beautiful actress and a recovering addict. Her primary role in the movie is as a kidnap victim whose plight will spur a depressed Holmes to return to detection. She then will join him in a hiatus from his work. This liaison was not an outcome in Meyer's book but was presumably introduced to appeal to big screen audiences. Once again, an Adler reincarnation is the incentive to encourage Holmes to leave his career, though presumably temporarily.

Adler has also appeared repeatedly in her own original identity and name but still relegated to being a romantic partner for Holmes. The 1965 Broadway musical, *Baker Street,* received four Tony Award nominations and garnered one for scenic design. It incorporated plot elements and the character of Adler from "A Scandal." Adler is an actress who has incriminating letters from an admirer, a Palace Coldstream Guard. The captain's dilemma is actually part of larger nefarious scheme orchestrated by Moriarty. Holmes initially believes that Adler is part of Moriarty's plans, but after he realizes she is not, he spends the rest of the musical resisting her overtures, declaring (singing) about his dilemma:

> I have waited in vain
> For someone to explain
> What love conceivably can offer
> The cerebral type of man [Coopersmith 63].

By the conclusion of the play this "cerebral type of man" succumbs to emotion, following Adler to America. Holmes is accepting her offer of romance: "I could have given you an adventure beyond your wildest dreams.

In feelings you have never known before" (Coopersmith 116). Presumably this will be a permanent alliance and defection from crime solving: Adler's charms have seduced Holmes away from being The Master Detective.

There is also a pattern of having the Holmes/Adler relationship culminate in a child (a son), which means Adler (her body) is enlisted to ensure a multi-generational Holmes legacy, after which Holmes resumes an uninterrupted life. For instance, in 1969, noted Sherlockian Baring-Gould's monographic "biography" of fictional New York detective, Nero Wolfe (who first appeared in 1934), postulated that he was the offspring of Holmes and Adler (*Nero Wolfe of West Thirty-fifth Street*).

The 1976 made-for-television movie *Sherlock Holmes in New York* is another example that uses the theme of a multi-generational Holmes legacy, which requires Adler to be the matriarch. It was nominated for a 1977 Mystery Writers of America Edgar Award for Best Television Feature or Miniseries. The movie reunites Holmes and the actress Adler in New York. Adler's son, Scott (Holmes's son), has been kidnapped by the villainous Moriarty as part of a plot to wreak vengeance on Holmes and also to (apparently) steal the world's gold reserves. Once again, Adler, in her role as inamorata, is the weak link that places Holmes at risk of being eliminated as a viable antagonist for evildoers. At the finale, in spite of Adler's suggestion that he linger, Holmes returns the next day to London, citing "so many things in London that require my attention" and the siren song of the "unknown mystery, the unknown peril." As he and Watson depart, he responds to Watson's suggestion that there is not much appealing about New York, with "Perhaps not." And with a melancholy look at the pictures of Adler and Scott in his watch, he closes it. There is no place for them in the daily life of a Consulting Detective.

There is also no place for a child and his mother in Laurie King's contemporary, ongoing book series about Holmes's female detective protégé, Mary Russell. The series began in 1994 with *The Beekeeper's Apprentice,* and titles in it have appeared on the *New York Times* Best Seller Lists, and one (*A Monstrous Regiment of Women*) received a 1996 award for literary excellence in mystery from the Nero Wolfe Society. In the series, Russell ultimately becomes Holmes's wife and detective partner, but the series also has a multi-book thread about Holmes's affair with Adler during his three-year hiatus from London and detection. And, the relationship produces a son. While this series offers the singular approach of romantically partnering Holmes with a female (wife) whose own detective skills equal his talent, that woman is not Adler. "The only woman he had allowed himself to love had been as jealous of her independence as he: Irene Adler had loved him for a time and then sent him away" (*A Monstrous* 267). Adler also keeps secret the existence of their son so that Holmes will not be "distracted" (*The Language of Bees* 23); that is, "she had not forced him to re-shape his life, his career, around a child" (25). She makes a major sacrifice to avoid inconveniencing Holmes's career, including depriving her son of a father with whom he does not reconcile until adulthood. This sacrifice is in marked contrast to the self-preservation instincts of the canonical Adler. Because of the affair with Adler, Holmes spends the next three decades without romantic entanglements. This subsequent avoidance of relationship could be construed as a negative consequence of Holmes's relationship with Adler, since Watson believes Holmes is languishing to the point of death at the time that he meets Russell, but he immediately begins to thrive in this new Pygmalion relationship (*The Beekeeper's* 37).

A 2001 Hallmark Channel presentation of *The Royal Scandal* (one of a four episode Canadian television movie series) combined "A Scandal in Bohemia" with "The Adventure of the Bruce-Partington Plans" (Conan Doyle, 1930). The production was nominated for a 2002 Canadian Society of Cinematographers Award for Best Cinematography in a TV Drama and also for a 2002 Gemini (Academy of Canadian Cinema & Television) Award for Best Costume Design.

This presentation is unique in having the Holmes/Adler romance occur prior to the events of the storyline. That past history includes the familiar elements of Adler's non-canonical character: seductive, deceptive, criminal. As a talented opera singer, she entices Holmes to a performance, where she entrances him with, as he says, "that face, that voice." He confesses that after he had "fallen completely and hopelessly under Miss Adler's spell," she tricks him into helping her to abscond with her patroness's large diamond. She subsequently defrauds her collaborator in the caper. Little wonder that this Holmes characterizes Adler as the "foremost consulting criminal" (*The Royal*). However, years later, Adler possesses an embarrassing photograph of herself and the future German Kaiser, and Holmes seeks to retrieve it for his client. Eventually, he will save Adler from one of the Prince's murdering henchmen, whereupon Holmes learns that her deception is multi-faceted. She is actually a double agent spying for Britain, and while that knowledge does not destroy his career, it makes a serious dent in his relationship with his brother Mycroft, Chief of Intelligence for the country.

At the end, after Adler leaves, Holmes is left staring sadly at her photograph, reminiscent of the last scene in *Sherlock Holmes in New York*. If she stayed, this "exquisite" woman who had "the most profound effect" (*The Royal*) on Holmes would import what Hall (1991) terms the "sensational" into Holmes's "rational world" (302). The sensational is what "make his cases exciting," but it is also what Holmes as detective brings under control (Hall 302). An alliance of the sensational and the rational would create too much tension for continued co-existence.

The Adventures of the Woman Today

The three contemporary and currently ongoing media series productions of Ritchie's *Sherlock Holmes* movies, the BBC's *Sherlock* television series, and the CBS television series of *Elementary* continue the long tradition of diminishing Adler's original role in the nineteenth-century story of "A Scandal." She is no longer "*the* woman" who can best Holmes at his own detective game and thrive independently in the life of her choice, while also gaining Holmes's admiration for her skills and leaving him philosophical about his defeat even as he proceeds to whatever the next case might be.

It is true that initially all three of these twenty-first century Adlers are depictions of beautiful, intelligent, independent women capable of self-preservation and who flaunt society's social norms and its law. However, unlike the original Adler, they are actual criminals, which is all the more justification for the Holmes characters to best them. Their introductions in these storylines are as equals for Holmes's cognitive and physical exceptionalism. But, they rapidly become foils to affirm Holmes's sexuality, or more specifically, his heterosexuality, and to reinforce his superiority of deductive (cognitive) powers compared to their own. At the same time, romantic involvement with Adler is depicted as being to Holmes's disadvantage, threatening his well-being and his career, and it also turns out badly for Adler. Adler's presence in Holmes's life will serve to weaken/emasculate him, since his identity is The Master Detective, who has asserted that "love is an emotional thing, and whatever is emotional is opposed to that true cold reason which I place above all things" (Conan Doyle, "The Sign of Four" 157). And, as part of their threat to Holmes, the Adlers' flexibility in self-presentation is represented as deception, something to be condemned rather than applauded as clever. However, the canonical Adler's disguise in "A Scandal" was viewed in that plot as artful, as Holmes' own canonical and non-canonical impersonations are universally seen as canny. Also, as the roles of the various Adlers in the new narratives rapidly degenerate to victims who need Holmes to literally rescue them, they are depicted as pawns used by Holmes's perpetual nemesis, Moriarty, to destroy the detective (although this aspect does have an interesting twist in *Elementary*).

Director Ritchie's two-movie franchise of Sherlock Holmes is set in the Victorian time period of the Conan Doyle stories. The first movie, *Sherlock Holmes* (2009), introduces Adler as a self-confident thief, and now without, as she says, her "boring and jealous" husband. She visits Holmes as a client, wanting him to find a missing man. Adler and Holmes obviously have a previous romantic history. He has her framed picture on a table; she mentions that her hotel gave her "our old room." And, Watson sketches that past relationship when he asks Holmes, "Why is the only woman you've ever cared about is a world-class criminal? Are you a masochist?" Watson reminds Holmes, "She's the only adversary who ever outsmarted you—twice. Made a proper idiot out of you." Here the canonical Adler's keen sense of justice that guides her circumvention of legalities is reduced to "criminal" activity. And there's an implicit challenge to Holmes in Watson's description, which could be phrased as "Are you going to continue letting this lawbreaking woman make a proper idiot out of you again?" In order to avoid this outcome, Holmes must defeat Adler.

In this adaptation Adler and Holmes spar in an odd courtship ritual in attempting to outwit each other. She catches him trying to break into her hotel room, invites him in, parades around nude and then in a dressing gown, drugs him, kisses him passionately, and leaves him handcuffed, nude, to the bed. Her overt sexuality is a weapon used with the intent and result of disorienting Holmes and making him appear foolish, an emasculating. This Adler uses her female nudity as a disguise/deception to best Holmes, rather than assuming the canonical Adler's disguise as a young man to accomplish the same goal.

Adler is actually working for Moriarty, whom she fears, and which Holmes realizes. Holmes warns Adler of the danger that faces her and attempts to get her to leave the situation or to go into protective custody, which she ignores since apparently she isn't really all that astute.

She initially appears self-sufficient. For example, she uses a weighted crop and a knife to thwart two men who accost her in an alley. Holmes, who is secretly following her, declares, "That's the Irene I knew." Yet, further along in the plot, Holmes and Watson rescue a chained and gagged Adler from a giant sawblade, thus saving this endangered woman in a melodramatic scene reminiscent of the silent movie series, *The Perils of Pauline*. Because the villain can hold Adler hostage or threaten her, she is also the vulnerability (emotional attachment) used to render Holmes ineffective as a crime fighter. In the background of the sawblade scene, the second villain in the movie, Blackwood, announces, "She followed you here, Holmes. You led your lamb to slaughter."

In the end of the movie, Blackwood holds Adler at sword point on the end of a bridge, to thwart Holmes's retrieval of what is supposed to be a highly dangerous machine. This scene evokes a common trope in superhero adventures: the protagonist declares that he eschews romance because a woman would be at potential risk from his enemies, thereby thwarting his mission to do good.

As Holmes's affection for Adler puts him at risk, Adler's feelings for Holmes also endanger her. When Adler attempts to leave Moriarty's employment, he refuses, telling her, "Your job was to manipulate Holmes's feelings for you, not succumb to them." He demands that she finish her job "or the next dead body will be Sherlock Holmes." Thus he is exploiting what has become a weakness for Adler, her emotions. Her adroit intelligence will not trump that vulnerability. In contrast, the canonical Adler's emotional attachment to her husband was the spur for her adept besting of both Holmes and the King.

In the end of the movie, after rescuing her, Holmes handcuffs Adler, who tells him about Moriarty and also tells him "everyone has a weak spot, and he found mine." He leaves her with the key to the handcuff, and she declares, "You'll miss me Sherlock," and he responds, "Sadly, yes," and leaves her with a chaste kiss. The handcuffing seems a payback for Adler's having handcuffed him earlier in the movie and demonstrates that he is now in control of her body. Holmes has defeated Adler on multiple levels, including wreaking havoc in her collaboration with Moriarty and proving that he is cleverer than she is. Holmes establishes that he is the one with the power to save her when she is incapable of that. He imprisons her body but leaves her with the key to escape, demonstrating his power to free or not free her. He can also easily disregard the weakness of emotional attachment to her, including resisting her sexuality, and thus preserve his role as the totally focused detective who does not need women, at least not this woman.

In the beginning of second movie, *A Game of Shadows* (2011), Adler is once again thwarted by Holmes in a mission to retrieve a package for Moriarty. She then recovers it with the assistance of several burly assistants. When she delivers a payoff package from Moriarty, Holmes shows up to disrupt this transaction, greeting Adler with what is now his signature chaste kiss. She attempts to retrieve an evidential letter from him by planting one of her trademark passionate kisses on him, but he is not tricked. Because she does not have the letter, Moriarty tells Adler, "It's been apparent to me for some time that you had succumbed to your feelings for him." For that betrayal, Moriarty poisons her with a biochemical agent and then leaves with her blood stained handkerchief. She has paid the ultimate price for indulging her emotions. The handkerchief evidence of her demise is shown to Holmes by Moriarty, who tells him that her death is "damage of a collateral nature" and declares, "Two gentlemen find themselves at cross purposes, a young woman torn between them." She was simply a pawn, "an object of desire in need of protection" (Hennessy and Mohan 401, 1994) whom Holmes failed to protect. Then Moriarty asks Holmes if he wants to "play this game." Holmes leaves with the handkerchief and later tosses it overboard the ship on which he's traveling—so much for Adler as Holmes continues the game. Adler loses her life both because she has not been savvy enough to thwart Holmes and to anticipate Moriarty's reactions and because of her weakness, her emotional connection to Holmes. In turn, his emotional weakness for her threatens to lose him his profession and his life. Adler's presence may verify Holmes's heterosexuality, but her continued presence would threaten his identity as the unequaled detective.

Season two of the BBC's *Sherlock* includes the episode "A Scandal in Belgravia," a variation of "A Scandal in Bohemia" (Conan Doyle). As in the canonical "A Scandal" (Conan Doyle), Adler initially appears as the adversary for Holmes's royal client. Then, she becomes a client for Holmes, but she is actually working with Moriarty, and her motivation is profit. In her first meeting with Holmes, who seeks to retrieve information embarrassing to the royal family, this professional dominatrix (who will tell Watson that she is gay) appears in the nude, or what she calls her "battle dress." In preparing his outfit for the meeting, Holmes refers to selecting the "right armor," which is the garb of a clergyman. Each is attempting to assume camouflage that will trick the other. The surprise is that Adler is using the guise of her unclothed body to gain advantage, since Holmes is unable to deduce anything about her from her appearance. As with the first Ritchie film (*Sherlock Holmes*), this Adler is also using female nudity as disguise to defeat Holmes, rather than adopting the male garb of the canonical Adler. However, Holmes is not so misled that he fails to note that her measurements, which will later prove to be the combination to her wall safe.

The Adler/Holmes relationship of this episode continues as cell phone texts, most of which are from Adler. Watson describes this interchange as "flirting." However, per Kestner's premise that the canonical Holmes had "the qualities gendered masculine ... science, reason, system and principle" (28), Adler's use of technology and of a secret system (password) to hide her secrets disguise her as masculine, thus thwarting Holmes's "powers of observation" since those will "fail when it comes to meeting Adler on his own masculine ground when she is cross-dressed" (Hoffman 84).

In this series, Holmes's sexual orientation is a topic for on-going speculation. In the first episode of season one, "A Study in Pink," Watson attempts to determine Holmes's relationship status, asking if he has a girlfriend or boyfriend. Holmes's response is that "I consider myself married to my work." In the season two episode "A Scandal in Belgravia" Watson asks Mrs. Hudson, the landlady, if Holmes "ever had a girlfriend, boyfriend—a relationship—ever?" She does not know. In this same episode, Holmes's brother Mycroft says to him, regarding Adler's profession of dominatrix, "Don't be alarmed. It's to do with sex." Holmes snaps, "Sex doesn't alarm me." Mycroft responds, "How would you know?" Along the same lines, Adler informs the Holmes brothers that Moriarty's nickname for Holmes is "the virgin." Per Atkinson (49), Holmes maintains power with his abstinence, his distance from Adler. But he is not immune to heterosexual attraction. When Adler reappears, supposedly seeking help for an unbreakable code, Sherlock was, as his brother Mycroft will eventually tell him, "One lonely naïve man desperate to show off. And a woman clever enough to make him feel special." And thus for Adler Holmes has broken the key to vital information belonging to his own government.

But how deeply is he attracted to Adler? When Adler had led Holmes to believe that she is dead, Watson reports Holmes's reactions as "He's writing sad music, doesn't eat, barely talks.... I'd say he was heartbroken. But, he's Sherlock. He does all that anyway." And, in the final confrontation with Adler, Holmes chides her for her "sentiment," which he defines as "a chemical defect found in the losing side." He says that "I imagine that John Watson thinks that love is a mystery to me. But the chemistry is incredibly simple and very destructive." Holmes reveals that the code to access Adler's own cell phone's critical information is based on her attraction to him. As he tells her, this was a mistake; she should have used a non-personal code. Her merging of the male/cerebral/technological disguise of her information with the female/emotional/personal code defeats her. He knows her interest in him is genuine since when she had been flirting with him in person, he was secretly taking her pulse and observing the dilation of her pupils. Even in a potentially romantically charged moment, Holmes remains the aloof intellectual. In contrast, Adler's body, once used as disguise, has now betrayed her. Adler tells Holmes, "I was just playing the game." Holmes responds, "I know. And this is just losing." Her loss is his triumph, and he revels in it.

Holmes tells Mycroft to either lock Adler up or let her go, since she is unlikely to survive without her store of compromising information. She asks Holmes, "Are you expecting me to beg?" and he responds, "Yes." She then says, "Please. You're right." His reply is along the lines of "Sorry." This modern Holmes bests Adler and saves his reputation and career. She, on the other hand, has lost the information that would have generated a fortune and protected her as well—a significant difference from the canonical Adler's successful retention of valuable information (the contested photograph) that would give her protection from the King.

However, in spite of Holmes thwarting Adler, the episode's ending shows Holmes dramatically saving a bound Adler from beheading by terrorists in Karachi, and it is quite noticeable that he wields a very large scimitar while doing so. Douglas has taken note of the irony of the threat of beheading ("castration-like threat") for "*the* woman" who, until the episode's denouement, was Holmes's intellectual equal ("Why" 27). Adler is reduced to being a convenience for demonstrating Holmes's truly astounding superiority. After all, his own brother has asserted to Watson that the only person who could possibly have saved her is Holmes, who could not have been there—but he was, because of course he is exceptional.

The last scene of Holmes smiling and chuckling as he contemplates the memento of Adler's cell phone before he places it in a drawer, while repeatedly saying "*the* woman," suggests possible conclusions to this convoluted relationship. Perhaps there was more to this encounter post–Karachi. Perhaps by saving her Holmes has now finished with the Adler episode and is back to his game and wins yet again. Regardless, it is Holmes whose intellectual prowess has proven superior, with Adler being defeated because she allowed emotion and her body to trump her intellect. Holmes, on the other hand, was able to maintain focus even during emotionally charged moments, including the pulse-taking incident. And, per Kestner's masculinity manifested as science and practical application (29), by retaining the technology of her now useless cell phone, Holmes has, in one sense, retained the symbolic emasculation of Adler, paralleling Douglas' reading of the potential beheading/castration threat to Adler in Karachi (27).

Adler appears very briefly in the third season of the *Sherlock* series, but literally as memories. In the first episode, "The Empty Hearse," Holmes returns from his presumed death after a two-year hiatus. In the second episode, "The Sign of Three," Holmes uses his mind palace as he grapples to make sense of many disparate clues, including who knew Watson's middle name. Holmes recollects, "And *the* woman, she knew." But he adds, "God knows where she is." At this point, a nude Adler appears in his memory and strokes his face, to which Holmes declares, "Out of my head. I am busy!" Adler, as a naked woman making overtures, is a distraction who will interfere with

Holmes' detection, but he easily dismisses her. Her reduction to an "amatory" role is reiterated in the third episode, "His Last Vow," when Holmes once again reverts to his mind palace. In his mind palace instances in episode two, Holmes is coached through deductions by his brilliant brother, Mycroft. In the third episode, Holmes retreats to his mind palace in an instance of near death. There he is coached through survival by Mycroft, by Molly Hooper, the morgue lab assistant who helped him fake his death, and by Philip Anderson, formerly with the police forensics and antagonistic to Holmes but now a Sherlock fanboy. Holmes also sees Moriarty, who reminds him that Holmes' death would mean "Mrs. Hudson will cry. And Mummy and Daddy will cry. And *the* woman will cry. And John will cry." Thus, Adler appears in Holmes' mind palace as potential seductress and as someone with an emotional connection to Holmes; she does not appear as someone who can assist Holmes in his cerebral endeavors and work.

This theme of Adler as the romantic interest who serves to both introduce a weakness for Holmes that threatens his career and to demonstrate his superiority reappears in CBS's *Elementary* series. Recovering addict Holmes is relocated to contemporary New York, where most of the mysteries he solves are in his new role as an unpaid consultant to the New York City Police Department (NYPD). In another example of the gender role flexibility that characterizes other recent Holmes sagas, Dr. Watson is portrayed by a woman. And, in this rendition, Holmes is training Watson to be his detective partner. As was done with King's Russell character, Holmes uses an apprenticeship to create the intellectual equal that he wants, in contrast to the parallel talent already inherent in the independent Adler characters. King's and *Elementary*'s Holmes characters have new female partners who are women "owing" their success to his mentorship. In contrast, these series' contemporary Adlers do not start the relationship with him as subordinates, but they end as such. As with the King book series, *Elementary*'s Holmes eventually has a partner whose cleverness rivals his detection skills, but it is not Adler, who is once again merely the distracting "amatory" interest.

The *Elementary* series has a multi-episode thread focused on Adler. In the "M" episode, Watson has discovered that there was a romantic interest named Irene in Holmes's past. Holmes reveals to Watson details about his relationships with Adler, who was a talented artist, and with the serial killer known as M. Watson grasps that "M killed her," and Holmes continues, "I have no intention of capturing M. I have every intention of torturing and murdering him." So, his entanglement with Adler has now reduced Holmes to extreme criminal action. Holmes continues explaining the depth of his emotional involvement with Adler: "Suffice it to say I was quite smitten. Up to that point in my life, I'd found most women quite boring ... Irene was different." Her murder/loss had serious consequences for his well-being and career since "prior to her murder, my drug use had been recreational.... After Irene, well I lost control. I used various stimulants as I tried to help the authorities identify M.... When the trail finally went cold, I turned to opiates." This series' Holmes has an active sex life before and after the loss of Adler. However, in these encounters he is engaged in physical passion but not emotional passion that might cloud his intellect, so in that sense he adheres to Atkinson's requirement of purity for power, since "mind holds complete sway over matter for Holmes" (49). *Elementary's* Holmes emphasizes his boundaries between emotional and cerebral, even with sexuality, when he declares to Watson: "You're well aware that I view sex as an exercise. As do the women I entertain" ("Corpse de Ballet"). No emotional entanglements need apply.

Thus Adler, because of Holmes's emotional involvement with her, is responsible for Holmes's potential total physical self-destruction, which includes institutionalization for addiction and which wrecked his former stellar career in Britain. His seeking to avenge her demise, by capturing and torturing M in the episode of that name, leads to a major career setback in the U.S. when Lestrade severs Holmes's consultancy with the NYPD.

The flexibility of gender roles in this series is manifested in Adler's appearance in the series as initially a hostage of Moriarty ("Risk," "The Woman"), followed by the shocker that she is Jamie Moriarty ("The Woman," "Heroine"). Adler, as Moriarty, is a criminal mastermind. She uses male disguise but is not garbed in it. Her male disguise is her persona as the villain, Moriarty, who is blamed first for her death and then her abduction. Her supposed murder was faked because she did not want to kill Holmes (an emotional decision), even though his detective work was interfering with her enterprises ("Heroine"). It was sufficient for him to be disabled as an addict. She returns as an abductee because she has learned of his recovery. As Holmes says, "We both made a mistake. We fell in love" ("Heroine"). Holmes's mistake resulted in time lost in the throes of addiction and in the destruction of his original career. But, his detection skills trump Adler's schemes when he deduces that the surgical change in a birthmark on her shoulder means that she has been lying about Moriarty. Her body has once again betrayed Adler. Adler/Moriarty's mistake sends her to prison, the direct consequence of her "gendered masculine" foray into the "exact knowledge, logic and system" (Kestner 29) required to manage an international criminal enterprise. In prison, she spends her time painting, which could be considered gendered feminine activity. Holmes resumes his career and his relationship with the NYPD and his collaboration with Watson, the intellectual equal that he has cultivated.

Even after Adler/Moriarty is in prison, her influence continues to negatively impact Holmes. In the episode "Ancient History," Holmes tells a new widow, "When the one that you love is revealed to have a dark heart ... well, it's excruciating." He also has maintained a correspondence with Adler/Moriarty, and at the end of one second season episode ("We"), he is reading a letter from her, and he is not smiling. His power will be at risk as long as he has any emotional tie to this woman who is a "sensation," a disruption.

Adler/Moriarty and Holmes reunite in the second season episode of "The Diabolical Kind." Holmes has maintained a correspondence with Adler, and Watson tells him that he still has feelings for her, which he initially denies but later admits, also saying that he hoped she could change. A tense collaboration between Adler and Holmes is forced when a young girl is kidnapped, and then it is ultimately revealed that the child is Adler's (but not Holmes') daughter. In the finale, a gravely wounded Adler admits to him that she has refrained from killing her prison guard because of Holmes' influence, because she cares what he thinks of her actions. Holmes carries her outside the building to a waiting ambulance; he has saved her not only physically, but to a certain extent, spiritually. In the end of this episode, he is still keeping Adler's letters, but since she is imprisoned, she is, conveniently for Holmes, out of his way.

Conclusion

The canonical Adler was a woman of purpose who used her intelligence and talents to shape the life that she wanted, whatever others might think. But the passage of time has not preserved those attributes. Instead, Adler has been repeatedly cast as a convenient romantic interest for Holmes, and using Douglas' description, has been both sexualized and criminalized in the process (26). Moving into the second decade of the twenty-first century, the widely seen continuing sagas of Holmes in Ritchie's Sherlock Holmes movies, the BBC *Sherlock* and CBS television's *Elementary* series follow a long-standing convention of not getting Irene Adler "right," per Douglas' phrasing (26).

The Adlers of all three franchises and series share more with each other than they do with the canonical Adler. As with the canonical Adler, all three successors are beautiful, intelligent, and talented. But there the resemblance ends. These contemporary Adlers are active lawbreakers, and two of them are allied with Holmes's nemesis, Moriarty, while the third is Moriarty. Unlike the canonical Adler, the Ritchie and CBS Adlers have an overt romantic interest in Holmes. The BBC Adler says she is gay, but she has a bisexual history, and the plot conveys the impression she is fascinated by Holmes (such as texting him in what seem to be her last minutes of life). Holmes's interest in the Ritchie and the CBS versions of Adler is both emotional and (hetero) sexual. For the BBC Adler, Holmes has enough emotional investment to be tricked by her faked death and by her need to have a code broken and finally to save her from beheading. All three Adlers use their bodies, rather than male disguise, to distract Holmes, but it is their bodies/emotions that betray them, so that Holmes, ever the intellectual, is ultimately not bested by any of these three Adlers. Holmes also demonstrates his (masculine) superiority by saving all three Adlers (repeatedly so for the BBC version) from physical or moral destruction (the latter for the CBS Adler). However, the presence of all three Adlers threatens Holmes's physical safety and/or career, so they are removed from active participation in all of these franchises/series. The Ritchie Adler is murdered, Holmes does not know where the BBC Adler is after her near-death in Karachi, and the CBS Adler is in prison.

From the nineteenth to the twenty-first century, adaptations of Holmes's adventures have retained the familiar attributes of his canonical characterization as The Master Detective. These include an extraordinary intellect, amazing powers of deduction, a talent for disguise, and an idiosyncratic sense of justice. However, his peer in these arenas, Irene Adler, has been translated by these three popular current media presentations from a Victorian woman of independence to a modern supporting act for headliner Holmes, rather than to a modern heroine deserving of her original portrayal.

Notes

    1. For example, the 2005 collection for juvenile audiences, *The Adventures of Sherlock Holmes*, retold by Chris Sasaki (Conan Doyle), omits all references to the canonical Adler as an "adventuress" who is of "dubious memory."

    2. The first *Sherlock Holmes* (2009) movie, directed by Ritchie, was nominated for two 2010 Oscars. In 2010, its Holmes, Robert Downey, Jr., won a Golden Globe and an Irish Film and Television Award. The film was nominated for eight different 2010 Academy of Science Fiction, Fantasy, and Horror Films Saturn Awards and received nominations for two *Empire* film magazine awards, receiving one.

    Ritchie's second *Sherlock Holmes* (2011) film received a 2010 ASCAP award from the American Society of Composers, Authors and Publishers. It was nominated for two 2012 Golden Trailer awards and won one. It was also nominated for a 2012 *Empire* film magazine Best Thriller Award and for two Academy of Science Fiction, Fantasy & Horror Film awards. It received three nominations for Fox television network's 2012 Teen Choice Awards (selected by popular vote).

The BBC's *Sherlock* show has accumulated more than fifty media awards and more than eighty nominations for its three series. These include four 2011 Primetime Emmy nominations, thirteen 2012 Primetime Emmy nominations, five 2014 Primetime Emmy nominations, and seven 2014 Primetime Emmy awards from the Academy of Television Arts & Sciences. It also received a 2013 Golden Globe nomination for Benedict Cumberbatch's Holmes. In 2011, the series received three BAFTA (British Academy of Film and Television Arts) awards and was nominated for four others. In 2012, it won four BAFTA TV awards and was nominated for two others. The series was also nominated in 2011 and 2012 for the BAFTA YouTube Audience Award, which is given by popular audience vote. In 2013 it received the Mystery Writers of America's Edgar Award for Best Television Episode, for "A Scandal in Belgravia," the episode that introduces Adler.

Per *TV Guide*, *Elementary* ranked fifteenth in the top twenty-five most watched shows of the 2012–2013 season, but it was ranked the highest among new series when it came to numbers of viewers (Schneider, 2013). In 2013, it was nominated for the Outstanding New Program of the Year award from the Television Critics Association. One episode was nominated for a 2013 Mystery Writers of America Edgar for Best Television Episode in a TV Series. The series received three 2013 nominations for Teen Choice Best Choice awards, and the series' Watson, Lucy Liu, received the award for Choice TV Actress: Action. It also received the 2013 President's Award from the Entertainment Industries Council, which acknowledges authenticity in entertainment industry portrayals of mental illness and substance abuse and recovery. In 2014, *Elementary* received two Emmy nominations and also received a GLAAD Media Award from the Gay & Lesbian Alliance Against Defamation.

Works Cited

"Ancient History." *Elementary: The Second Season*. Perf. Jonny Lee Miller and Lucy Liu. Paramount, 2014. DVD.
Atkinson, Michael. *The Secret Marriage of Sherlock Holmes and Other Eccentric Readings*. Ann Arbor: University of Michigan Press, 1996. Print.
Baker Street. By Jerome Coopersmith. Dir. Harold Prince. Perf. Fritz Weaver, Inga Swenson, Raymond Jessel. Broadway Theater, New York. 16 February 1965. Performance.
Baring-Gould, William S. *The Annotated Sherlock Holmes*, Vol. 1. New York: Clarkson N. Potter, 1967. Print.
_____. *Nero Wolfe of West Thirty-fifth Street: the Life and Times of America's Largest Detective*. New York: Viking, 1969. Print.
"Bromance." *The Oxford English Dictionary*. Web. 14 Sept. 2014. http://www.oed.com.
Brough, James. *The Prince & The Lily*. New York: Coward, McCann & Geoghegan, 1975. Print.
Conan Doyle, Arthur. "The Adventure of Charles Augustus Milverton." *The Complete Sherlock Holmes*. Garden City, NY: Doubleday, 1930. 572–82. Print.
_____. "The Adventure of the Blue Carbuncle." *The Complete Sherlock Holmes*. Garden City, NY: Doubleday, 1930. 244–57. Print.
_____. "The Adventure of the Bruce-Partington Plans." *The Complete Sherlock Holmes*. Garden City, NY: Doubleday, 1930. 913–32. Print.
_____. "The Adventure of the Devil's Foot." *The Complete Sherlock Holmes*. Garden City, NY: Doubleday, 1930. 954–70. Print.
_____. "The Adventure of the Lion's Mane." *The Complete Sherlock Holmes*. Garden City, NY: Doubleday, 1930. 1083–95. Print.
_____. "The Adventure of the Mazarin Stone." *The Complete Sherlock Holmes*. Garden City, NY: Doubleday, 1930. 1012–22. Print.
_____. "The Adventure of the Red Circle." *The Complete Sherlock Holmes*. Garden City, NY: Doubleday, 1930. 901–913. Print.

____. *The Adventures of Sherlock Holmes*. Retold by Chris Sasaki. New York: Sterling, 2005. Print.
____. "The Boscombe Valley Mystery." *The Complete Sherlock Holmes*. Garden City, NY: Doubleday, 1930. 202–17. Print.
____. "The Five Orange Pips." *The Complete Sherlock Holmes*. Garden City, NY: Doubleday, 1930. 217–29. Print.
____. "The Red-Headed League." *The Complete Sherlock Holmes*. Garden City, NY: Doubleday, 1930. 176–90. Print.
____. "A Scandal in Bohemia." *The Complete Sherlock Holmes*. Garden City, NY: Doubleday, 1930. 161–175. Print.
____. "The Sign of Four." *The Complete Sherlock Holmes*. Garden City, NY: Doubleday, 1930. 89–158. Print.
____. "A Study in Scarlet." *The Complete Sherlock Holmes*. Garden City, NY: Doubleday, 1930. 15–86. Print.
____. "The Valley of Fear." *The Complete Sherlock Holmes*. Garden City, NY: Doubleday, 1930. 769–866. Print.
Conan Doyle, Arthur, and William Gillette. *Sherlock Holmes: A Drama in Four Acts*. The Diogenes Club, 1999. Web. 13 Nov. 2013. http://www.diogenes-club.com/sherlockplay.htm.
Coopersmith, Jerome. *Baker Street*. New York: Doubleday, 1966. Print.
"Corpse de Ballet." *Elementary: The Second Season*. Perf. Jonny Lee Miller and Lucy Liu. Paramount, 2014. DVD.
Cullen, Rosemary, and Don B. Wilmeth. *Plays by William Hooker Gillette*. Cambridge: Cambridge University Press, 1983. Print.
"The Diabolical Kind." *Elementary: The Second Season*. Perf. Jonny Lee Miller and Lucy Liu, Paramount, 2014. DVD.
Douglas, Carole Nelson. *Good Night, Mr. Holmes*. New York: Doherty, 1990. Print.
____. "Why Can't They Get Irene Adler Right?" *Mystery Scene* Summer 2013: 26–27. Print.
"The Empty Hearse." *Sherlock: Season Three*. Perf. Cumberbatch, Benedict, and Martin Freeman. BBC Worldwide, a Hartswood Films Production for BBC, 2014. DVD.
Erisman, Fred. "If Watson Were a Woman: Three (Re)visions of the Holmesian Ménage." *Clues* 22 (2001): 177–188. Print.
Fernald, Anne E. "The Domestic Side of Modernism." Rev. of *The Marriage Paradox: Modernist Novels and the Cultural Imperative to Marry*, by Davida Pines, and *Modernism and the Architecture of Modern Life*, by Victoria Rosner. *Modern Fiction Studies* 54 (2008): 827–36. Print.
Garber, Marjorie. *Vested Interests: Cross-Dressing & Cultural Anxiety*. New York: Routledge, 1992. Print.
Gunn, Drewey Wayne. *The Gay Male Sleuth in Print and Film: A History and Annotated Bibliography*. Lanham, MD: Scarecrow Press, 2005. Print.
Hall, Jasmine Yong. "Ordering the Sensational: Sherlock Holmes and the Female Gothic." *Studies in Short Fiction* 28 (1991): 295–303. Print.
Hennessy, Rosemary, and Rajeswari Mohan. "'The Speckled Band': The Construction of Woman in a Popular Text of Empire." *Sherlock Holmes: The Major Stories with Contemporary Critical Essays*. Arthur Conan Doyle. Ed. John A. Hodgson. Boston: Bedford, 1994. 389–401. Print.
"Heroine." *Elementary: The First Season*. Perf. Jonny Lee Miller and Lucy Liu. Paramount, 2013. DVD.
"His Last Vow." *Sherlock: Season Three*. Perf. Cumberbatch, Benedict, and Martin Freeman. BBC Worldwide, a Hartswood Films Production for BBC, 2014. DVD.
Hoffman, Megan. "Strategies of Drag in Laurie R. King's Mary Russell Series." *Murdering Miss Marple: Essays on Gender and Sexuality in the New Golden Age of Women's Crime Fiction*. Ed. Julie H. Kim. Jefferson, NC: McFarland, 2012. 81–100. Print.
"Jude Law Offers an Update on Guy Ritchie's 'Sherlock Holmes 3'." *Digital Spy*. Hearst Magazines, 4 Nov. 2013. Web. 25 Nov. 2013. http://www.digitalspy.com/movies/news/a527468/jude-law-offers-an-update-on-guy-ritchies-sherlock-holmes-3.html.
Kestner, Joseph A. *Sherlock's Men: Masculinity, Conan Doyle, and Cultural History*. Aldershot: Ashgate, 1997. Print.

King, Laurie R. *The Beekeeper's Apprentice, or on the Segregation of the Queen.* New York: St. Martin's, 1994. Print.
_____. *The Language of Bees.* New York: Bantam Books, 2009. Print.
_____. *A Monstrous Regiment of Women.* New York: Bantam Books, 1997. Print.
Krumm, Pascale. "'A Scandal in Bohemia' and Sherlock Holmes's Ultimate Mystery Solved." *English Literature in Transition* 39 (1996): 193–203. Print.
"Langtry, Lillie." *Oxford Dictionary of National Biography.* Web. 25 Nov. 2013.
"Lola Montez." *Oxford Dictionary of National Biography.* Web. 25 Nov. 2013.
"M." *Elementary: The First Season.* Perf. Jonny Lee Miller and Lucy Liu. Paramount, 2013. DVD.
Meyer, Nicholas. *The Seven-percent-solution, Being a Reprint from the Reminiscences of John H. Watson, M.D.* New York: Dutton, 1974. Print.
Morgan, Eleanor. "The Film that Changed My Life: Mark Gatiss." *The Observer* 6 Nov. 2010. Web. 29 Nov. 2013. http://www.theguardian.com/film/2010/nov/07/mark-gatiss-sherlock-holmes.
Payne, David S. *Myth and Modern Man in Sherlock Holmes: Sir Arthur Conan Doyle and the Uses of Nostalgia.* Bloomington, IN: Gaslight, 1992. Print.
The Private Life of Sherlock Holmes. Dir. Billy Wilder. Perf. Robert Stepehens, Colin Blakely, Geneviève Page. MGM, 2003. DVD.
Professorfangirl. "Holmesosexuality: On Mark Gatiss's Camp." *One Hell of a Steep Learning Curve: Because Every Pleasure Deserves to Be Taken Seriously,* 23 Sept. 2013. Web. 29 Nov. 2013. http://professorfangirl.tumblr.com/post/61772278860/mid0nz-holmesosexuality-on-mark-gatisss-camp.
Redmond, Christopher. *In Bed with Sherlock Holmes: Sexual Elements in Arthur Conan Doyle's Stories of The Great Detective.* Toronto: Simon & Pierre, 1984. Print.
"Risk Management." *Elementary: The First Season.* Perf. Jonny Lee Miller and Lucy Liu. Paramount, 2013. DVD.
Rocha, Mona, and James Rocha. "A Feminist Scandal in Holmes's Generalizations." *Sherlock Holmes and Philosophy: The Footprints of a Gigantic Mind.* Ed. Josef Steiff. Chicago: Open Court, 2011. 147–55. Print.
Rosenberg, Samuel. *Naked Is the Best Disguise.* Indianapolis: Bobbs-Merrill, 1974.
The Royal Scandal. Dir. Rodney Gibbons. Perf. Matt Frewer, Kenneth Welsh, and Liliana Komorowska. Echo Bridge, 2007. DVD.
"A Scandal in Belgravia." *Sherlock: Season Two.* Perf. Cumberbatch, Benedict, and Martin Freeman. 2 entertain Video, a Hartswood Films Production for BBC, 2011. DVD.
Schneider, Michael. "America's Most Watched: The Top 25 Shows of the 2012–2013 TV Season." *TV Guide* 10 June 2013. Web. 1 Dec. 2013. http://www.tvguide.com/News/Most-Watched-TV-Shows-Top-25-2012-2013-1066503.aspx.
The Seven Percent Solution. Dir. Herbert Ross. Perf. Nicol Williamson, Robert Duvall, Alan Arkin, and Vanessa Redgrave. Universal, 1976. DVD.
Sherlock Holmes. Dir. Guy Ritchie. Perf. Robert Downey, Jr., Jude Law, and Rachel McAdams. Warner, 2009. DVD.
Sherlock Holmes: A Game of Shadows. Dir. Guy Ritchie. Perf. Robert Downey, Jr., Jude Law, and Noomi Rapace. Warner, 2011. DVD.
Sherlock Holmes in New York. Dir. Boris Sagal. Perf. Roger Moore, John Huston, Patrick Macnee, and Charlotte Rampling. NBC, 1976. DVD.
The Sherlock Holmes Society of London. "The Private Life of Sherlock Holmes—with Mark Gatiss." *The Sherlock Holmes Society of London, n.d.* Web. 29 Nov. 2013. http://www.sherlock-holmes.org.uk/event_info.php?id=257.
Sherlock Series 1. Writ. Mark Gatiss and Steven Moffat. BBC. 2010. Television.
Sherlock Series 2. Writ. Mark Gatiss and Steven Moffat. BBC. 2012. Television.
Sherlock 2: Fan Q & A in New York. 13 May 2012. PBS. Web. 1 March 2014. http://video.pbs.org/video/2232626419/.
"The Sign of Three." *Sherlock: Season Three.* Perf. Cumberbatch, Benedict, and Martin Freeman. BBC Worldwide, a Hartswood Films Production for BBC, 2014. DVD.
Sir Arthur Conan Doyle Literary Estate. "Biography Page 8." *The Official Web Site of the Sir*

Arthur Conan Doyle Literary Estate. Oxford Web Applications, 2000. Web. 29 Nov. 2013. http://www.sherlockholmesonline.org/Biography/biography8.htm.
"A Study in Pink." *Sherlock: Season One.* Perf. Cumberbatch, Benedict, and Martin Freeman. 2 entertain Video, a Hartswood Films Production for BBC, 2010. DVD.
Tierney, Tom. *Sherlock Holmes Paper Dolls.* Mineola, NY: Dover, 2009. Print.
"We Are Everyone." *Elementary: The Second Season.* Perf. Jonny Lee Miller and Lucy Liu. Paramount, 2014. DVD.
"The Woman." *Elementary: The First Season.* Perf. Jonny Lee Miller and Lucy Liu. Paramount, 2013. DVD.

"Of dubious and questionable memory"
The Collision of Gender and Canon in Creating Sherlock's *Postfeminist Femme Fatale*

Maria Alberto

It is perhaps one of the most recognizable openings Arthur Conan Doyle has left his readers, Watson's declamation from the 1891 "A Scandal in Bohemia": "To Sherlock Holmes she is always the woman.... In his eyes she eclipses and predominates the whole of her sex" (187). Critics and apologists have argued many meanings into this introduction, ranging from disbelief in Watson's claims that Holmes couldn't love Adler to support for Holmes's supposed misogyny, but in spite of these differences, most will return to its final line: "And yet there was but one woman to him, and that woman was the late Irene Adler, of dubious and questionable memory" ("A Scandal in Bohemia" 205). In having Watson label Adler "of dubious and questionable memory" for her part in a scandal that could have disgraced a king, Conan Doyle is already contributing to a certain tradition of female characters in detective fiction. Though Janet Staiger contends that the femme fatale was only formalized as a type during the late nineteenth century (32–3), Conan Doyle's choice of words—negative but also faintly admiring—already recalls the type. Although the femme fatale is arguably one of the most recognizable types in cinema and literature, let alone the detective and noir genres she has helped to popularize, she is distinguishable by her sense of threat and allure to the male protagonist as much as by the sexualized appearance most audiences will recognize.

Despite the fact that they precede the femme fatale type, though, Conan Doyle's Irene Adler and Mary Morstan are remarkable for additional reasons:

although each woman appears only briefly in Conan Doyle's Holmesian narrative, both have come to occupy liminal but unmistakable spaces in Holmesian studies due to the unique place of privilege and power each holds in relation to the dynamic duo of Holmes and Watson. Adler is unmistakable as the only woman who both fascinates and bests Holmes, and Morstan is unambiguous as the woman who removes Watson from Holmes's life at Baker Street. The lack of explicit detail about either woman in Conan Doyle's writing has never hindered reader speculation: Christopher Redmond notes that the first few issues of the canonical *Baker Street Journal* were dedicated to speculations about Adler, placing her variously as Holmes's fellow schemer in surviving the Reichenbach fall, as Holmes's first and only lover, or even as Holmes's wife. Similarly, Holmesian scholars often speculate that Morstan was only one of sometimes as many as three or four successive wives and ephemeral marriages who periodically engaged the doctor's attention away from crime-solving with Holmes, citing Watson's bereavement for both Holmes and a wife in "The Empty House" (1891–1894) but also Holmes's insistence in 1903's "Blanched Soldier" that Watson had "deserted" him for a wife as well as other dating indiscrepancies.

The BBC show *Sherlock* revisits this interminable interest, acknowledging Holmesians' long-standing fascination with the adventuress Adler and the orphan governess Morstan by reincarnating them as the dominatrix Irene and the disguised assassin Mary. In doing so, the show specifically acknowledges the influence of readers' fascination with the canonical characters: writer Steven Moffat says that the entire second season was created to "do the three big things, and the three big things are the Hound, the Woman and the Professor," and actor Benedict Cumberbatch notes that the show was addressing "the [stories] that seem to have the most amount of resonance when people mention Sherlock Holmes" (*Sherlock* "Sherlock Uncovered").

However, I intend to argue that although *Sherlock* appears to elevate Irene and Mary beyond Adler and Morstan, placing these women in more pivotal roles closer to the epicenter of the Holmesian narrative, the ultimate effect is actually rather different. Even the most casual viewer can tell that the episodes "A Scandal in Belgravia" and "His Last Vow" do not feature quite the same women as "A Scandal in Bohemia" and "The Sign of the Four": what may be harder to discern, though, is that the proud and powerful Irene and Mary portrayed in *Sherlock* actually work against the remarkable accomplishments of Conan Doyle's Adler and Morstan.

Despite Victorian trappings and limitations that so easily disguise the fact, the Adler and Morstan of Conan Doyle's Holmesian narrative are remarkable, resilient women who retain ongoing fascination and vitality because of their credible involvement in a male-centered account of a male-dominated tradition. In her 1995 *The Woman Detective: Gender & Genre*, for instance, Kathleen Gregory Klein notes that from its inception the detective genre has privileged males, characters as well as readers, largely because expected genre characteristics such as logic, reasoning, and violence were relegated to "sex-role definitions [that] allocated all the detectives' usual talents to men" (4). Moreover, Lawrence Frank contends that the historical context of Conan Doyle's stories plays an especially crucial part in his depictions of women, as Conan Doyle was writing during a time of political debates over divorce law, married women's rights, and the regulation of prostitution, where "each controversy involved a denial of the status of woman as genuine legal subjects with corresponding rights of their own" (Frank 54). Adler and Morstan are thus doubly remarkable, as they retain considerable influence over the actions of Holmes and Watson in both a narrative time and a narrative space where women's power was negligible at best—though this complicated feat is often overlooked due to the superficial appearances of the stories' Victorian setting and Conan Doyle's own traditional mindset.

However, although *Sherlock*'s Irene and Mary appear to outstrip their predecessors' accomplishments through more predominant roles in the show's Holmesian narrative, their narrative functions ultimately emphasize the appearances of female prominence rather than holding their own pivotal significance. While named and situated to reference the Adler and Morstan of Conan Doyle's stories, *Sherlock*'s Irene and Mary actually prioritize access to a singular typecasting phenomenon, a hybridic cross between the image of a candidly-sexual/sexualized female and the pre-emptive claims of the postfeminist space. I will call this new archetype the postfeminist femme fatale, for it references many aspects of that older and more recognizable type even as it refutes them. A representative of this new type will still access the openly commercial sexuality of the femme fatale, but through her the illusion of power is rather different because sexuality has become simply the gateway to a much larger and arguably more worrisome transaction—the suggestion of agency in exchange for any place in the narrative at all.

In *Sherlock*, Irene and Mary function as postfeminist femme fatales because their femaleness allows the show to access a narrative shorthand that shortcuts any genuine explanation of them as female *characters*, and instead prioritizes them as female *narrative devices*. Both Irene and Mary are important more for the histories, blindsides, and possibilities of their female bodies than for any genuinely interesting or unique human characteristics, thus conceding to the postfeminist femme fatale's role as an instrument of narrative advancement beneath the smokescreen of female agency.

"She is always the woman": Positing the Presence of a Postfeminist Femme Fatale

Any argument about the type is all too easily reduced to bromidic declarations about the useless phrase "strong women," but a closer examination will reveal that the femme fatale's singular power is actually derived from the men around her. While in her 1991 *Femmes Fatales* Mary Ann Doane notes that one of the femme fatale's main functions is to disrupt male homosocial bonds, and by extension male interpersonal relationships (1–3), she also contends that overall cinema "can only conceptualize the woman as subject of discourse in relation to a masculine role" (34). Staiger, though, further complicates the femme fatale's source of power by noting that the type habitually acts as a complicated manipulator of agency, motivation, and commercialization. For Staiger, the stakes of a femme fatale lie in her reversal of the inherent places in a sexual "property" system, since she is aware of herself as a sexual commodity and enters the typically male-only player system to "negotiate and, even more significantly, aggressively participate in the business" (32).

However, the femme fatale is notable for her interventions as well: instead of simply entering the sexual playing field, she also dominates it, neutralizing her male opponents by overturning the demands of their sexuality. Stephen Kolsky notes that one of the type's more overlooked attributes is her apathy, since despite the conscious and purposeful manipulation of her own sexuality, the femme fatale herself is rarely sexually interested in the male protagonist. Kolsky notes that a female of this type may either fake an interest or play up her disinterest, but either way she is disorienting and playing the male(s) to increase her own advantage and emasculate their apparent sexual authority (47). This ability to challenge, so inherent in the femme fatale's modus operandi, is especially damaging to the detective genre's male protagonist(s) because it carries the potential to annihilate the homosocial bonds defined by Eve Kosofsky Sedgwick in her 1985 *Between Men*.

According to Sedgwick, such bonds operate as societal ties between men—sometimes specifically homosexual, but more often "the presence of male heterosexual desire, in the form of a desire to consolidate partnership with authoritative males in and through the bodies of females" (38). Sedgwick also notes that this male-male-female "triangle" is not a random ahistorical form, "but [rather] a sensitive register precisely for delineating relationships of power and meaning" (27). Under this definition, then, a properly-functioning homosocial bond features the woman as a receptive medium who simply channels the more important "partnership" at stake, but Kolsky notes that the double threat of the femme fatale's commercialized yet ultimately unattainable sexuality has the power to nullify these bonds (46). As Michael Flood observes that the homosocial bond and its obligations must be prioritized in order to maintain their authority (344), the femme fatale's ultimate threat to male characters is that she can isolate them from one another, and thus the homosocial community that validates them in the traditionally male-centered detective profession (Klein 4). Consequently, a femme fatale's narrative value derives from her trial of masculine motivation and agency as much as from her enactment and ratification of female agency, but ultimately the type remains flawed because both types of critical power actually stem from the male characters and their values. At its most basic level, this under-read dissemination of the femme fatale's actual strength epitomizes the main disparity between Conan Doyle's Adler and Morstan and the show's Irene and Mary—the former are women whose narrative presence and power can be seen accentuated by the male characters, where the latter are more accurately femme fatales whose narrative power ultimately comes from these male characters.

Inevitably, Staiger contends that whether a victimizing aggressor or an aggressive victim, the femme fatale's complicity in the narrative cannot be taken at face value, since potential complications include her role (protagonist, antagonist, or foil), the true nature of her actions (agency or reactive/protective instinct), and the high possibility of narratorial bias in reporting her circumstances and actions (52). In addition, this potential for the further distortion of female agency, especially the misrepresentation of necessity as malevolence, also marks the sexual transaction as the first aspect of the femme fatale that a postfeminist reshaping would overhaul. To understand this necessity, though, it must also be understood that postfeminism is different enough from its (feminist) predecessor to necessitate a complete transformation. Hawkesworth in particular notes that although many believe feminism has evolved or "been transformed into some more advanced stage of existence" (965), various definitions of the term "postfeminism" encompass a retreat to traditional gender roles (965), a return to "pre-feminist" scholarly suppression of women and erasure of queer theory (966–7), or an appropriation and revision of second-wave feminism and its precepts (967–8). The common aspect that unites these otherwise comically-different definitions, though, is the idea of postfeminism's distance from feminism in some fashion. Hawkesworth notes that "invocations of postfeminism, then, could be read as banishments, commanding us to imagine gender relations, higher education, individual psyches, and contemporary culture at large as spatial and temporal zones in which feminism has been eclipsed" (969).

Depending on which of Hawkesworth's three definitions is being referenced, then, a postfeminist thinker might imagine that either (a) all will as be treated according to the "proper" traditional gender roles that feminism had temporarily occluded, or (b) all will be treated as "proper" social equals despite differences in sex, gender, orientation, and identification thanks to feminism as a now thankfully-outdated concept.

Consequently, the intersection between the concepts of the femme fatale and of the postfeminist rationale might seem ambiguous, but a brief survey of the current cinematic climate will prove that a similar trend has already been noticed. Heldman and Cahill, for instance, note the rise of a "disturbing trend of appropriating female agency and power for male pleasure" (9) in the films from the decades circa 1990–2010. Similar to the intersection that I posit between the femme fatale and a postfeminist space, Heldman and Cahill contend that filmmakers have "co-opted the ideals of self-identification and authentication from the most recent feminist movement [to contribute] to the proliferation of woman-as-body" (9). They contend that the woman-as-body is depicted as an autonomous female character of deceptive strength, but ultimately signifies just a 'perfect' and often super-human body that exists only to please male viewers. In short, they argue that a character of this type "has become the ultimate Fighting Fuck-Toy (FF-T). Her autonomy spills over into presentations of consensual hypersexuality that allow filmmakers to unabashedly present female characters as sex objects in ways that would have previously been thought of as offensive" (9).

While the characteristics of this "woman-as-body" cinematic type are similar to those of the postfeminist femme fatale in a number of ways—both types *appear* to advance female agency, for instance—the main difference lies in each type's ultimate purpose. As Heldman and Cahill note, the woman-as-body advances objectification—so as a glorified sex object weakly disguised by apparent power, this new cinematic type prioritizes the sexual aspect of the traditional femme fatale while diminishing her already-limited agency and enhancing what Doane calls male-driven conceptualization (34).

The postfeminist femme fatale, however, will reverse the same elements in order to create the opposite equation. Where the woman-as-body type references the traditional femme fatale's overt sexuality as it overemphasizes the trappings of power to try and disguise hypersexuality, the postfeminist femme fatale type references the femme fatale's commercialization as it emphasizes the trappings of femininity and sexuality to disguise narrative function as agency. Likewise, just as neither the femme fatale nor the woman-as-body is quite able to produce true female agency, the postfeminist femme fatale type also falls short of the mark since she is not structurally valuable for herself. Whatever motives, beliefs, or actions this type might display, the agency behind them is the narrative's rather than her own: she is only female so that the male protagonist(s) can move forward, usually without her.

Despite her avoidance of the term "femme fatale," Antonia Primorac observes a comparable phenomenon concerning female agency in the neo–Victorian results of appropriating literature such as Conan Doyle's. Primorac notes that the literary trend she calls "aftering" primarily involves the retroactive "sexing up" of Victorian characters in order to attract contemporary audiences (90), but she also contends that this "sexing up" actually destroys the agency of female characters by exchanging their credibly-limited power in the original work for sexual-only material in the adaptation (90–1). While Primorac is defining the occurrence rather than the type involved, though, she does observe that Conan Doyle's Irene Adler is a prominent victim of this "aftering," calling attention to the way both the 2009 and 2013 Warner Bros. films and the 2010–present *Sherlock* utilize Irene Adler as a form of sexual shorthand. While Primorac doesn't apply the same "aftering" lens to Conan Doyle's Mary Morstan or any of her adapted successors, the concept is not difficult to connect to *Sherlock*'s Mary as well, since here both females are important for *what* they are rather than *who* they are.

Throughout *Sherlock*, Irene and Mary are instantly and constantly visible, and each holds some matter of power in, and over, the life of title character Sherlock Holmes in a way that seems to expose and transcend the limited agency of Conan Doyle's Adler and Morstan. When coupled with her physical presence, for instance, Irene's exchanges with Sherlock seem to outdo Adler's match of wits with Holmes, and Irene certainly "beats" Sherlock more soundly than even Adler manages with Holmes: in the same fashion, Mary's literal displays of power over both John and Sherlock certainly surpass Morstan's more conventional connubial separation of Holmes and Watson.

Neither increased visibility nor a "sexing up," though, can quite cover the cracks in any claim that Irene's and Mary's literal narrative power makes them more noteworthy female characters than Adler and Morstan. When considered in light of the episodes in which they appear, and in comparison to their canon counterparts, it becomes clearer that Irene and Mary function more as narrative shorthand to drive the show's plot forward—and thus they can add little to their canon counterparts' triumphant histories because their place in *Sherlock*'s Holmesian narrative *demands* that they are female, rather than Adler's and Morstan's remarkable participation in a male-dominated narrative *despite* the fact that they are female. As will be shown in the next sections, Irene's narrative authority stems from her conscious manipulation of overtly-dominant female sexuality, without which she would be powerless, and similarly, Mary's narrative authority stems from her constant references to heteronormative ideals of the female as wife, lover, and mother, without which she seems to be portrayed with neither credible motive nor sufficient protection.

"Beaten by a woman's wit": Conan Doyle's Adler and Sherlock's Irene

In Conan Doyle's "A Scandal in Bohemia," Holmes and Watson are hired by the King of Bohemia to steal a photograph from Adler, an American-born opera singer and a "well-known adventuress" ("A Scandal in Bohemia" 192) the King met during his youth: the King claims that Adler, jealous of his recent engagement to a Scandinavian princess, is blackmailing him with a photograph that has the potential to break off this engagement. Holmes tails Adler and inadvertently serves as sole witness to her marriage, and Adler inadvertently reveals the photograph's location when Holmes tricks his way into her home before a false fire alarm. However, Adler is gone when Holmes, Watson, and the King arrive to confront her the next day, and Holmes's newfound respect for the woman is sealed by the letter she leaves for him, which explains how she was actually aware and a step ahead of him the entire time.

The Adler of this "Scandal" already seems different from the Irene of "A Scandal in Belgravia" (2012), the *Sherlock* episode in which Sherlock is coerced into trying to steal the woman's smartphone, which supposedly contains explicit photos of a young female member of the royal family. Though Sherlock initially fails to recover the phone, Irene later leaves it at Baker Street before her apparent death at an anonymous enemy's hand: distressed, Sherlock tries and fails to unlock it for several months. Irene later appears, alive and unharmed, to reclaim the phone, and in trying to show off,

Sherlock solves a cypher that results in the termination of a high-stakes MI6 mission. Irene then threatens Mycroft Holmes with the promise of additional high-stakes information that Sherlock had been unable to reclaim, but at the last moment, Sherlock finally guesses the passcode he has been unable to generate for months. Irene is later pronounced dead again, and Sherlock appears to mourn her, though the episode's final scene reveals that he in fact rescued her.

Any comparison between Conan Doyle's Adler and *Sherlock*'s Irene thus becomes the attempt to place an opera-singer adventuress and her protective instincts alongside a lesbian dominatrix and her criminal connections, an endeavor that establishes how significant differences in female advantage/male disadvantage and motive reduce *Sherlock*'s Irene to the typecast of a postfeminist femme fatale.

The matter of female advantage/male disadvantage serves as the first indicator that Irene is not truly a female character with increased agency. Although Conan Doyle's Adler and Holmes cannot quite contend as true equals because of the era's restrictions upon female agency, "A Scandal in Bohemia" features a contention of speed, disguises, wit, and personal information networks played out between its main male and female characters. By contrast, the contentions between the main male and female characters in "A Scandal in Belgravia" are characterized by a distinct series of advantages and disadvantages that privilege Irene simply for her sex. In addition, although this unbalanced series of advantages and disadvantages privileges Irene as the female over Sherlock as the male, many of its implications do not quite make sense from a character standpoint, and this failure is the one of the main reasons Irene functions more as a plot device than as an actual character.

One of the most visible female advantage/male disadvantage dichotomies present with Irene is the treatment of her occupation as a dominatrix. While Irene is presented as primarily and unapologetically sexual, her identity and significance are often reduced even beyond this overt sexuality, instead shrunk to an incredibly narrow focus on the way she supposedly uses it. Audiences' first visual of her features red nails, sheer lace, "Brazilian knickers," and a riding crop as Irene sends a text, strides down a short hallway, strikes the crop against the door frame of a room that contains a bed and someone restrained upon it, and then slams the door behind herself ("A Scandal in Belgravia"). Her face is not shown during this short exchange: after she sends the text, the shot focuses on her body from the waist down. Similarly, the first lines that audiences hear from *Sherlock*'s Irene cannot be mistaken for anything other than dominantly sexual, as she asks, "Well, now. Have you been wicked, Your

Highness?" and walks towards the person restrained as a demure female voice answers, "Yes, Miss Adler" ("A Scandal in Belgravia").

This initial focus on overtly-dominant female sexuality quickly becomes Irene's main advantage when dealing with Sherlock, or even other male characters such as John Watson and Mycroft Holmes. Whenever the detective attempts to question or learn about her, for instance, Irene responds by alluding to some aspect of her profession and the experience she has gained through it. Queries about her knowledge, means, or connections are consistently met with Irene's rejoinder "I know what he/she likes" ("A Scandal in Belgravia"), a deliberate reference to the power she is used to holding over others. This experience and the superior position it provides Irene give her a unique angle from which to approach her male opponent: where Sherlock is applying his intelligence, and continually extending her the option to do the same, Irene counters by foregrounding her sexuality and the double shock factors of its being both female and dominant. For instance, when Sherlock arrives at her Belgravia home to try and trick her into revealing where her phone is hidden, Irene is waiting for him and walks in on him to reveal her naked body instead ("A Scandal in Belgravia"). She relies on the taboo shock of this action to fluster Sherlock enough to keep him from finding the phone, which is later revealed to be protected by a safe whose passcode comprises her bust-waist-hip measurements ("A Scandal in Belgravia").

There are dual downsides to Irene's use of the advantage/disadvantage dichotomy concerning her own sexual dominance, though. Most visibly, it allows her to prioritize herself in a way that would never be countenanced from a male in her position. She continuously violates the confidentiality of clients who have paid for her discretion as much as her sexual services, name-dropping their professions and submissive sexual preferences as she tries to shock and outdo Sherlock. Where Conan Doyle's Adler reveals that she learned about Holmes from her own network, probably connections maintained from her days as an opera singer ("A Scandal in Bohemia" 203–4), *Sherlock*'s Irene gains her knowledge from her clients, but in a way that exploits their trust, and from Moriarty, as a male character who in turn is using her as another way to get at the Holmes brothers. Irene also ignores the imperative concept of consent that would be observed and respected by a professional BDSM practitioner. In drugging and then beating Sherlock to force him drop her phone, Irene seems fully aware that she is misusing various tools of her profession. After Sherlock has been overcome, she goes so far as to tell him, "It's been a pleasure. Don't spoil it. This is how I want you to remember me—the woman who beat you" ("A Scandal in Belgravia"), and when John comes in to find him unconscious, Irene makes the doctor aware of the potential danger with the warning, "Make sure he doesn't choke on his own vomit. It makes for a very unattractive corpse" ("A Scandal in Belgravia"). Her flippancy verifies how casually she views her occupation and its potential fatality if misapplied, a casual apathy that would be termed abuse from a male sadomasochist but is apparently acceptable from Irene as a female.

A later downside to Irene's sexual advantage/disadvantage is that it also enables her to avoid using a significant intellect in any way that could threaten Sherlock's. Her dependence on the shock of her body and her dominant sexuality is continually bested by his use of his mind, as when his intellect enables him to open the safe concealing her phone and thus surprise and overcome their attackers ("A Scandal in Belgravia"). Although Irene proves her own considerable intellect by solving the hitchhiker case almost as quickly as Sherlock had and by fully planning out how to encrypt and booby-trap her phone to withstand even its owner's potential torture ("A Scandal in Belgravia"), she never fully switches to using this intellect against her male opponents, returning again and again to her sexual modus operandi even after it has been proven flawed.

In addition to the advantage/disadvantage dichotomy, though, the other point that reduces *Sherlock*'s Irene to a figure of the postfeminist femme fatale typecast is the issue of motive and the male role in such motivation. Conan Doyle's Adler is continuously underestimated by Holmes, who misjudges her protective intentions, her ability to see through his ruse, and her feelings for new husband Godfrey Norton. Primorac notes that "in the course of the narrative, [Adler] is transformed from a suspected villain into a wronged woman" (94): although the King of Bohemia vilifies Adler, her letter to Holmes reveals that *she* was wronged, and Holmes recognizes his inadvertent complicity when he "coldly" tells the King, "From what I have seen of the lady she seems indeed to be on a very different level to your Majesty" ("A Scandal in Bohemia" 204). This reversal is convincing because it reveals both Adler and Holmes as interesting and credible human characters: Adler's victory is motivated by her fear for a loved one and enabled by her abilities as a veteran performer during an era that made the accomplishment difficult for a female, and Holmes's defeat is driven by his era-typical underestimation of female agency and his own unique inability to rate emotion as strong a driving factor as logic.

By contrast, the motives of *Sherlock*'s Irene fluctuate wildly and are not completely her own, factors that make her less credible than Adler and that never quite line up with her initial appearance as an autonomous agent. This contradiction becomes apparent when Irene reappears to collect her phone from Baker Street. When Sherlock had first tried to extract the phone, she had called it "her life" and protection, telling him that he should inform her previous client "that sweet little posh thing the pictures are safe with me. They're not for blackmail, just for insurance" ("A Scandal in Belgravia"). However, the show never offers a credible explanation for this initial requirement for insurance unless it was a lie from the start, since when she returns, Irene starts to use the phone's contents for blackmail instead. The reversal is made even less convincing when Irene reveals "I can't take all the credit. Had a bit of help ... Jim Moriarty sends his love" ("A Scandal in Belgravia"). The disclosure that she has actually been working with Sherlock's archenemy and had left the phone with the detective to prove that it couldn't be compromised if even he couldn't access its information reveals a near-complete lack of agency for Irene. When she admits "I had all this stuff, never knew what to do with it. Thank God for the consultant criminal [Moriarty]" ("A Scandal in Belgravia"), Irene is also inadvertently admitting that she has been acting on a male character's motives and agenda all along.

This complete and completely-incomprehensible reversal is crowned by the last scenes of "A Scandal in Belgravia," which reveal that a major disparity between *Sherlock*'s Irene and Conan Doyle's Adler is not so much that Irene "loses," but instead that she loses in such an inexplicable manner. This incomprehensible defeat begins with her phone, which Sherlock finally realizes is protected with a passcode derived from his own name: SHER LOCKED ("A Scandal in Belgravia"). In explaining how he finally arrived at this conclusion, Sherlock reveals "I took your pulse" and registered the elevated rate that registered sexual arousal—though earlier Irene herself admits that she is gay, in response to John's protests that he is not ("A Scandal in Belgravia"). In other words, Irene's sexuality and sexual orientation seem intended for shock value—a *lesbian* dominatrix is the only thing more scandalous than a dominatrix—since they are also mutable when it serves the narrative's purpose, where a male character's (John's) are not.

Irene's farcical "defeat" concludes with a rescue in what has been called the infamous "Sherlock of Arabia" scene. In the beginning of this scene, Mycroft Holmes informs John that Irene has been killed, "captured by a terrorist cell" and beheaded in Karachi, Pakistan—but when John informs Sherlock, a series of flashbacks reveals that a disguised Sherlock actually saved Irene's life ("A Scandal in Belgravia"). Leaving aside the unanswered questions of Irene's presence in Pakistan and the improbability of a late-night, single-victim beheading in one of Pakistan's largest metropolises, especially when compared to the greater possibility of terrorist activity along the country's more turbulent northern and eastern borders with Afghanistan, the scene makes little sense. Irene is reduced to crying on her knees without hope of salvation before her deliverance comes in the form of the selfsame male character she has "wronged," and thus the agency that has already diminished throughout the course of the episode is completely gone.

Irene's narrative power in the Holmesian narrative of "A Scandal in Belgravia" is thus exposed as a combination of exploited and uncontrollable circumstances, including her continual misuse of an already-vilified profession and the eventual revelation that her agency in fact stems from a male character. Combined with her inconsistent fixation on Sherlock as well as her sudden dependence on external salvation in the final scene, Irene's importance as a narrative force is dependent on the fact that she is female. Her female body and the weight of history that apparently comes with it are used to variously disguise and excuse her abuse of her occupation and to serve as an acceptable shorthand for Sherlock's male/virginal/moral bafflement. As a result, the multiple, palpable differences between *Sherlock*'s Irene and Conan Doyle's Adler all derive from the disparate types of power these women hold over Sherlock and Holmes, respectively. Adler's power stems from Holmes's underestimations of her as a female of the period and as an opponent, while Irene's power stems from Sherlock's lack of information about her as a female sadomasochist and as a manipulative criminal accessory. Put differently, Holmes thinks of Adler as "simply" a woman and comes away the worse for the underestimation, while Sherlock considers Irene as an intellectual equal but comes away the worse for a little while because he cannot quite respond to the way she uses her female body to counter his intellect.

"As a lover in a false position": Conan Doyle's Morstan and Sherlock's Mary

The Mary Morstan introduced and portrayed in the third season of *Sherlock* is particularly complicated to untangle since her narrative role can be traced to two particularly difficult characters from Conan Doyle's stories: mainly Mary Morstan, the young woman Watson intends to marry at the end of "The Sign of the Four," but also with a substantial nod to the anonymous woman who shoots her blackmailer in "The Adventure of Charles Augustus Milverton."

In "The Sign of the Four," orphan governess Mary Morstan hires Holmes to help her discover the fate of her missing father and the identity of an anonymous "friend" who sends her a pearl every May. Holmes and Watson discover that Morstan's father had been killed in an altercation over a stolen treasure hidden in Agra during the 1857–58 Indian Mutiny and eventually dedicate themselves to recovering this treasure from Jonathan Small, the final survivor of the four vagabond soldiers who had originally stolen it. Over the course of the narrative, Watson is drawn to Morstan and despairs of his chances because the Agra treasure will elevate her beyond his reach, but when Small throws the treasure overboard rather than let another benefit from his hard-earned gains, Watson is free to court and then marry Morstan. "Sign" concludes with Holmes reaching for his sustaining bottle of cocaine after Watson reveals that Morstan has accepted his proposal of marriage. By contrast, "The Adventure of Charles Augustus Milverton" features Holmes hired not to solve a case, but to negotiate with notorious blackmailer Milverton. When Milverton demands a price beyond the means of Holmes's client, Holmes and Watson break into his home to steal the documents—only to observe Milverton's death at the hands of a masked woman who claims that he ruined her.

Since both her predecessors hold some power of destruction—the former figuratively ends a comfortable "bachelor life" where the latter actually ends a man's life—*Sherlock*'s Mary accesses the narrative shorthand of a female body to further extend and display this power while also remaining protected from its logical consequences. This dual purpose is most obvious in the episode "His Last Vow" (*Sherlock* "His Last Vow" 2014), which features Sherlock hired to negotiate a deal with notorious blackmailer Charles Augustus Magnussen. When Magnussen refuses to negotiate, Sherlock uses a ruse of engagement to the blackmailer's PA to get himself and John into the man's office, where the detective then finds Mary threatening Magnussen. Mary shoots Sherlock in the chest, and when he is in the hospital, warns him not to tell John, but Sherlock later engineers a dramatic revelation that leaves John furious for the lie and Mary scared for her marriage. After a Christmas dinner where John says he forgives her, Sherlock drags his friend to Magnussen's home, Appledore, to trade state secrets for all incriminating evidence Magnussen has on Mary's past as a freelance assassin, but Sherlock ultimately shoots and kills Magnussen when the blackmailer reveals that there are no hard copies of the information.

Consequently, similar to the Irene/Adler case, the comparison between Conan Doyle's Morstan and *Sherlock*'s Mary entails a comparison of wildly-disparate contradictions—this time, the orphan governess alongside the freelance assassin. Also likewise, the comparison quickly establishes how significant differences in female advantage/male disadvantage and motive reduce *Sherlock*'s Mary to the typecast of postfeminist femme fatale.

Comparably to Irene's case, the interplay of female advantage/male disadvantage throughout "His Last Vow" is an immediate indicator that *Sherlock*'s Mary functions as more of a narrative device than a female character with truly increased agency. Although Conan Doyle's Morstan and Holmes are never explicit antagonists, the conclusion of "The Sign of the Four" makes it obvious that both want Watson's companionship, and that for one to win it, the other must lose it. The competition, though, is implicit rather than taking up any overt place in the narrative, and it passes completely above the good doctor's head. By contrast, though, the contention between Mary and Sherlock in "His Last Vow" is characterized by a distinct series of advantages that privilege Mary for her sex alone.

For instance, Mary's narrative power in "His Last Vow" is immediately established as the consequence of one substantial and unmistakable advantage: her pregnancy, and by extension but to a lesser degree, her heteronormative marriage. The pregnancy, a possibility open to her alone as a female, acts as a type of narrative shorthand by presuming certain principles of 'fair' treatment, much like assuming that audiences can overlook if not outright excuse any action from Mary because she's a pregnant wife. At the beginning of the episode, for instance, viewers are treated to a snippy exchange between John and Mary as John prepares to find and drag a neighbor's son from a drug den. John displays a shortness and certain turns of speech he's obviously learned from Sherlock, though he admits he hasn't seen his friend in a month ("His Last Vow")—his reluctance and obvious discomfort give the impression that he is not completely happy in his new life. The reason behind this sulky constancy, though, is solidified through more than just his marriage when Mary uses her pregnancy to guilt John into bringing her along to the den: he protests, "You can't come. You're pregnant" and she returns with "You can't *go*. I'm pregnant" ("His Last Vow"), and apparently that reminder is enough for her to win the argument.

This immediate focus on a factual capacity of the female body rapidly becomes Mary's greatest advantage in dealing with the episode's male characters. Due to her pregnancy, even the narrative shorthand inherent to Mary's role as an apparent assassin—attributes such as attempted murder and dual/mistaken identity—can be condoned and its consequences negated. For instance, because of the gunshot wound's placement on Sherlock's chest, John posits that "he was facing whoever it was," and that the detective hasn't shared the identity of his shooter because "he's tracking them down himself ... or protecting them ... protecting *someone*, then. But why would he care? He's *Sherlock*. Who would he bother protecting?" ("His Last Vow"). Sherlock's actions and Magnussen's explanation of the detective's "pressure point" later prove that the detective had been protecting John, but the weak chain in the link is Mary—John's morals are too traditionally-oriented to let him expose or leave his pregnant wife, and thus the female capacity for pregnancy serves as a shorthand explanation for the secondhand loyalty that eventually leads Sherlock to confront Magnussen.

"His Last Vow's" dependence on the female advantage/male disadvantage of Mary's pregnancy offers significant downsides for Mary as a character, though. Most damningly, it reduces her ostensible agency to a desperate but compulsory bid for continued consideration from a male character, husband John Watson. Repeatedly, Mary acts not from concern for her survival, her welfare, or even her loved ones', but in fear of her continued place as John's wife. This difference in motive is yet another way in which Sherlock's Mary is proved a postfeminist femme fatale who cannot quite live up to her canon counterpart—not only is Mary's agency actually proven tied to a male character, but also her motive to exercise that agency is as well. Where Conan Doyle's Morstan is certainly interested in Watson as a potential husband, she also actively participates in the mystery's solution by preserving potential clues ("The Sign of the Four" 107), serving as a witness at the Sholto manse ("The Sign of the Four" 121–2), and keeping calm and steady in the face of the same dangers Holmes and Watson face ("The Sign of the Four" 122), actions that remain both understandable and credible. *Sherlock*'s Mary, on the other hand, seems to act far less rationally. Though she says that she acts "because John can't ever know that I lied to him. It would break him and I would lose him forever—and, Sherlock, I will *never* let that happen.... There is nothing in this world that I would not do to stop that happening" ("His Last Vow"), Mary's actions surrounding her shooting Sherlock are neither consistent nor explicable. For instance, she admits that she only shot Sherlock and not Magnussen in order to keep John from becoming a suspect ("His Last Vow"), but then doesn't kill Sherlock in the hospital when John steps away, though her line "You won't tell John" seems to show that she had been alone with Sherlock at some point ("His Last Vow"). If she were meant to be understood primarily as an assassin, it is hard to imagine why she did not take this opportunity, but there is certainly room for an explanation of some kind. Instead, though, the contradiction of motive continues to grow: Mary's apparent ruthlessness returns with a perfect shot through a fifty-pence piece during the shadowed confrontation with Sherlock at Leinster Gardens ("His Last Vow"), yet only moments later, she is seated with bowed head at Baker Street awaiting a decision not on her life, but on her role in John's life.

Thus, where Conan Doyle's Morstan draws Watson away from bachelorhood at Baker Street of her own accord and attractions, *Sherlock*'s Mary is acting under unexplained external influences and contingent desirability to keep John away from Sherlock and Baker Street. This difference is only further highlighted by the dual narrative shorthands discussed above, those of Mary's pregnancy and her past as an assassin, which are combined as if to forestall any need for explanation. The slapdash application of certain keywords seems intended to make audiences assume that John must stay with Mary because she's apparently pregnant with his child and that Mary must have an inexplicable secret past because she was an American CIA agent and then a freelance assassin, rather than even attempting to provide any more context or backstory.

Hope yet remains for the tangled mesh of cinematic-cultural histories that surrounds her female body and reduces Mary to the sum of this body and its narrative function, but only because the third season of *Sherlock* ended upon such a confusing and climactic note with Jim Moriarty's apparent survival. Hopefully the fourth season will provide some more background, context, and/or explanation for Mary's actions than the season three conflation of the narrative shorthands for scared lover-wife and hyper-powerful vengeful assassin—and also instead of going overboard trying to rationalize and validate her actions.

"Of dubious and questionable memory": The Potential for Female Characters in Sherlock

While Conan Doyle does introduce both Adler and Morstan as secondary fixtures in their respective stories, these female characters' relevance and reputations in fact stem from the way in which they both manage to act despite the limitations of era and narrative. However, since *Sherlock*'s Irene and Mary derive their significance from the way they advance certain episodes' narratives rather than from their genuine part in those narratives, they must be judged separately from their canon counterparts. This treatment is especially interesting in terms of other female characters from *Sherlock*, who show that referencing the postfeminist femme fatale type is not necessary in order to create genuinely interesting and credible female characters, even antagonistic ones.

Such female characters are palpable presences throughout the show. A brief survey will most prominently reveal Martha Hudson, John and Sherlock's landlady; Sally Donovan, a lieutenant at New Scotland Yard; Molly Hooper, a pathologist at St. Bartholomew's Hospital; Kitty Riley, a journalist; and Janine Hawkins, a media specialist and personal assistant. Despite their distance from the center of the Holmesian narrative and their relatively small amounts of screen time, all five of these female characters are presented with legitimate, credible, and explicable reasons to work either with or against Sherlock and John, and simultaneously, three of the five are difficult to pin as either antagonists or protagonists. Martha Hudson plays a mediatory role in many cases, and in the short time that viewers have access to the other four, Sally Donovan is shown thanklessly dealing with an antagonistic Sherlock in a consultant role that must break some of the laws she is sworn to uphold; Molly Hooper is shown quietly dealing with an exasperating Sherlock as he alternately preens and ignores her; Kitty Riley is shown struggling to push past the detective archetype in search of the story that will help her break through a journalistic glass ceiling; and Janine Hawkins is shown enduring an unintentional bridesmaid/beard dilemma alongside Sherlock with uncommon poise. Furthermore, Martha Hudson is directly drawn from the landlady in Conan Doyle's Holmesian narrative.

Yet although these female characters are typically overlooked in favor of Irene and Mary, either for their comparative marginality or because they have no predecessors in Conan Doyle canon, they are also more convincing participants in *Sherlock*'s Holmesian narrative. Because Irene and Mary have been subjected to a version of Primorac's "aftering," or the sense that Conan Doyle's canon must be outdone in order to be updated, their reasons for working against Sherlock are likewise arbitrary or only patchily explained because such reasons come secondary to the narrative functions both must fulfill. By contrast, though, Martha Hudson and the four original female characters who have no canon counterparts to outdo, update, or 'sex up' are given legitimate reasons for their more realistically-credible interactions with Sherlock Holmes and John Watson.

Works Cited

Conan Doyle, Arthur. "The Illustrious Client." 1924. *The Complete Sherlock Holmes, Volume II*. New York: Barnes and Noble Classics, 2004. 497–515. Print.

_____. "A Scandal in Bohemia." 1891. *The Complete Sherlock Holmes, Volume I*. New York: Barnes and Noble Classics, 2004. 187–204. Print.

_____. "The Sign of the Four." 1887. *The Complete Sherlock Holmes, Volume I*. New York: Barnes and Noble Classics, 2004. 3–96. Print.
Doane, Mary Ann. *Femmes Fatales: Feminism, Film Theory, Psychoanalysis*. New York: Routledge, 1991.
Flood, Michael. "Men, Sex, and Homosociality. How Bonds Between Men Shape Their Sexual Relations with Women." *Men and Masculinities* 10.3 (2008): 339–59.
Frank, Lawrence. "Dreaming the Medusa: Imperialism, Primitivism, and Sexuality in Arthur Conan Doyle's 'The Sign of Four.'" *Signs: Journal of Women in Culture and Society* 22.1 (1996): 52–85.
Hawkesworth, Mary. "The Semiotics of Premature Burial: Feminism in a Postfeminist Age." *Signs: Journal of Women in Culture and Society* 29.4 (2004): 961–985.
Heldman, Caroline, and Michael Cahill. "The Beast of Beauty Culture: An Analysis of the Political Effects of Self-Objectification." The Western Political Science Association Conference, Las Vegas. 8–10 March 2007. 1–39. Conference paper.
"His Last Vow." *Sherlock*. Dir. Nick Hurran. Writ. Steven Moffat. Perf. Benedict Cumberbatch, Martin Freeman, and Amanda Abbington. BBC, 2014. DVD.
Klein, Kathleen Gregory. *The Woman Detective: Gender & Genre*. Urbana: University of Illinois Press, 1995. Print.
Kolsky, Stephen. "Male Homosociality, the Femme Fatale, and Gender Relations in Andrea Camilleri's *Il campo de vasaio*." *Romance Studies* 31.1 (2013): 41–52.
Primorac, Antonija. "The Naked Truth: The Postfeminist Afterlives of Irene Adler." *Neo-Victorian Studies* 6.2 (2013): 89–113.
Redmond, Christopher. *In Bed with Sherlock Holmes: Sexual Elements in Arthur Conan Doyle's Stories of the Great Detective*. Toronto: Simon & Pierre, 1984.
"A Scandal in Belgravia." *Sherlock*. Dir. Paul McGuigan. Writ. Steven Moffat. Perf. Benedict Cumberbatch, Martin Freeman, and Lara Pulver. BBC, 2012. DVD.
Sedgwick, Eve Kosofsky. *Between Men: English Literature and Male Homosocial Desire*. New York: Columbia University Press, 1985. Print.
"Sherlock Uncovered." *Sherlock: Season 2*. BBC, 2012. DVD. Disc 2.
Staiger, Janet. "*Les Belles Dames Sans Merci*, Femme Fatales, Vampires, Vamps, and Gold Diggers: The Transformation and Narrative Value of Aggressive Fallen Women." *Reclaiming the Archive: Feminism and Film History*. Ed. Vicki Callahan. Detroit: Wayne State University Press, 2010. 32–57. Print.

"Feeling Exposed?"
Irene Adler and the Self-Reflective Disguise
KATHARINE MCCAIN

When fans think of "*the* woman" they think of the one person who beat Sherlock Holmes ... and they recall that she did so by dressing in drag (Klinger, 5). Disguise is a crucial element of Sir Arthur Conan Doyle's short story "A Scandal in Bohemia" (2007), the first of fifty-six short stories to feature the great detective. Irene Adler of the BBC *Sherlock* (2010) adaptation, "A Scandal in Belgravia" (2012), places equal emphasis on concealment but the modern TV show handles disguise in an entirely different manner from its literary counterpart. This essay closely examines BBC Irene's pronouncement that a disguise is a "self-portrait"—that it paradoxically reveals more than it conceals—and attempts to determine not only whether such an argument holds up under scrutiny but also the ways in which these two vastly different Irenes apply such knowledge. Indeed, Conan Doyle's Irene chooses to disguise herself as a man, revealing an inherently "masculine" nature (according to Holmes' fictional 19th century standards) while BBC Irene's series of "disguises"—nakedness and purloining Sherlock's clothes—presents a far more complex series of revelations that are centered around a desperation to keep her secrets. By the time both women have shed their masks it is clear who comes out on top: she who is willing to embrace the disguise as a self-portrait reaps its benefits, while she who tries to use self-reflection as a means of hiding from the world ultimately fails.

Just a third of the way through the second season episode of *Sherlock* our title character kicks off this theme of disguises by conning his way into Irene's house, dressed as a vicar, and sporting a bruise he antagonized John into giving him. He plans to use this disguise in order to spin a story about being mugged in the hopes of gaining information regarding some compromising photographs in Irene's possession. However, Sherlock quickly discovers that Irene is not so easily fooled. Instead of being taken in by his getup she confidently enters the room naked, taunts Sherlock, and proceeds to make a grand pronouncement regarding the true nature of a disguise.

> IRENE: Do you know the big problem with a disguise, Mr. Holmes? However hard you try, it's always a self-portrait.
> SHERLOCK: You think I'm a vicar with a bleeding face?
> IRENE: No, I think you're damaged, delusional, and believe in a higher power. In your case, it's yourself ["A Scandal in Belgravia"].

There is a great deal to unpack in this exchange, the most significant of which is this labeling of Sherlock's disguise as a "self-portrait." Irene takes Sherlock's literal appearance—a vicar costume and a "bleeding face"—and strives to find meaning behind these details—that he is "damaged," not only physically but emotionally, and that like the clergy he believes in a "higher power" which ultimately makes him "delusional" (a cynical view that in-and-of-itself says a great deal about Irene's character). This definition of a disguise is conflicting at best; surprising that a tool designed to conceal instead proves to be revealing. Yet it is a contradiction that, as we will later see, Irene is initially a master at utilizing.

However, prior to this BBC production disguises were highlighted as significant within Conan Doyle's stories and the implications of a person's looks or how they dressed were discussed well before any actual costumes were donned. In "A Scandal in Bohemia" Conan Doyle chooses to introduce Irene through the King's striking description of her:

> I know that she will [send the photographs]. You do not know her, but she has a soul of steel. She has the face of the most beautiful of women, and the mind of the most resolute of men. Rather than I should marry another woman, there are no lengths to which she would not go—none [Klinger 18].

This is a surprising characterization as the King is arguing that although Irene may *look* like a woman (and a very fine one at that) in every significant way she is akin to a man. This is hardly the first time that the sex and/or gender of a character within the canon has been challenged, with perhaps the most infamous instance being Rex Stout's assertion that Watson's writings about Holmes were clearly a "woman speaking of a man," or C. Bradley and William Sarjeant's controversial book, *Ms. Holmes of Baker Street: The Truth About Sherlock* (2004), which asserted that Holmes himself was actually the woman (Stout). However, little has been said about how the way in which a character presents his/her sex or gender can act as a disguise. In Irene's case, the disguise is her femininity that hides the "mind" of a man and potentially the soul of one as well—at least by these fictional, 19th century standards.

Indeed, there is a connection drawn between Irene's mind and her soul through the King's use of similar, descriptive adjectives; ones that convey hard, unyielding natures: Irene has a "resolute" will and her soul is made of "steel." If Irene's mind and soul are in agreement and if her mind is that of a man's, it seems to go without saying that Irene's soul must also bear masculine qualities. In more modern terms, the King implies that our antagonist is perhaps something akin to a contemporary understanding of transgendered. Although Irene's body is female, she expresses "a gender identity that differs from the one that corresponds to [her] sex at birth" ("Transgender"). One might immediately question, however, whether this description of the King can be trusted given that he is presented as somewhat of a buffoon; with a comical air for dramatics and the inability to judge his own intelligence in comparison to others. This is true particularly in his interactions with Holmes as the King initially believes, foolishly, that he's succeeded in tricking the detective: "'I may confess at once that the title by which I have just called myself is not exactly my own.' 'I was aware of it,' said Holmes drily" (Klinger 15). Indeed, the reader may conclude that this "transgendered" Irene is as inaccurate as the King's reading of her motives (that is, his narcissistic assumption that she holds on to their photograph not for her own safety but "to ruin" the King just as he is about to be married). Perhaps Irene is *only* a woman—biologically, psychologically, spiritually—and there is no implication of duplicity, leaving her disguise merely that ... a costume and nothing more.

Yet there is another perspective that coincides with the King's. It helps that this added perspective is one that the reader can trust. It is Holmes himself, revered as the most logical, objective, and critical of all observers. Should Holmes agree with the King's description of Irene as "transgendered" then there can be little doubt that it is true—or at least, that it is highly likely. Indeed, the King's first statement, that "she has the face of the most beautiful of women," is reinforced when Holmes tells Watson of his time spent outside Irene's home. "I only caught a glimpse of her," he says, "but she was a lovely woman, with a face that a man might die for" (Klinger 23). Holmes, who once assured Watson that "the fair sex is your department" and who has only caught one "glimpse" of Irene, nevertheless agrees that she is "lovely." This agreement helps to build a foundation of trust in the King's words. It may be a little thing but if even Holmes, who Watson at one point describes as "an automaton—a calculating machine," is moved enough by Irene's looks to make note of them then she must truly be "the most beautiful of women," making at least that one part of the King's description true (Klinger 235). If we can believe *both* these men's words when it comes to Irene's looks, perhaps we can begin to trust their judgment of her in other matters as well.

The issue of defining Irene's mind—and perhaps also her soul—is a little trickier. After all, it is quite a leap to declare that Irene, a paradigm of feminine beauty, nevertheless has the "mind of the most resolute of men," let alone that her adoption of such a strikingly feminine demeanor is a mere façade. And what evidence does the King give us for this assertion? None really, other than an implication that only someone with the characteristics of a man would be so audacious as to blackmail a king. In the style of a true detective Holmes provides the King with the evidence he needs to back up his exceptional statement. Despite never making so bold an assertion as claiming that Irene is more man than woman, Holmes unknowingly makes a distinction between the mind and the instincts of a woman, inadvertently strengthening the King's argument. Throughout the story Holmes lectures on the characteristics of women—and thus the characteristics of Irene—all of which *seem* to hold true as the tale progresses. He claims, "Women are naturally secretive, and they like to do their own secreting ... [the photograph] must be where she can lay her hands upon it. It must be in her own house" and indeed, Holmes discovers that the photograph has been hidden behind a panel in Irene's living room (Klinger 30). Later when Watson gives the cry of fire, Holmes knows that Irene will retrieve the photograph because, as a woman, "her instinct is at once to rush to the thing which she values most," and as an unmarried woman who lacks a child, the photograph is her most precious possession (Klinger 33). Just as before, Irene "responded beautifully" and thus the implication is that as someone who adheres to the "rules" of womanhood, Irene must very much be a *woman*.

Thus, according to Holmes' (incredibly flawed) beliefs, a woman is biologically geared towards behaving in a certain way; certain actions are instinctual for her. However, even if the reader accepts this they are only *instincts* and a woman still possesses the ability to overcome them with higher thinking. Holmes believes it is only natural that Irene is influenced by these instincts since she is, biologically, female. Yet every time she falls slave to them she immediately fights back, consciously choosing to think like a man despite her supposed, natural psychology pressuring her to act otherwise. Yes, Irene does keep the photograph in her house and proving that she is "secretive," but this is also the most logical hiding place and one that a man would likewise have chosen. Holmes himself says that a banker or a lawyer is out of the question for "she could not tell what indirect or political influence might be brought to bear upon a business man" (Klinger 30). The other option would be for

Irene to hide it on her person which Holmes dismisses because the photograph is "too large for easy concealment about a woman's dress." Yet, as we'll see later, Irene is not averse to wearing men's clothes. Why then not hide the photograph in a man's coat or a vest? Most likely because twice now "she has been waylaid" and the King "diverted her luggage when she travelled" (Klinger 18). Her person, then, does not seem the safest place to keep such a valuable item, not when the King is so determined to retrieve it. Irene's home is also the most logical place for anyone, male or female, to hide the photograph, despite that being the location where a woman supposedly *would* hide it. Somewhat hypocritically, in later adventures Holmes often chooses his own home as his bank, keeping such valuable items as the Countess of Morcar's blue carbuncle in his Baker Street strong-box (Klinger 207).

Furthermore, Irene's response to the call of fire is, surprisingly, equally representative of her masculine thinking. She reaches for the photograph just as Holmes knew a woman would, but immediately afterwards Irene is thinking ahead in a manner worthy of the detective himself. In her later note she compliments Holmes, saying:

> You really did it very well. You took me in completely. Until after the alarm of fire, I had not a suspicion. But then, when I found how I had betrayed myself, I began to think. I had been warned against you months ago. I had been told that, if the King employed an agent, it would certainly be you. And your address had been given to me. Yet, with all this, you made me reveal what you wanted to know [Klinger 38].

Irene admits that her instincts and Holmes' plot "took [her] in completely" but unlike another woman who may have panicked or even ignored the situation in the hopes that she was mistaken, Irene *immediately* begins to rectify it by "[beginning] to think." She not only realizes that she has been tricked, Irene also identifies who has tricked her, thinking back to the warning she had been given months ago. With these thoughts in mind Irene rushes upstairs to don a new disguise— men's clothing—that will prove so successful it fools even the great Sherlock Holmes. Time and time again the reader of Conan Doyle's stories has seen Holmes rush into his own bedroom, choosing the perfect disguise to aid him in his quest. Here, Irene acts out the same sequence of events, proving that although others may view her instincts as feminine and although she chooses to play up that femininity with her looks, her thought process is very much that of a man's. This distinction is truly driven home at the end of the story when the King exclaims: "What a woman—oh what a woman! ... Is it not a pity that she was not on my level?" To which Holmes "coldly" replies, "From what I have seen of the lady, she seems, indeed, to be on a very different level to your Majesty" (Klinger 38). Irene may biologically be female but Holmes makes it clear that she has the intelligence of a man, having proven herself equal to one exceptional man, Holmes himself, and far superior to another, her royal ex-lover.

Thus it would seem that we *can* accept the King's declaration that Irene has "the face of the most beautiful of women, and the mind of the most resolute of men," and it is this description that establishes Irene as a paradigm of BBC Irene's beliefs in regard to disguises. Recall that BBC Irene claims that a disguise is a "self-portrait," paradoxically implying that it reveals more than it hides. What could be more perfect then but that canon Irene disguises herself as a man? She chooses to do just that when, having realized that it was Sherlock Holmes who started the fire within her home, Irene proceeds to follow him and Watson to their flat at 221B Baker Street dressed in her hurried male garb:

> We had reached Baker Street and had stopped at the door. He was searching his pockets for the key when some one passing said: "Good-night, Mister Sherlock Holmes." There were several people on the pavement at the time, but the greeting appeared to come from a slim youth in an ulster who had hurried by. "I've heard that voice before," said Holmes.... "Now, I wonder who the deuce that could have been" [Klinger 35–6].

Here, Irene's decision to disguise herself as a man ends up reaffirming the King's belief that she has a masculine mind and quite possibly a masculine soul as well. For Irene does not merely wear the disguise, she embodies it, well enough that she manages to fool the very thing she is imitating. Watson, who is most assuredly a man (despite what Rex Stout might have to say about it) looks at Irene and sees only a "slim youth in an ulster," never doubting his impression that he is looking at a boy. And although the term "youth" is not always gender specific, in this case the implication is most certainly of a "young man between adolescence and maturity" ("Youth"). More significantly, Irene manages to fool Sherlock Holmes who is not only a man but also one of the most observant men in his literary world. As Irene passes him by Holmes wonders "who the deuce that could have been," highlighting that he is unsure about the identity, not the sex, of his greeter (Klinger 36). Irene is so well disguised that she fools not only other men but even the most discerning of men and the reason for this success is that Irene *is*, in many respects, a "man." It may also help that she has had ample practice at passing as male, admitting that "male costume is nothing new to me. I often take advantage of the freedom which it gives," perhaps further implying that this freedom Irene experiences is not merely societal but personal as well (Klinger 38). We have been shown that Irene is a "man" throughout the entirety of the story, in both her actions and her thought process, as she proceeds to react to situations in a masculine manner as defined by her literary world, despite her supposed feminine instincts. This "disguise" then is actually a revelation of what truly hides beneath Irene's feminine exterior and the exterior itself is concealing, suggesting that BBC Irene was right: in this case the disguise is far more revealing than one might imagine.

However, the original question still remains—does this theory hold for BBC Irene? One would imagine that it would. She is after all the one who comments on it. Yet it is worth our time to forgo this assumption and work our way through the evidence as Holmes himself would have us do, for if BBC Irene does *not* adhere to her own beliefs then this will help to confirm that she is a remarkably different Irene from her canon counterpart. Perhaps even a lesser Irene.

To start, it should be noted that at the very least Irene's rule regarding disguises is active in the rest of the BBC *Sherlock* world. After being pulled from what proves to be a crime scene with a transparent solution, Sherlock and John find themselves in Buckingham Palace. The scene opens with them trading jokes about their situation, allowing the camera time to take in the palace's layout and décor. Certainly it is impressive, posh enough that John fights the impulse to "steal an ashtray" (*Sherlock* "A Scandal in Belgravia"). However, what is truly notable about the palace is that it is dominated entirely by two colors: red and more significantly, gold. Everything in the room from the ceiling to the floor has at least a hint of gold, from the couches' pattern to the moldings on the walls. Literally everything has a touch of it, making it *the* color of Buckingham Palace (and truly, is that any surprise?) What this sets up then is an association: gold equals wealth, power, royalty, and authority. It may catch the viewer's notice then that both Mycroft and their "illustrious" client's employee—introduced only as Harry—both come in wearing yellow and gold ties.

What BBC Irene fails to mention in her definition of a disguise is that often the best disguises are those that are not strictly intended to be disguises at all. Both of these men are dressed in suits which, while looking like normal clothes (if a bit on the expensive side) can actually be read as a kind of camouflage. The suits act as both armor and diversions, allowing their owners to present the world with an image of an authoritative male while simultaneously protecting those weaknesses that the wearer would prefer remain hidden. When Moriarty cracks a code the British government has been trying desperately to keep from him, he sends a text to Mycroft celebrating his victory: "Jumbo Jet. Dear me, Mr. Holmes, dear me" ("A Scandal in Belgravia"). The resulting shots show Mycroft dealing with the aftermath but it is not the glass of brandy at his side, or his head in his hands, or even the enormous hall he sits in—that makes him appear terribly small—that conveys just how anxious he is about this situation. Rather, it is the removal of his suit jacket, no doubt put away carefully in a closet somewhere off-screen. For a man who is *always* impeccably dressed, even when he is alone (take note of Mycroft's Christmas Eve earlier in the episode, alone by the fire, yet not even his tie has been loosened) the fact that he would remove an article of clothing now speaks volumes about his emotional state. Or, think again of Moriarty, calmly smoothing out his own jacket after being attacked by John and saying only, "*Westwood*" (*Sherlock* "The Great Game"). Ironing out the wrinkles of his jacket is akin to ironing out the wrinkles of the situation. John may have proven to be a bit of a wild card and Sherlock may be pointing a gun at his head but at the very least Moriarty can make sure that his clothes, his disguise, remains untarnished. A suit then, simply put, makes one appear in control regardless of whether or not he actually is. Thus Mycroft's rejection of his suit is also an acknowledgement of his failure while Moriarty's careful smoothing of his is a nod to the fact that, yes, he believes that he still has the upper-hand.

It is significant then that when Mycroft and Harry enter the palace they are both dressed to the nines and as Irene has argued, their choice of clothing is quite revealing. As mentioned previously, each wears a gold/yellow tie, immediately drawing an association between their clothes and their environment. It is also worth mentioning that each has chosen a tie with a bit of blue in it: Mycroft with a delicate, almost invisible pattern while Harry sports bold diagonal stripes. These suits, their "disguises," reveal a great deal about how these men want to be viewed. The choice to wear gold represents their need to be seen as powerful and dignified—everything that Buckingham Palace represents—while the bit of blue speaks to their desire to be connected with other, powerful figures—namely each other. Mycroft would like to link himself with Harry, employed to such an "illustrious" client, while Harry can certainly benefit from Mycroft's reputation, considering that he "*is* the British government" (*Sherlock* "A Study in Pink"). As Irene rightly points out, even the tiniest details—like a bit of cardboard playing at a clerical collar, or the color of one's tie—can say much about a man or a woman.

This scene helps to establish that Irene's theory holds in the world of BBC *Sherlock* but the characters begin to diverge when Irene does away with the male/female disguises that her counterpart chose. Instead she opts for her "battle suit," more commonly known as a "birthday suit." For the majority of her first conversation with Sherlock, Irene is naked but for some makeup, diamond earrings, and a pair of heels, literally baring all. Though this is obviously an attempt to make "the virgin" uncomfortable, and thus perhaps lessen his ability to deduce, Irene's nakedness benefits her in another way as well ("A Scandal in Belgravia"). As Sherlock confronts the dominatrix he attempts to deduce something, anything about her and all he can come up with is "????" ("A Scandal in Belgravia"). However, Sherlock's sudden difficulty stems more from nakedness used as a *disguise* rather than nakedness as a sexual tool.

It should first be noted that Sherlock's skills are not on the fritz for they work just fine on John, deducing that he has a date that night, recently used an electric razor, and other minor, personal details. Rather paradoxically there is something about being naked—literally revealing everything—that works as a disguise. We can compare this to the King's costume that, in contrast, is so elaborate that it takes Watson half a page to describe, yet Holmes sees through it with just a glance (Klinger 16). Why does this work? How can the paradox of a revealing disguise possibly sustain itself? A large part of the success seems to rely on the character's motivations in combination with the detective's purpose. The detective, simply put, is meant to deduce things. When someone like the King enters wearing a "black vizard mask" he creates the perfect scenario for the detective to thrive in, for he only exists to unveil that which is hidden (Klinger 14). Compare this then to Irene who refuses to give Sherlock anything to unravel. She has taken the mystery away, given everything to him freely, and suddenly, our detective has no purpose. The brilliant bit is that instead of handing Sherlock every bit of knowledge about her, by denying him his usefulness Irene simultaneously denies him his deductions. By revealing everything—"everything" here being her feminine body—she ensures that she reveals nothing at all.

Here then Irene is able to make use of her own theory. She reveals so much of herself that her disguise becomes impenetrable, just as Conan Doyle's Irene "revealed" her true self by wearing men's clothes. Unlike canon Irene however, BBC Irene's success does not last. Things begin to fall apart the moment she gets dressed; specifically, when Irene bypasses her own clothes in favor of Sherlock's coat and, later, his dressing gown. Now instead of having a "disguise" that reveals a part of her innermost self, as was the case with canon Irene, this clothing works in reverse, with BBC Irene adopting the characteristics of the clothes' owner. Sherlock himself mentions early on that his clothing has the ability to be misleading, explaining to Harry that he looks taller in his photographs due to a "good coat and a short friend" (*Sherlock* "A Scandal in Belgravia"). Now, Irene literally becomes more logical when dressed in his things. While naked she demands that Sherlock explain to her the solution to his latest case but the moment she puts on his coat Irene is solving the mystery for herself. Later, sporting Sherlock's dressing gown—significantly an article of clothing that both canon and BBC Holmes wear while doing much of their thinking—Irene manages to trick Sherlock, convincing him that he's succeeded in acquiring her phone's pass-code. This little bluff, a feat in and of itself, earns her the compliment, "Oh you are rather good" ("A Scandal in Belgravia"). What Sherlock fails to acknowledge is that these successes are not actually products of Irene herself but are rather the work of her "disguises," *his* clothes.

This is not the only time that wearing another's clothes produces characteristics generally alien to the person in question. In season three's "The Empty Hearse" (*Sherlock* 2014) Mycroft and Sherlock compete in a battle of deductions, each attempting to deduce more than the other about a hat that has come into Sherlock's possession. It should first be noted that Mycroft is canonically the more observant of the two, with Conan Doyle's Holmes admitting, "My dear Watson.... When I say, therefore, that Mycroft has better powers of observation than I, you may take it that I am speaking the exact and literal truth" (Klinger 638). This characterization is shown as canonical within *Sherlock* as well when Mycroft reminds his brother that he always wins these little deduction battles. He then quickly backs up his words. Having been tossed the hat just a second before and after taking only one sniff, Mycroft spouts off that he finds "nothing irresistible in the hat of a well traveled, anxious, sentimental, unfit creature of habit with appalling halitosis ... damn" ("The Empty Hearse"). It is that "damn" at the end that is particularly interesting. The curse, along with Mycroft's expression, informs the audience that he had no intention of actually playing this game. Yet he has, implying that his deduction skills aren't just incredible but nearly instinctual as well; they happen automatically. In the matter of drawing conclusions, Mycroft is clearly Sherlock's superior.

How then is Sherlock able to win? By the time they've finished their deductions—nearly two minutes later—Sherlock has stumped his brother by concluding that the hat's owner is "isolated" and "lonely" ("The Empty Hearse"). It seems unlikely that Sherlock would have a better understanding of human emotion than Mycroft, as Mycroft is the one involved in the more social career of civil servant/British government while Sherlock, prior to befriending John, reveled in his self-description as a "high functioning sociopath" ("A Study in Pink"). Yet, here Sherlock is able to easily recognize and understand this man's isolation while Mycroft is irrevocably blind to it. The only way in which they deduce differently and the only advantage Sherlock has against his brother's superior observation skills is that Sherlock actually puts the hat *on*. Placing it jauntily atop his head—happily ignoring the stench and the chewed bits—Sherlock is able to see the owner's loneliness because, for just a moment, Sherlock is a recipient of that characteristic in the same way that Irene briefly receives a watered down version of his deductive skills. The transference is strong enough that Sherlock is able to recognize loneliness within Mycroft as well, at least until the hat is removed. After that, Mycroft's loneliness is (as of yet) not mentioned again.

Thus disguises, even those not necessarily intended as such, not only reveal aspects of a person but can also briefly alter the details of who that person is. They act as a cover nearly as well as complete disclosure, such as Irene's nakedness, for indeed it is hard to see "Irene" when she is masquerading as "Sherlock" or to recognize "Sherlock" when he is channeling an isolated man with an obsessive attachment to his hat. It is telling that Irene becomes far better at deceiving Sherlock while wearing his garments and that Sherlock is suddenly able to understand a sibling's loneliness while wearing a hat. But this power, if you will, that disguises possesses becomes nearly conclusive when one observes the clothing being removed. Mycroft is a recurring character destined for season four. Thus any analysis of his loneliness (or lack thereof) is ongoing. However, Irene's story is, supposedly, complete and she *does* loose her deductive abilities as soon as she changes back into her own clothes. The next time we see Irene she is once more wearing the sort of sexy dress that's appropriate for her dominating lifestyle and this is also the time when Irene is finally outwitted by Sherlock.

Standing in a room with the Holmes brothers, Irene gloats about her and Moriarty's victory. Just like her canon counterpart she's done it all: fooled the detective, blackmailed the government, and ensured herself a flawless escape route. Then all at once she finds her success crumbling. Sherlock takes her hand, explaining that earlier he took her pulse, and thus deduced her greatest secret— she likes him. This here is BBC Irene's downfall. Halfway through the episode she develops a secret she needs to hide and thus the revealing disguise no longer *feels* like an option. We have certainly seen this before; the King of Bohemia desperately wants to hide his identity and thus immediately fails at doing so. Canon Irene, in contrast, attempts to hide nothing at all. She makes it clear that she has the photographs they seek, she freely admits to marrying Mr. Norton, and, most important of all, her disguise does not conceal but rather reveals her inherent, masculine nature. BBC Irene was right at the start. Best to reveal herself in a more literal manner than Conan Doyle's Irene, but she is unable to utilize this "self-portrait" for long. While being accused of loving Sherlock, Irene instantly makes the mistake of trying to *hide* her feelings. "Oh dear god," she says, "look at the poor man. You don't think I was actually interested in you...?" and Sherlock retorts with the cynical belief that sentiment is a "chemical defect found on the losing side" ("A Scandal in Belgravia"). Whether or not this is true is a discussion for another time but it is not the existence of Irene's sentiment that dooms her, rather, it is her blatant attempts to hide it. She denies her interest verbally and tucks the evidence away in a place that she thinks is safe, her phone. But instead of her infatuation remaining hidden, the scene ends with Sherlock dramatically entering the pass-code "I am SHER-LOCKED," revealing both Irene's feelings and the information she was using as blackmail ("A Scandal in Belgravia"). Irene would have done better to remain naked, baring it all both figuratively and literally, for it seems that it is only the concealed secrets that have a tendency to come out.

This then is indeed a very different Irene from the one Conan Doyle gave us. She, like her predecessor, understands the importance of a revealing disguise. Yet unlike canon Irene she is incapable of adhering to her own rules. At the end of "A Scandal in Belgravia" Irene has undergone numerous trials that Conan Doyle's Irene never had to face, all of which stem from her inability to paradoxically reveal more than she hides. This Irene has *lost* to Sherlock, fallen in love with him, and has had her affections rejected. She has worked alongside Moriarty (disrupting the dynamic of a *woman* attempting to beat Sherlock Holmes, no matter how she dresses), put herself at the mercy of the British government, and nearly loses her life in the process. Is this Irene a more clichéd woman than her original—issues of masculine minds and spirits aside? After all, it can be argued that she failed, stereotypically fell in love with a man (despite being presented as a lesbian), needed the help of another man to even attempt going after Sherlock, and ultimately needs Sherlock to save her. Are we moving backwards? Is this Irene, despite her assertive nature and the stunning mind that matches her stunning body, a far less progressive Irene than Conan Doyle's? She who beyond her masculine qualities is still "*the* woman"? Perhaps. But we should also be wary. As Holmes continually reminds us, "there is nothing more deceptive than an obvious fact" (Klinger 108).

Works Cited

Alan Bradley, C., and William A. S. Sarjeant. *Ms Holmes of Baker Street: The Truth About Sherlock*. Edmonton: University of Alberta, 2004. Print.

"The Empty Hearse." *Sherlock*. BBC One. London. 1 Jan. 2014. Television.

"The Great Game." *Sherlock.* BBC One. London. 8 Aug. 2010. Television.
Klinger, Leslie. "The Adventure of the Blue Carbuncle." *The New Annotated Sherlock Holmes vol. 1.* New York: W.W. Norton, 2007. 197–223. Print.
_____. "The Boscombe Valley Mystery." *The New Annotated Sherlock Holmes vol. 1.* New York: W.W. Norton, 2007. 101–132. Print.
_____. "A Scandal in Bohemia." *The New Annotated Sherlock Holmes vol. 1.* New York: W.W. Norton, 2007. 5–40. Print.
_____. "The Sign of Four." *The New Annotated Sherlock Holmes: The Novels.* New York: W.W. Norton, 2005. 209–379. Print.
"A Scandal in Belgravia." *Sherlock.* BBC One. London. 1 Jan. 2012. Television.
"A Study in Pink." *Sherlock.* BBC One. London. 25 Jul. 2010. Television.
Stout, Rex. "Was Watson a Woman?" *Sacrilege!* Baker Street Irregulars Meeting. 1941. Web. http://www.hwslash.net/stout.html.
"Transgender." Def. 1. *Merriam-Webster.* Encyclopedia Britannica, n.d. Web. http://www.merriam-webster.com/dictionary/transgender.
"Youth." Def. 2. *Merriam-Webster.* Encyclopedia Britannica, n.d. Web. http://www.merriam-webster.com/dictionary/youth.

I Am Sherlocked
Adapting Victorian Gender and Sexuality in "A Scandal in Belgravia"

Lindsay Katzir

The BBC series *Sherlock* (2010–) closely draws on Arthur Conan Doyle's Sherlock Holmes stories and features well-known characters such as Dr. Watson, Mycroft Holmes, and Moriarty. Reviewers and fans have variously criticized or praised "A Scandal in Belgravia" (2012), the premiere of *Sherlock*'s second series, for its portrayal of Irene Adler. Adler, Conan Doyle's original character in "A Scandal in Bohemia" (1891), is a clever, gender-bending protofeminist who uses her wits and flair for performance against Holmes. She is one of the original series' few antagonists to earn Holmes's esteem and evade his capture. "Belgravia," written by *Sherlock* co-creator Steven Moffat, transforms Conan Doyle's adventuress, who leaves "Bohemia" happily married, into a lesbian dominatrix. Critical reactions to *Sherlock*'s Irene, played by Lara Pulver, often either confirm or dispute the character's status as a feminist archetype. While some viewers object to Pulver's on-screen nudity, others herald Irene as a strong female character, and Pulver herself attests to having felt empowered in shedding her clothes in order to confound the sexually inexperienced Sherlock (Jeffery).

"Bohemia" takes place during a period of inquiry regarding sex and gender. In her influential work *Sexual Anarchy*, Elaine Showalter characterizes the Victorian fin de siècle as a period "when all the laws that governed sexual identity and behavior seemed to be breaking down" and argues that marginal figures "redefined the meanings of femininity and masculinity" (3). Mainstream Victorians realized that "sexuality and sex roles might no longer be contained within the neat and permanent borderlines of gender categories" (9). Megan Hoffman calls attention to gender anxiety in Victorian detective fiction, which "in spite of its apparent glorification of masculinity, makes [the genre] a prime site for examination of the potential flexibility of gender roles" (81). And in *Sherlock's Men* Joseph Kestner acknowledges that masculinity was a constructed, contested, and negotiated category in late nineteenth-century society and contends that Conan Doyle probes ideas of manliness and masculinity throughout his Sherlock Holmes series.

Like Moffat's *Sherlock*, other recent screen adaptations of nineteenth-century literary works have reimagined their Victorian characters in twenty-first-century settings, often producing paradoxical readings of familiar texts, especially where issues of sex and gender are concerned. Neil McCaw perceives this particular phenomenon in Holmes adaptations: these afterlives of Conan Doyle's series appear "to both reinforce and challenge the prevailing status quo in a host of ways, sometimes within the same text" (36). Imelda Whelehan views neo–Victorian texts as contradictory, noting that such "fiction offers a ... 'safe' examination of gender, class, and other social concerns depending on whether narrative strategies are interpreted as involving a challenging reflection on our own times, or whether transplanting gender and class politics to a previous era neutralizes current political issues" (278). Antonija Primorac highlights the "blatant and much overlooked loss of Victorian female characters' agency that takes place in the process of "updating" Victorian texts in contemporary screen adaptations through the—now almost routine—"sexing up" of the proverbially prudish Victorians" (90). Moffat's "Belgravia" illustrates Primorac's theory of the postmodern breakdown of female agency, curtailing the agency that Conan Doyle originally invested in Irene Adler.

In this essay I look to Conan Doyle's "Bohemia," examining the interplay of sexual difference and gender performance within the narrative in order to unearth a fundamental problem with the portrayal of both Irene and Sherlock in the BBC's "Belgravia." Drawing on the arguments of McCaw, Whelehan, and Primorac, I interrogate intersecting experiences of gender and sexuality in the two texts, underscoring the adaptation of Holmes and Adler's relationship. Markedly different from Conan Doyle, Moffat grounds Irene in a hetero- and gender normative system. The Victorian Adler not only eludes Holmes's capture, but also resists gender identification through performance and cross-dressing. Holmes is similarly indicted in normative gendering, and contemporary revisions of the detective portray Conan Doyle's nonconformist as a model of masculinized rationality. Normative gendering in Moffat's "Belgravia" reinforces heteronormative sexuality, undermining the sexual and gender ambiguity of Conan Doyle's characters.

Conan Doyle's Model Masculinity

Scholars often present the detective's universe as perfectly controlled, ordered, and above all, rational based on Holmes's repeated affirmations of universal continuity and his emphasis on unemotional logic. For example, in "The Illustrious Client," when accounting for his failure to provoke an emotional response from Violet de Merville, Holmes locates "the head," in contradistinction to "the heart," as the site of rational procedure. "I use my head, not my heart," he reminds Watson (Conan Doyle 2: 525). Holmes's system relies on the fundamental truth of "the science of deduction." The detective believes he can arrive at the correct answer to a problem by observing connections between events and drawing reasoned conclusions from such sequences.

Critics interested in gender relations within the Holmes series often argue that normative masculinity is inscribed in Holmes's logical methodology and that Conan Doyle portrays the feminine as other. Patrick Morgan marks a distinction between "the traditionally feminine qualities of emotion and heated passion" and "the male world of cold reason" in Conan Doyle's Holmes stories (26). Andrew Smith underscores the critical tendency to identify an ever-present "masculine intellect" contrasted with "images of feminine irrationality" in the series (47). Jasmine Yong Hall declares that stories featuring female clients help to establish the "rational detective as a powerful, patriarchal hero" (295). Some critics, working from the premise that Holmes and Watson uphold a patriarchal societal structure, render Holmes as a "paragon of masculinized rationality" who actively "polices gender roles and social order" (Hoffman 81). Many readings of "Bohemia" examine the tension between Holmes's attempts to reinforce normative gender roles and Adler's subversion of such gender dynamics; however, both characters destabilize conventional sex and gender categories. Conan Doyle's story presents sexual liminality and gender performance in both the gender-bending adventuress Adler and the bohemian celibate Holmes.

"Bohemia" narrates Holmes's attempts to retrieve a photograph from Adler. The king of Bohemia hires Holmes to secure an incriminating photograph of himself with his former lover. Holmes trails Adler, participates in her wedding to solicitor Godfrey Norton, employs disguise and deception to infiltrate her house, tricks her into revealing the concealed photograph, and finally, congratulates himself on defeating her. However, Adler catches on to his scheme and safeguards the photograph before leaving the country with her new husband. By the time Holmes, Watson, and the king arrive to confront

Adler, she has vanished with the evidence, leaving a letter and a different photograph—of herself alone—in its place.

The king first describes Adler as "the well-known adventuress" (Conan Doyle 1: 215). Victorian readers would have understood "adventuress" to mean an unscrupulous woman seeking social or financial advantages through questionable, often sexual, means. Holmes's index identifies Adler as an American-born opera singer, retired and living in London. Marjorie Garber explains that "a career in European opera was for American women of the period often both professionally lucrative and socially liminal" (192). In addition to training her in acting and costume, an opera career would have granted Adler social flexibility.

Many scholars agree that Adler's profession intertwines her social and sexual categorization, positioning the actress as adventuress. Garber suggests that "retired from operatic stage" implies "kept woman" (192). According to Tom Bragg, the text intimates that Adler is Norton's mistress, a "sexual adventuress" who lives "outside of conventional and sanctioned norms" (22). Pascale Krumm reasons that she fits squarely into the "harlot" category of the Victorian paradigm of "housewife or harlot" but overlooks Adler's capacity for penetrating seemingly fixed borders, especially considering that she eventually becomes Norton's legitimate wife (194). Rather than place Holmes and Adler in opposition, the "adventuress" classification aligns Adler more closely to the categorically transgressive Holmes.

Adler's final letter assures that she will not send the photograph to the king's bride, but rather keep the photograph as protection against future harassment. For Randall Warren, Adler's refusal to sell the photograph indicates personal, not professional, interest in the king; in other words, Adler's heart guides her actions (234). She married Norton for love, and the king wronged her, presumably in matters of love and marriage. In assessing Adler's exceptionality, Christopher Redmond draws a similar conclusion, remarking on the extraordinariness of Adler's marrying "a solicitor who shows no evidence, as far as the reader is aware, of riches or exceptional style" (62). But Conan Doyle's Adler acts deliberately with intelligence and foresight throughout the story, and her capacity for love does not preclude her from executing her plans and achieving her desired ends. Conan Doyle's Adler transcends Warren's definition of "adventuress" just as the character blurs the distinction between wife and harlot. Adler's liminal position between gendered binaries and social boundaries affords her complete personal autonomy.

Although Holmes and Adler both perform character and gender, Holmes fails to register Adler's gender duality until the end of the story. Adler's exhibition of both feminine and masculine characteristics first confounds, and then intrigues, the detective. At first Conan Doyle represents Adler's beauty as especially feminine. When familiarizing Holmes with the details of his case, the king readily describes Adler's remarkable beauty: "she has the face of the most beautiful of women" (Conan Doyle 1: 216). When Holmes finally sees her he tells Watson that she is "a lovely woman, with a face that a man might die for," and he pronounces her "the daintiest thing under a bonnet," a diminutive that reinforces a singularly feminine identity (1: 220). Adler is a paragon of feminine beauty, and her femininity reassures Holmes that she is ultimately definable.

Though disguised himself when he first meets Adler, Holmes fails to consider that the uncommonly beautiful woman's face might mask "a soul of steel" (Conan Doyle 1: 216). Adler's "mind of the most resolute of men" (1: 216), according to the king, enables her to carry out her threats. Like Holmes, Adler goes to great lengths to achieve her goals. Jill Galvan notes that Holmes takes offense at the king's undervaluation of "so formidable a companion" (139), presumably because by the end of "Bohemia" Holmes considers the woman who beat him to be an intellectual equal. Adler's defeat of Holmes is made possible by her knack for playing roles—in this case, playing with prescribed gender roles.

Several critics read Adler as actively subverting Holmes's normatively gendered system by usurping the authority centralized in the figure of the male detective. Ronald Thomas asserts that Adler "challenges the detective's perceptions of her and her conformity to certain gendered codes of behavior" (149); and Smith determines that "Adler is a deeply disturbing presence for Holmes because she confounds his preconception that women are not able to think rationally and so challenges his own claims for the dominance of a superior, masculine and rational gaze" (51). Hoffman champions Adler, stating that Conan Doyle provocatively depicts the detective "matching wits with a worthy female antagonist and failing due to his underestimation of her abilities" (83). However, others are less complimentary of Adler. Richard Kellogg argues that she must "assume 'masculine' traits in order to outwit a man" (115); and Krumm disavows her savvy altogether, concluding that it is Holmes's overconfidence, and "not Adler's exceptional cleverness," that causes him to lose the case (199). For some writers, then, "Bohemia" holds to the Victorian concept of gendered spheres, and Adler's gender duality disrupts Holmes's strict distinction between masculinity and femininity.

However, Adler's gender duality and her expertise in costume complement Holmes's own sexual ambiguity and skill in assuming and performing various roles, forging a connection between play and gender in the text. This is evident in the way Holmes refers to Adler. In the first line of "Bohemia," Watson recalls that "to Sherlock Holmes she is always *the* woman" (Conan Doyle 1: 209). Watson observes that he has "seldom heard [Holmes] mention [Adler] under any other name" (1: 209). Krumm attributes Holmes's reluctance to name Adler to his embarrassment at losing a case to a woman (193). On the other hand, Galvan maintains that Holmes intends the phrase as an honorific, that "*the* woman" at once acknowledges his previous misconception of female mental acuity and indicates his respect for Adler as an intellectual equal (139). But underlying these claims is the assumption that "*the* woman" functions as a marker of singular gender identity. Adler bests Holmes at his own game of intrigue and disguise, and her cross-dressing points to fin-de-siècle gender performativity in "Bohemia" and throughout the series.

When writers cite Adler's besting of Holmes, they refer to two moments in the narrative, both of which rest on Adler's gender duplicity. First, she regains the upper hand. Adler admits the detective—disguised as a clergyman—into her house, in accordance with his plan to discover the location of the photograph. When Watson stages a fire in her parlor, Adler rushes to secure the photograph, her most valuable possession, and reveals its hiding place. In so doing, she undermines control over her own space. However, Adler quickly recuperates, and as Victoria Rosner asserts, reclaims the "masculine liberty" of controlling the space by safeguarding the photograph (107).

Second, Adler utilizes a disguise to deceive the detective. After the fire, Holmes prematurely revels in his victory over Adler while walking home with Watson. When they stop at the door of 221B Baker Street and Holmes fishes for his key, a "slim youth in an ulster" utters, "Good-night, Mister Sherlock Holmes," in passing (Conan Doyle 1: 226). Though the male voice is familiar to Holmes, he does not recognize it as Adler's. In her parting letter, Adler writes that Holmes's performance of the clergyman would have completely fooled her, had she not been trained as an actress (1: 228). Adler admits that the two are *almost* an intellectual match, with one caveat: her cross-dressing fools Holmes. The woman informs him that "male costume is nothing new to [her]"—presumably because she played pants roles during her time on the stage—and that she "often take[s] advantage of the freedom which it gives" (1: 228).

"Bohemia's" conclusion with Adler's letter exemplifies, for Rosner, Adler's usurpation of the detective's (masculine) role. Adler "unpacks additional obscure details" of the case, effectively "supplanting Holmes's chain of reasoning with her own" (Rosner 109). Kellogg claims that "the usual power relationship between males and females during the Holmes era is dramatically reversed in 'A Scandal in Bohemia'" (115). But it is important to recall Lawrence Frank's point, that "in 'Bohemia' and elsewhere in his Sherlock Holmes stories, Conan Doyle was not merely reverting to some ahistorical archetype of the phallic woman" (54), that Adler is not simply a sexually aberrant disruption in Holmes's strictly normative system. I argue that "Bohemia" cannot be reduced to an example of gender role reversal, as "reversal" implies the presence of stable categories. Adler eludes classification, which for Frank, is predicated on her position as an "adventuress" (54), a term that is, itself, unclear in definition and application.

Conan Doyle similarly portrays Holmes as androgynous. *A Study in Scarlet* (1887), the first Holmes novel, describes the detective in feminine terms. Watson characterizes Holmes's reaction to his praise of his abilities as womanly: "My companion flushed up at my words.... I had already observed that he was as sensitive to flattery on the score of his art as any girl could be of her beauty" (Conan Doyle 1: 29). Watson also reports that Holmes suffers from occasional bouts of "nerves," a condition explicitly coded as feminine. And later in the series, in "The Mazarin Stone," Holmes solves a case by cross-dressing. Masculinity functions as performance for both Adler and Holmes; notably, Holmes's two costumes in "Bohemia," a groom and a clergyman, evoke different notions of masculinity.

Holmes is well known as a master of disguise. Despite his cognizance of Holmes's "amazing powers in the use of disguises," Watson nearly mistakes his friend for a "drunken-looking groom ... with an inflamed face and disreputable clothes" (Conan Doyle 1: 218). Holmes then vanishes and promptly emerges "tweed-suited and respectable, as of old" (1: 218). Shortly after, Watson relates Holmes's transformation into "an amiable and simple-minded Nonconformist clergyman" and muses on the detective's ability to convincingly perform even the most wildly different characters: "It was not merely that Holmes changed his costume. His expression, his manner, his very soul seemed to vary with every fresh part that he assumed" (1: 222–23). Watson then remarks that the detective might have been a successful stage actor. Here, Conan Doyle not only immortalizes the detective as a performer, but also draws a comparison between Holmes and Adler, the preeminent stage actress.

The tendency to position Holmes as enforcer of Victorian gender norms stems from the idea that he embodies quintessentially masculine qualities. For Kestner, Holmes "constitute[s] a contestation of masculinity, as well as an advocacy, [endowed] with elements that mark him as both paradigm and outsider" (37). In "Bohemia" Watson contrasts his own marital bliss with

Holmes's capricious nature and enduring discontent: "My own complete happiness, and [my] home-centred interests ... were sufficient to absorb all my attention, while Holmes, who loathed every form of society with his whole Bohemian soul, remained in our lodgings in Baker Street" (Conan Doyle 1: 209). According to Kestner, the "Bohemian" Holmes represents both normative and exceptional masculinity. Bragg argues, despite Holmes's "sexual ambiguity" or status as a "troubled, fitful degenerate" (19), the detective's ability to "reconcile differing models of masculine behavior," such as his preference for scientific reasoning and his predilection for music and art, enables him to become the series' policeman of gender normativity (4). Although Kestner and Bragg both acknowledge the complicated nature of Holmes's masculinity, each respectively returns to the view of that character as, to some extent, normatively gendered.

However, Holmes, like Adler, destabilizes cultural norms in part because his sexuality is situated between homo- and heterosexuality. Holmes's disinterest in women as sexual or romantic objects originates in the early stories, during the fundamental systematizing of his concept of rationality. In "The Second Stain" Holmes forswears sexual and romantic interest in women, reminding the bourgeois heterosexual Watson that "the fair sex is your department" (Conan Doyle 1: 911). And Watson begins his account of "Bohemia" by introducing Holmes's dispassionate view of Adler, and of romantic love generally:

> It was not that he felt any emotion akin to love for Irene Adler. All emotions, and that one particularly, were abhorrent to his cold, precise but admirably balanced mind.... For the trained reasoner to admit such intrusions into his own delicate and finely adjusted temperament was to introduce a distracting factor which might throw a doubt upon all his mental results [1: 209].

Instead of suggesting Conan Doyle's Holmes acts as a stabilizing force for gender and sexual norms, I read Holmes as a celibate, a figure that, according to Benjamin Kahan, works "between sexuality and asexuality" and unsettles familiar binaries of hetero- and homosexual (2). Throughout "Bohemia" Holmes's celibacy is contrasted with Watson's and Adler's respective heterosexual marital intimacies. In "The Lion's Mane" Holmes affirms his celibacy: "women have seldom been an attraction to me, for my brain has always governed my heart" (2: 681).

Some scholars and fans favor a romance between the detective and the woman. Redmond introduces a more intriguing possibility: "what makes Irene Adler fascinating, it seems, is that rather than cuddling up to Sherlock Holmes she fights him, and she wins" (69). Audiences often appreciate, even expect, the introduction of a heterosexual love interest for Holmes in their favorite version of Conan Doyle's series, and adaptations rarely depict Adler as capably outwitting the master of deduction without falling in love with him. Screen adaptations of the Sherlock Holmes stories, including the Warner Brothers film *Sherlock Holmes* (2009), the CBS series *Elementary* (2012–), and the BBC series *Sherlock*, cast Adler as a romantic leading lady. However, in the original story, the two characters frustrate audience expectations, failing to form a romantic attachment. Adler may be "*the* woman" in Holmes's index, but Watson assures his reader that Holmes's memory of her is not colored by romance. Holmes's celibacy absolves him of the hero's duty to romance Adler, and he instead fondly remembers her as his intellectual match, as the woman who beat him. "*The* woman," then, is an ironic signifier—the woman who circumvented Holmes in male dress.

Conan Doyle's Holmes stories undermine gender- and heteronormativity even as these texts variously appear to uphold Victorian beliefs about gender and sexuality. Holmes classifies himself as sheer intellect, incapable of love: "I am a brain, Watson. The rest of me is a mere appendix" (2: 561). But Watson paints a different Holmes in "The Three Garridebs": "It was worth a wound—it was worth many wounds—to know the depth of loyalty and love which lay behind that cold mask.... For the one and only time *I caught a glimpse of a great heart as well as of a great brain*" (emphasis added) (2: 624–25). Though Holmes conceives of himself as a brain alone, Conan Doyle blurs the head/heart distinction here and elsewhere in the series. Holmes categorizes his world, and rather than indexing based on gender difference, he admires and catalogues skill, irrespective of gender—or morality. Even the most respected woman in the Holmes stories is memorialized as "dubious and questionable" (Conan Doyle 1: 209). Ultimately, Conan Doyle's characters disturb categorized notions of gender presentation and sexual orientation.

The Disappointing Conservatism of a Lesbian Dominatrix

"A Scandal in Belgravia," the premiere of *Sherlock*'s second series, adapts the basic premise of "Bohemia" and incorporates specific elements from Conan Doyle's original story, including parallel scenes and verbatim lines. In his review for *Radio Times*, David Brown claims that the episode "follow[s] the heartbeat of Conan Doyle's original," citing similarities such as "the clergyman disguise, the ruse of a potential fire, the use of Adler's 'goodnight,

Mr. Sherlock Holmes,' and a keepsake by which the detective could remember his adversary—only here it was a phone rather than a photograph." Viewers familiar with the original stories often praise this adaptation's commitment to textual authenticity. Keeping in continuity with their first series, co-creators Steven Moffat and Mark Gatiss use Conan Doyle's text as a point of departure for their vision of a modern-day Holmes adventure, complete with mobile phones, sex scandals, and Islamist radicals.

Whelehan asserts that "adapting the Victorian in the past two decades has been all about sexing up the past, so that risqué content is almost routine and rarely shocking" (277). However, Moffat's decision to include a scene foregrounding Irene's naked body provoked some debate over adapting the Victorian woman. According to Paul Revoir in his review for the *Daily Mail*, some British viewers voiced concern over Pulver's appearing almost completely naked on screen, complaining that "the BBC had gone too far with the raunchy scenes." Some *Sherlock* fans took to the web to denounce the nude scene. For example, Esther Inglis-Arkell criticizes modern media incarnations of the Irene Adler character because in the Richie and Moffat versions she "takes off her clothes in front of Holmes to rattle him into making a mistake." Why craft a complex feminist character, Inglis-Arkell concludes, "when Irene Adler can get naked on camera?"

While some viewers expressed dissatisfaction with Irene stripping down for Sherlock, multiple reviewers for British news outlets, including *The Independent*, *Radio Times*, and *Digital Spy*, applaud Moffat's interpretation of Irene Adler. Tom Sutcliffe argues, "her nudity is a mind-game, not a desperate bid for attention." Laura Pledger admires Irene for employing her "feminine wiles" in furtherance of her ambition. Morgan Jeffery characterizes Pulver's Irene as confident and powerful rather than degraded and antifeminist. In an interview with Stuart Jeffries, Moffat rejects antifeminist charges, claiming, "In the original, Irene Adler's victory over Sherlock Holmes was to move house and run away with her husband. That's not a feminist victory." Here, Moffat insults Adler's agency in Conan Doyle, ignoring that character's bodily autonomy. His "liberation" of the Victorian female character restricts Irene, and consequently, Sherlock, in several ways. Moffat's adaptation curbs the gender and sexual transitivity of Conan Doyle's "Bohemia," effectively reinforcing gender and sexual singularity. "Belgravia" rigidly distinguishes masculinity from femininity and repudiates non-normative sexuality even though *Sherlock* categorizes both Sherlock and Irene as queer.

The "scandal" alluded to in the episode title refers to the surfacing of compromising, presumably sexually explicit, photographs of Irene with a

British royal woman. Mycroft explains that Irene works as a professional dominatrix known as "the Woman." Rather than Holmes's personal use of the phrase as a nod either to Adler's intellectual prowess or her male dress, "the woman" becomes a clear marker of unambiguous gender; she is a woman notable for her expansive sexual experience. Whereas Redmond defines the term "adventuress" as a liminal position "between a social climber and a high-class tart," this Irene services the socially significant, but demonstrates no interest in social mobility, which erases that ambiguity, leaving her as the singular "high-class tart" (58). Moffat's "Belgravia" negates the narrative flexibility of Conan Doyle's "Bohemia" from its opening scenes.

Pulver's Irene wears costumes, but unlike her literary, film, and television forebears (including Gayle Hunnicutt in Granada Television's "A Scandal in Bohemia" from the series *The Adventures of Sherlock Holmes* [1984–1985] and Rachel McAdams in the Warner Bros. film *Sherlock Holmes*), she never dons the more "freeing" male-style clothing. Rather, Irene appears variously in tight designer dresses, lingerie, nothing at all, and a burka, none of which serve any practical purpose in the narrative. The only functional piece of clothing Irene wears, Sherlock's coat, covers her nakedness and facilitates her temporary escape from the detective. But Irene's brief usurpation of Sherlock's distinctive coat proves a provisional solution to the episode's greater problem of constraining female characters. The elision of cross-dressing confirms the finality of Irene's fixed, knowable identity. Garber asserts that, in detective fiction, "the cross-dresser ... must always elude a final capture" (209). Assigning Irene a singular identity, revoking gender transitivity, eliminates her hope for final escape.

"Belgravia" depicts Irene as hyper-feminine, perhaps because, as Redmond suggests, "for many Sherlockians Ms. Adler has gone beyond being the character who appears in 'Scandal,' and has become an archetype, the absolute incarnation of femininity" (66). Irene builds her professional reputation around the sexual fantasy of a dominant femme. When Sherlock and Irene first meet in her sitting room, she has applied red lipstick, connoting her as a "bad girl," and shed her clothes to undermine the detective's confidence, momentarily stunning him. Primorac argues, "the elision of female agency takes place through a paradoxical representation of Adler as supposedly strong and in control because of her overt sexuality and reliance on using her body as a weapon" (98). In an interview with Morgan Jeffery, Pulver describes her on-camera nakedness as empowering, but, as Primorac observes, in many "screen adaptations of classic Victorian texts and themes, the spectacle of the nude or scantily clad female body draws viewers' attention away from diminished rather than enhanced female agency in these contemporary renditions of female characters" (93).[1]

"Belgravia" portrays the physical body as tantamount to identity. Revealing the code to the safe that holds her most valued commodity, her phone, Irene gives her bust/waist/hip measurements. Later, Sherlock misidentifies a dead body as Irene's based partially on these measurements. The similar body fools even Sherlock Holmes because the episode depicts Irene as nothing but a body. Furthermore, the scene alluding to Conan Doyle's line, "how the best plans of Mr. Sherlock Holmes were beaten by a woman's wit" (1: 229), shows Irene physically disarming Sherlock by stabbing him with a syringe filled with a sleeping draught and repeatedly beating him with her riding crop in order to retrieve her phone. The altered line, "the woman who beat you," highlights the extent to which "Belgravia" identifies Irene with physicality. Instead of besting Holmes by outwitting him, Irene literally beats Sherlock.

The focus on female physicality extends to the spaces women occupy. Lesli J. Favor claims, "Conan Doyle devises plots that depend upon women who ... are controlled, contained, and marginalized" (398). While I disagree that Favor's argument is borne out in the original Holmes stories, her point sheds light on *Sherlock*'s female characters. The narrative safely contains each of the primary female characters: Molly Hooper, Mrs. Hudson, Sally Donovan, Mary Morstan, and Irene each act within the boundaries of specific spaces. Moreover, *Sherlock*'s female characters wield power only within their assigned spaces. For example, Molly is useful at St. Bart's, but Sherlock finds her an inadequate substitute for John outside of the hospital in "The Empty Hearse." And Mary holds her own against Sherlock, except in scenes where Sherlock controls the space. For example, "His Last Vow" contains a number of scenes wherein Sherlock easily dominates Mary, including the empty house in Leinster Gardens (a meeting that he contrived), the living room at Baker Street, and his parents' house. Irene successfully manipulates Sherlock in two places, her house and his flat, either in bedrooms or intimate spaces where her overt sexuality impedes his deductive abilities. For example, after turning up in his bedroom wearing nothing but his dressing gown, Irene kisses Sherlock to compel his revelation of a secret government initiative spearheaded by Mycroft.

Although "Belgravia" concludes with the restoration of his masculine authority, these failures emasculate Sherlock. After disclosing Irene's betrayal, Mycroft ridicules Sherlock's naiveté. Upon her arrival to negotiate with the elder Holmes, Irene undercuts Sherlock's intellect, the seat of masculine authority, by dismissing and insulting him, forcing him to realize she has deceived him. And the scene aboard the grounded plane reveals Sherlock's exclusion from systemic information; unlike Conan Doyle's Holmes, the chief categorizer of information, Sherlock is momentarily cast as an amateur, "stumbling around the fringes" of a system over which he has temporarily lost control (*Sherlock* "A Scandal in Belgravia").

Because Sherlock's strong, singularly masculine character rests upon rationality, Moffat renders disguise ineffectual. In "Belgravia's" transposition of the scene in which Holmes infiltrates Adler's parlor, Sherlock attempts to discover Irene's mobile phone, which contains the incriminating royal photographs. However, in this rendition, Irene is made aware of Sherlock's plan and is able to prepare for his arrival. Meanwhile Sherlock searches frantically for an appropriate costume. After John and Sherlock leave for Eaton Square, John notes that Sherlock did not actually change clothes, a striking difference from Watson's observations of Holmes's transformative abilities in "Bohemia." And unlike Conan Doyle's Holmes, Sherlock is a terrible actor, unable to perform the clergyman convincingly. Irene remarks, the "problem with a disguise" is that "however hard you try, it's always a self-portrait" (*Sherlock* "A Scandal in Belgravia"). Indeed, Sherlock fails to shed his own character in order to successfully play a role.

Throughout Conan Doyle's Holmes stories, the detective often, though not invariably, fails to deduce the motives of women. Holmes usually attributes these failures not to his own oversights, but to women's inscrutableness or insolubility. Holmes's inability to understand women never prevents the series from depicting powerful female characters, and as Laurie Langbauer claims, "rather than being some hidden and subversive deconstructive principle, the power of women's inexplicableness is part of what made these stories so popular" (148). Langbauer further remarks that the attraction of "Bohemia" lies in "finding that Holmes can be just like everybody else," that Holmes makes mistakes (150). However, although he commits minor missteps during "Belgravia," Sherlock bests Irene at the end of the episode.

Hall argues that women in the Holmes stories function as "a conduit for male power," explaining, "as the object of sexual dominance, they are necessary to release that power. But they do not acquire power themselves; it is, instead, passed on to Holmes" (301). Hall's argument strikes me as more relevant to "Belgravia," and one scene in particular demonstrates Irene's transfer of power to Sherlock. After coercing from Sherlock details of the British government's secret project, Irene propositions him. The two clasp hands; Irene believes she unsettles Sherlock's sense of control, when in reality, she unknowingly reveals data that Sherlock will later use to destroy her plans. Sherlock is able to deduce Irene's motives because Moffat's narrative limits women to singular bodies, singular spaces, singular identities. Additionally, the narrative is also reductive to Sherlock, who has gone from the observant cataloguer of Conan Doyle's story to a veritable deity, emphasizing the potentially godlike qualities of the male sex. Moffat depicts both characters as singularly gendered.

The moment Irene believes she has succeeded in her game and extorted from Mycroft all her demands, "Belgravia" reinforces normative gender roles by granting Sherlock control over Irene's body. Given the episode's fixation with the limitations of the body, it follows that Irene fears bodily injury. Her phone, or more precisely, the sensitive information stored within it, both protects and endangers Irene's body: its presence provides her with leverage to ensure her safety, and its loss exposes her to physical harm. Sherlock asserts dominance over Irene's body by finally unlocking her phone.

Having lost her phone and thus, her leverage, Irene is caught by an Islamist terror cell and sentenced to death by beheading. The narrative then invalidates the image of Irene as a dominating sex worker. In her final scene, Irene appears dressed in a burka, a garment that deemphasizes her visual gender and sexual allure. She appears weak, defeated, helpless, crying, and fearful of her impending death. Unlike Conan Doyle's Adler, who outwits Holmes, only the direct intervention of a godlike male figure can liberate Irene. Sherlock arrives to rescue Irene, the damsel in distress, at her execution, effectively reinforcing a conventional gender dynamic. Additionally, Sherlock reasserts his dominance over Irene, shown on her knees. Moffat's Sherlock even usurps Adler's securing of the last word in "Bohemia." The detective tidies up the scandal and safely compartmentalizes Irene, eliminating the possibility of her return. Irene's body is ejected from the series, only appearing again trapped in Sherlock's mind, under his control.

Despite Sherlock's masculine control over Irene's feminine body, "Belgravia" designates both characters as queer, which is the closest the episode comes to the gender reversal present in "Bohemia." Like NBC's *Dracula* (2013), which reimagines Lucy Westenra as a lesbian in love with Mina Murray, Moffat's revision appears to engage with queer and gender concerns, to "fill in what is unsaid in Victorian writings" (Whelehan 276). However, despite Irene's explicit self-identification as gay, "Belgravia" problematically issues little but innuendo. This episode ultimately fails to actualize these dispossessed figures.

Scholars and fans alike have praised the series for subverting heteronormative sexuality. Carlen Lavigne congratulates the series for making "no canonical commitments" to Sherlock's sexuality, insisting that his sexual orientation remains undefined (18). Lavigne suggests that Sherlock, John, and Moriarty are not *necessarily* queer, but "*can* be read that way" (20), despite John's objections and the creators' denial of homosexual subtext. Several critical works deal at length with the question of Sherlock's sexuality and the nature of his relationship with John.[2] Here, rather than discussing all queer representations in *Sherlock*, I examine significant scenes from the series to support my claim that the program marks Sherlock as queer.

In *Sherlock*'s debut episode, "A Study in Pink," John and Sherlock wait together in a restaurant for the appearance of a suspected serial killer. The proprietor, who makes it clear that he has known Sherlock for some time, assumes the two men are dating, prompting a foundational conversation regarding Sherlock's sexuality. When John asks Sherlock if he has a girlfriend, Sherlock caustically retorts, "No, not really my area." John then asks if Sherlock has a boyfriend, quickly adding, "Which is fine, by the way." Sherlock snaps, "I know it's fine." When John repeats the question, Sherlock simply responds, "No." Sherlock mistakes John's likening of their mutual single status for a come-on, and lets him down easily, remarking, although he's flattered, he considers himself married to his work, and is unavailable for a romantic relationship with John (*Sherlock* "A Study in Pink"). Sherlock's disavowal of sexual interest in women ("not my area") and noncommittal response regarding sexual interest in men ("I know it's fine") taken together strongly suggest same-sex preference. Queer allusion continues throughout the series, even during and after the introduction of Irene as a heterosexual romantic interest for Sherlock and the ruse of Sherlock's relationship with Janine in the third series finale. Later in the series Sherlock ignores, but does not refute, frequent insinuations that he and John are sleeping together.

In "The Blind Banker," an old university acquaintance, Sebastian, hires Sherlock to solve a case. Sherlock introduces John to Sebastian as "my friend," and a look of confusion passes over Sebastian's face. "Friend?" Sebastian asks, significantly. John immediately corrects him, "Colleague." Sebastian chuckles and replies knowingly, "Right" (*Sherlock* "The Blind Banker"). The three men then stand in uncomfortable silence for some seconds. Considering that the series has, at this point, established John and Sherlock as friends, I doubt that John would then deny their friendship. Rather, John suspects that Sebastian interprets "friend" to mean "lover," and Sebastian's knowing response affirms this assumption. John validates that suspicion by correcting "friend" to "colleague." It is unlikely that Sebastian would infer that the two men are sexually involved unless he has, since their university days, believed that Sherlock sleeps with men. Sebastian's conjecture mirrors that of the restaurant-owner in "Pink."

During a confrontation with Irene in "Belgravia," John denies sleeping with

Sherlock, a protestation Irene rebuffs because she speculates both men are, at least to some extent, attracted to other men. Exasperated, John insists he neither knows for certain Sherlock's sexual preference nor is he himself "actually gay." Irene smirks, declaring, "I am. Look at us both" (*Sherlock* "A Scandal in Belgravia"). Irene's equivocal confession confirms a series of suppositions: that she is a lesbian; that she cares for Sherlock; that John cares for Sherlock; and finally, that their mutual interest in Sherlock runs counter to their avowed sexual orientations. But the series suggests that Sherlock is equally devoted to John. For example, in his wedding toast to John and Mary in "The Sign of Three," Sherlock claims to be one of the two people John loves most, effectively occupying the role of John's lover by aligning himself with John's bride.

In "Belgravia" Moffat emphasizes Sherlock's sexual inexperience, a circumstance neither questioned nor relevant in the series again until "His Last Vow." Drawing on the concept, if not the language, of celibacy, Moffat temporarily displaces queer Sherlock in order to stage a heterosexual romance between Sherlock and Irene. Over the course of the episode, characters repeatedly and derisively label Sherlock a "virgin." Mycroft implies that Sherlock lacks sexual experience, and Irene, as a mouthpiece for Moriarty, refers to Sherlock as "the virgin," exposing his want of sexual competence or confidence (*Sherlock* "A Scandal in Belgravia"). In reading "Bohemia," Bragg affirms that Holmes's "virginity does not carry connotations of ineptitude and inexperience" (20–21), and Michael Atkinson holds that "Holmes draws his strength from his chastity" (67). Conan Doyle's Holmes performs confident, deliberate celibacy; but Moffat's Sherlock appears a clumsy virgin when contrasted with the sexually skilled Irene. "Virgin" connotes an unsatisfied lack, a desire for consummation, not the practice of intentional celibacy. But just as a man's coat provides imaginary self-determination, Irene's sexual dominance over Sherlock is illusory.

Throughout "Belgravia" Irene, assisted by Moriarty, engages in complex and sustained manipulation of Sherlock in order to obtain information she can barter for her own gain. Irene's threat to release compromising photos of a royal personage is a ruse concocted to bring her in contact with Sherlock. The episode, then, displaces Conan Doyle's focus on the adventuress and shifts it to the detective. Irene's game is, at first, strictly professional; but since the episode hinders the blurring of boundaries, falling in love with Sherlock intellectually cripples Irene.

In "Bohemia" love proves no hindrance for Adler. Here, love clouds Irene's judgment. Sherlock reveals that, when the two held wrists, he was taking Irene's pulse and observing her pupils, thereby "proving" her love for him, and also illustrating that he understands women's bodies, at least in a mechanical sense. The detective determines that the password to Irene's phone includes his name, and when the missing letters are supplied, the screen reads "I AM SHER LOCKED." Apart from the troubling implication that Irene belongs to Sherlock, the password is childish, akin to a school girl doodling her sweetheart's name in her notebooks. As he unlocks the phone, Sherlock smugly utters, "This is your heart, and you should never let it rule your head" ("A Scandal in Belgravia"). In this way Moffat rigidly upholds the head/heart division transgressed throughout Conan Doyle's stories. Sherlock uses Irene's heart to degrade her and send her body out into the world where it will likely be destroyed, reasserting his sense of superiority. The intersection of normative gendering *and* sexuality ensures that Sherlock's virulent masculinity overcomes Irene, the powerful lesbian dominatrix, who succumbs to her role as "weak woman." Not only is hetero-romance, at least for the Holmes character, contrary to the tenor of Conan Doyle's original stories, more importantly, it is contrary to the television series' non-normative sexual ethos.

Conclusion

Many readers criticize "Bohemia" for relegating Adler to the limits of action, alleging that the story affirms Victorian gender and sexual norms, and others aver that its adaptation portrays Irene as liberated from the confines of conventional gendering and sexuality. But as I have argued, the adaptation undercuts the performativity of the source text. Scholars often read Adler's marriage to Norton and their subsequent flight from London as both relinquishing her freedom and restoring the order centralized under Holmes's authority. Moffat insists that Adler's marriage undermines the character's status as proto-feminist. But as Hoffman observes, "Adler's most subversive act in the story, her cross-dressed foray into the streets of London, following Sherlock Holmes back to Baker Street, occurs *after* she is married," an act "not entirely consistent with the actions of a properly 'domesticated' Victorian wife" (84). And Langbauer counters antifeminist charges, arguing that Adler confounds Victorian gendered spheres "in part by doing what it least expects—joining it through her marriage to the respectable English lawyer" (150). Adler acts in accordance with her own desires and plays with Victorian conceptions of gender in order to gain these ends. Moffat repeatedly associates Irene with conventionally feminine attributes, not only feminine objects, but also the physical body. Consequently, the portrayal of Irene as weak reinforces the idea of the feminine as lesser.

In a way, Irene predicts Mary. Moffat, the writer of both "A Scandal in Belgravia" and "His Last Vow," concludes each episode by restraining and removing Irene and Mary, respectively, from the male world of action. Benedict Cumberbatch justifies Mary's early involvement in Sherlock and John's cases as "anti-misogynistic" because she is not "left behind" by the men ("Sherlock Uncovered"). Although Moffat depicts Mary as a capable assassin, and despite the fact of her already restrictive pregnancy, in the final scenes of "His Last Vow" Sherlock drugs Mary in order to prevent her from joining him and John in confronting Magnussen. Both instances indicate a systemic problem in Moffat's portrayal of women and other marginal figures.

Anything meant to seem subversive in "A Scandal in Belgravia" is insubstantial. Moffat's scripts hide behind pretend gender and sexual ambiguity to distract from conventional hetero-romance. Despite asserting artificial control in the bedroom, Irene never controls her own destiny. "Belgravia" further disappoints because it negates same-sex sexuality, a perplexing choice considering how sensitive many contemporary television series have become to gay inclusion. Irene, regardless of identifying as a lesbian, inexplicably falls in love with Sherlock. And Sherlock surprisingly capitulates. John and Mycroft assign sentiment to Sherlock's use of the phrase "the woman," implying that Irene is the one woman who has ever mattered romantically to Sherlock.

If, as Elaine Showalter remarks, the turn of each of the past two centuries signifies the breaking down of gendered and sexual binaries, then *Sherlock*, as the herald of a new century, attempts to reinscribe gender- and heteronormativity into contemporary social order. The gender and sexual dynamics of "Belgravia" inhibit performativity, circumscribe activity, and control identity. Conan Doyle's Holmes and Adler blur the lines between binaries such as body and mind, masculine and feminine, and hetero and homosexual. But Moffat's Sherlock reclaims dominance in a world organized by unemotional masculine reason, and Irene functions as a pawn in a game between men. In assessing the intersection of gender performance with non-normative sexuality, Moffat's singularizing gender presentation enforces the supremacy of hetero-romance. Further, Moffat, in revising the Victorian, asserts the superiority and dominance of masculine rationality.

Notes

1. Primorac takes up the issue of female nudity in recent Holmes adaptations in "The Naked Truth: The Postfeminist Afterlives of Irene Adler," and the analysis of diminished female agency elaborates on the issue in terms parallel to those I develop here, though with a different central focus.

2. Essays exploring Sherlock's sexuality and the relationship between Sherlock and John include Carlen Lavigne, "The Noble Bachelor and the Crooked Man: Subtext and Sexuality in the BBC's *Sherlock*," in *Sherlock Holmes for the 21st Century: Essays on New Adaptations*, ed. Lynnette Porter (Jefferson, NC: McFarland, 2012); Anissa M. Graham and Jennifer C. Garlen, "Sex and the Single Sleuth," in *Sherlock Holmes for the 21st Century: Essays on New Adaptations*, ed. Lynnette Porter (Jefferson, NC: McFarland, 2012); Bran Nicol, "Sherlock Holmes Version 2.0: Adapting Conan Doyle in the Twenty-First Century," in *Sherlock Holmes and Conan Doyle: Multi-Media Afterlives*, ed. Sabine Vanacker and Catherine Wynne (New York: Palgrave Macmillan, 2013); Benjamin Poore, "Sherlock Holmes and the Leap of Faith: The Forces of Fandom and Convergence in Adaptations of the Holmes and Watson Stories," *Adaptation* 6.2 (2013); and Stephen Greer, "Queer (Mis)recognition in the BBC's *Sherlock*," *Adaptation* 8.1 (2015).

Works Cited

Atkinson, Michael. "Virginity Preserved and the Secret Marriage of Sherlock Holmes: The Theory of Popular Romance Applied to a Detective Fiction." *Clues: A Journal of Detection* 2.1 (1981): 62–69. Print.
Bragg, Tom. "Becoming a 'Mere Appendix': The Rehabilitated Masculinity of Sherlock Holmes." *Victorian Newsletter* 116 (2009): 3–26. Print.
Brown, David. "A Scandal in Belgravia: full review." *Radio Times* 1 Jan 2012. *Radio Times*. Web. 27 Dec 2013.
Conan Doyle, Arthur. *Sherlock Holmes: The Complete Novels and Stories*. 2 vols. Ed. Loren Estleman. New York: Bantam, 1986. Print.
Favor, Lesli J. "The Foreign and the Female in Arthur Conan Doyle: Beneath the Candy Coating." *English Literature in Transition* 43.4 (2000): 398–409. Print.
Frank, Lawrence. "Dreaming the Medusa: Imperialism, Primitivism, and Sexuality in Arthur Conan Doyle's *The Sign of Four*." *Signs* 22.1 (1996): 52–85. Print.
Galvan, Jill. *The Sympathetic Medium: Feminine Channeling, the Occult, and Communication Technologies, 1859–1919*. Ithaca: Cornell University Press, 2010. Print.
Garber, Marjorie. *Vested Interests: Cross-Dressing and Cultural Anxiety*. New York: Routledge, 1992. Print.
Hall, Jasmine Yong. "Ordering the Sensational: Sherlock Holmes and the Female Gothic." *Studies in Short Fiction* 28.3 (1991): 295–304. Print.
Hoffman, Megan. "Assuming Identities: Strategies of Drag in Laurie R. King's Mary Russell Series." *Murdering Miss Marple: Essays on Gender and Sexuality in the New Golden Age of Women's Crime Fiction*. Ed. Julie H. Kim. Jefferson, NC: McFarland, 2012. 81–100. Print.
Inglis-Arkell, Esther. "Why Can't Any Recent Sherlock Holmes Adaptation Get Irene Adler Right?" *IO9*. 4 Jan. 2013. Web. 5 Aug. 2014.
Jeffery, Morgan. "'Sherlock' Lara Pulver interview: 'Playing Irene Adler is a privilege.'" *Digital Spy*. 29 Dec. 2011. *Digital Spy*. Web. 27 Dec. 2013.
Jeffries, Stuart. "'There is a clue everybody's missed': Sherlock writer Steven Moffat interviewed." *The Guardian* 20 Jan. 2012. *Guardian*. Web. 27 Dec. 2013.
Kahan, Benjamin. *Celibacies: American Modernism and Sexual Life*. Durham: Duke University Press, 2013. Web.
Kellogg, Richard L. "The Androgynous Ms. Adler." *Baker Street Journal: An Irregular Quarterly of Sherlockiana* 44.2 (1994): 114–16. Print.
Kestner, Joseph A. *Sherlock's Men: Masculinity, Conan Doyle, and Cultural History*. Brookfield, VT: Ashgate, 1997. Print.
Krumm, Pascale. "'A Scandal in Bohemia' and Sherlock Holmes's Ultimate Mystery Solved." *English Literature in Transition* 39.2 (1996): 193–203. Print.
Langbauer, Laurie. *Novels of Everyday Life: The Series in English Fiction, 1850–1930*. Ithaca: Cornell University Press, 1999. Print.
Lavigne, Carlen. "The Noble Bachelor and the Crooked Man: Subtext and Sexuality in the BBC's

Sherlock." *Sherlock Holmes for the 21st Century: Essays on New Adaptations.* Ed. Lynnette Porter. Jefferson, NC: McFarland, 2012. 13–23. Print.
McCaw, Neil. "Sherlock Holmes and a Politics of Adaptation." *Sherlock Holmes and Conan Doyle: Multi-Media Afterlives.* Eds. Sabine Vanacker and Catherine Wynne. New York: Palgrave Macmillan, 2013. 36–48. Print.
Morgan, Patrick. "The Subtle Ways of Watson: Sherlock Holmes and His Feminine Identity." *Baker Street Journal: An Irregular Quarterly of Sherlockiana* 58.3 (2008): 26–32. Print.
Pledger, Laura. "Ten Strong TV Women." *Radio Times* 8 Mar. 2012. *Radio Times.* Web. 27 Dec. 2013.
Primorac, Antonija. "The Naked Truth: The Postfeminist Afterlives of Irene Adler." *Neo-Victorian Studies* 6.2 (2013): 89–101. Print.
Redmond, Christopher. *In Bed with Sherlock Holmes.* Toronto: Simon and Pierre, 1984. Print.
Revoir, Paul. "Lara Pulver Naked in Sherlock Holmes: BBC Under Fire for Raunchy Pre-Watershed Scenes." *Daily Mail* 3 Jan. 2012. *Mail Online.* Web. 27 Dec. 2013.
Sherlock Holmes. Dir. Guy Richie. Perf. Robert Downey, Jr., Jude Law. Warner Bros., 2009. DVD.
Rosner, Victoria. *Modernism and the Architecture of Private Life.* New York: Columbia University Press, 2005. Print.
"A Scandal in Bohemia." *The Adventures of Sherlock Holmes.* Dir. Paul Annett. Perf. Jeremy Brett, David Burke. Granada Television, 1984. DVD.
Sherlock: Season 1. Writ. Mark Gatiss and Steven Moffat. Perf. Benedict Cumberbatch, Martin Freeman. BBC, 2010. DVD.
Sherlock: Season 2. Writ. Mark Gatiss and Steven Moffat. Perf. Benedict Cumberbatch, Martin Freeman, Lara Pulver. BBC, 2012. DVD
Sherlock: Season 3. Writ. Mark Gatiss and Steven Moffat. Perf. Benedict Cumberbatch, Martin Freeman, Amanda Abbington. BBC, 2014. DVD
"Sherlock Uncovered: The Women." *Sherlock.* BBC, 2014. DVD.
Showalter, Elaine. *Sexual Anarchy: Gender and Culture at the Fin de Siècle.* Boston: Little, Brown, 1992. Print.
Smith, Andrew. "Displacing Urban Man: Sherlock Holmes's London." *London Eyes: Reflections in Text and Image.* Eds. Gail Cunningham and Stephen Barber. New York: Berghahn, 2007. 47–58. Print.
Sutcliffe, Tom. "Last Night's TV: Sherlock, BBC 1." *The Independent* 2 Jan. 2012. *The Independent.* Web. 27 Dec. 2013.
Thomas, Ronald. "Making Darkness Visible: Capturing the Criminal and Observing the Law in Victorian Photography and Detective Fiction." *Victorian Literature and the Victorian Visual Imagination.* Eds. Carol T. Christ and John Jordan. Berkeley: University of California Press, 1995. 134–68. Print.
Warren, Randall. "Adventuresses: A Case of Hit and Myth: A Slander in Bohemia and Other Places." *Baker Street Journal: An Irregular Quarterly of Sherlockiana* 45.4 (1995): 232–36. Print.
Whelehan, Imelda. "Neo-Victorian Adaptations." *Blackwell Companion to Literature, Film and Adaptation.* Ed. Deborah Cartmell. Oxford: Blackwell, 2012. 272–92. Print.

The Woman and the Napoleon of Crime
Moriarty, Adler, Elementary

Joseph S. Walker

> "I have never loved anyone as I do you, right now, in this moment"—*Sherlock Holmes to Joan Watson,* Elementary *(episode one, "Pilot")*
>
> "We are the same, you and I. We both made the same mistake: we fell in love"—*Sherlock Holmes to Moriarty,* Elementary *(episode 23, "The Woman/Heroine")*
>
> "Ah, good—it's the new Sherlock Holmes"
> —*Pete,* Family Tree *(episode four, "Country Life")*

"Ah, good—it's the new Sherlock Holmes" are words we could imagine virtually anyone in the world saying in the more than a century and a quarter since the great detective was introduced to the world in *A Study in Scarlet*. What changes, over the course of time, is precisely what is meant by these words. For the first decades of his existence, "the new Sherlock Holmes" would denote a very specific kind of text—a fresh novel or short story by his creator, Sir Arthur Conan Doyle. Even before Conan Doyle's death, however, it became possible for "the new Sherlock Holmes" to indicate instead any one of the innumerable stories, novels, plays, radio dramas, comic books, films, pastiches, fan fictions or television dramas adapting, revising and expanding endlessly upon Holmes's adventures. Perhaps because of his appearance at the very moment when the mass media becomes inescapable, no individual has been "new" more frequently than Holmes, recognized by the *Guinness Book of World Records* as being played on film by more different actors than any other character. Often, in fact, the phrase "the new Sherlock Holmes" can be taken to mean not a literary or filmic text but rather the latest actor to take on the role—a list which in recent years has expanded to include Robert Downey, Jr., (in the *Sherlock Holmes* films directed by Guy Ritchie), Benedict Cumberbatch (in the BBC series *Sherlock*), Jonny Lee Miller (in the CBS series *Elementary*), and Jake Harders (in *Sherlock Holmes: The New Frontier*).

If this last name and title are less familiar than the others, it's because Harders's portrayal of Holmes is limited to two brief scenes glimpsed in the 2013 HBO/BBC comedy series *Family Tree*. The show's characters are obsessed with a number of television shows, and some of their greatest enthusiasm is reserved for *Sherlock Holmes: The New Frontier*. As seen in two episodes of *Family Tree*, this particular Holmes (a young white man) and Watson (a black man of similar age) wear costumes closely modeled on the Starfleet uniforms of the original *Star Trek* and, surrounded as they are by large computer displays and windows showing starfields, appear to be on a spaceship. *The New Frontier* is obviously a parody, spoofing the shifting of the Holmes mythology from Victorian London to a later period—the present day in *Sherlock* and *Elementary*, the distant future in *The New Frontier*. The science fiction trappings suggest that *Sherlock* is the particular mark here, as they evoke the strong associations between *Sherlock* and the rebooted *Doctor Who*. Both series, under the guidance of writer and producer Steven Moffat, have revived revered British heroes, using high production values, strong writing, and savvy, web-centered marketing to build and sustain a rabid worldwide audience. Despite the popularity of both shows, it is clear that *The New Frontier* should not be taken as a celebration of Moffat's version of Conan Doyle's hero. Consider the very first shot we see of Harders-as-Holmes: he is wearing a blue tunic and standing in front of a starfield, his eyes downcast thoughtfully, his mouth closed on the stem of a plastic and metal simulation of a calabash pipe with an electronic glow in its bowl. We don't really need to hear the watching character exclaim that this is "the new Sherlock Holmes"; the combination of his posture and the pipe, weighed down with almost a century's cultural association, tell us this immediately. The identification, however, is a problematic one, on at least two counts. First, to echo Magritte, the pipe is not a pipe; it produces no smoke and contains no fire. It simply takes the shape of a pipe and produces a similar light, and it is difficult to imagine what function it is meant to serve beyond carrying this resemblance. Second, the pipe itself is associated with Holmes not through Conan Doyle's work, but through stage and screen portrayals which established the calabash, along with the deerstalker cap, as definitive visual signifiers of the character. What we see in *The New Frontier*, then, is in essence a simulation of a falsehood—

a lie about a lie—and yet this allows our immediate and accurate identification of Holmes. Taken in the context of a parody, the "pipe" suggests that the new incarnations of Holmes—and specifically *Sherlock*—are similarly concerned with style and signifiers over substance, and similarly superficial in the employment of surface elements of the Holmes text to create something only seemingly "new."

The rabid devotion of millions of fans (many of whom express their appreciation in very sophisticated ways), along with the generally high level of production, would seem to argue that *Sherlock* is being unjustly mocked here, and that the series does have something tangible to contribute to the Holmes metatext. Ashley D. Polasek has argued, in fact, that by reimagining Holmes in the present day, *Sherlock* has rescued the character from generations of increasingly empty and inauthentic simulacra through the creation of a "fictional world in which none of the multitude of Sherlock Holmes referents that have built up within modern culture over the past century exist" (196). Polasek suggests that *Sherlock* be seen alongside other recent 'rebootings' of pop-culture franchises such as James Bond and *Star Trek* and that "By inventing fresh continuities that necessarily negate previous audience expectations and fan knowledge while writing their own cultural referents out of being, the simulacra falls apart and the sources are returned to their natural cycles of imaginative engagement" (196). In other words, by creating a world in which Sherlock Holmes and all associations with him were previously unknown, *Sherlock* allows the Holmes narrative to return to a form marked by originality and authenticity. Such an argument, however, ignores the fact that "fresh continuities" such as that created by *Sherlock* have been part of the Holmes pattern for some time. Polasek herself lists "Basil Rathbone as Holmes fighting the Nazis" alongside "Sherlock Holmes societies meeting all across the world year after year" and the "statue at the Baker Street tube station" as instances of the accumulation of empty simulacra, but is "Holmes in World War II" fundamentally different from "Holmes in the twenty-first century"? Perhaps the difference is only one of chronology, in which case the Cumberbatch series must through the passage of time eventually join the Rathbone films as another simulation which prevents, rather than enables, our "imaginative engagement."

Polasek's argument also requires us to ignore the fact that much of the pleasure of *Sherlock* comes precisely from its deliberate echoes of earlier manifestations of the narratives, particularly the Conan Doyle texts. Each episode of the series is a loose adaptation of a Conan Doyle story, with a teasingly altered title (thus "A Study in Scarlet" becomes the series' first episode, "A

Study in Pink"; "A Scandal in Bohemia" becomes "A Scandal in Belgravia"). The fundamental identities and relationships of the characters remain unchanged. The pleasure of the series derives primarily not from the creation of an entirely new experience unencumbered by the weight of Sherlock's history, but rather from our recognition of the playful engagement with that history (at one point Cumberbatch's Sherlock even dons a deerstalker in an effort to hide his face from photographers, saying "the last thing I need is a public image," only to become disgusted when images of him in the hat immediately become popular). This recognition depends upon the existence, not the negation, of "previous audience expectations and fan knowledge"; they acknowledge that the one thing Holmes cannot escape is his "public image." Part of the enormous global popularity of the series derives precisely from such moments; in asking its viewers to recognize and take pleasure from such echoes and allusions, the series rewards them for active engagement and for their understanding, thus encouraging still greater attention and devotion.

Ultimately, *Family Tree*'s implication that *Sherlock* is more concerned with style than substance is too harsh; however, Polasek's valorization of the series' ability to "reanimate texts that have become encumbered by the hyperreal" (196) also overstates the case. *Sherlock* is a valuable addition to the Holmes canon, if only because of the superb performances of Cumberbatch and of Martin Freeman as Watson. It is particularly remarkable that the series has generated such immense levels of fan and press attention on the strength of only three episodes per season, a testament to the canny ways in which the show has encouraged and manipulated the social media to build excitement. *Sherlock* is, for want of a more rigorous term, *cool*; the show has succeeded in creating a new incarnation of the character which will surely stand alongside Rathbone and Jeremy Brett in the short list of great Holmes performances, and in capturing the excited engagement of the kinds of fans more commonly devoted to science fiction and fantasy properties. It is inaccurate, however, to see the show as a completely "clean slate" allowing the wholesale reinvention of the Holmes narrative for a new age; the weight of the character's history is ultimately too great.

If *Sherlock*, then, is in the end limited in its ability to recreate Holmes, it would initially seem that *Elementary*, a creation of writer and producer Robert Doherty, would be even more limited. Certainly it remains largely unencumbered by any sense that it is *cool*. Initial response to the addition of the program to CBS's 2012–13 season treated the show as, essentially, a pale imitation of *Sherlock*, lifting the basic idea of Holmes operating in the present day. It seemed unlikely that the viewing public would embrace a parallel development of the same story, or view it as anything more than a trespasser on occupied ground. Moreover, the show's potential for innovation or imagination seemed limited by its place on an American broadcast network. While the big four (or, by some accounts, five) American networks still draw large audiences (albeit audiences which are, on the whole, older and less actively engaged in the act of viewership), it is indisputable that, over the last ten or fifteen years, most of the programs which fans, critics and academics have praised as most nearly fulfilling television's untapped potential for artistic achievement have come from cable channels or overseas sources. In this atmosphere the offerings of the broadcast networks are usually perceived as being too standardized, homogenized, familiar and formulaic to constitute real art. Broken up by too-frequent and too-long commercial breaks, confined to rigidly defined running times and structured by a mandate to reach the widest possible audience, network shows fall into a few highly conventional types. Specifically, it quickly became clear that *Elementary* would be one of a number of shows on CBS to fall under the umbrella of the case-of-the-week procedural. Following the dictates of this form, there would be a few plot elements continued from episode to episode, but the bulk of each episode would be dedicated to uncovering the solution to a single, isolated crime (contrast this with the sustained, season-long arcs that dominate shows such as *The Sopranos* or *Breaking Bad*). Balanced against these restrictions were the alterations the show made to the Holmes narrative, alterations that went well beyond *Sherlock* in changing the Conan Doyle template. This Holmes did not merely operate in the present day; unlike his counterpart in either the Conan Doyle stories or the BBC series, he is based in New York, not London. He works primarily as a police consultant, not a freelance consulting detective who sometimes assists the authorities and sometimes opposes them. Although names from the Conan Doyle stories occasionally occur, the individual episodes of the series are original cases, not adaptations of the stories. *Elementary*'s most prominent alteration, however, was reserved for Holmes's companion; this Watson is an Asian-American woman, Dr. Joan Watson.

The idea of a female Watson is not entirely new. In 1941, the mystery writer Rex Stout (whose character Nero Wolfe is regarded by many fans as an illegitimate son of Sherlock Holmes) gave a speech to the Holmes fan club, the Baker Street Irregulars, titled "Watson Was a Woman." In it, he proposed that various clues and seeming contradictions within the Conan Doyle stories can be decoded to reveal that "John Watson" was merely a pseudonym adapted by *Irene* Watson, who was in fact the (rather jealous and controlling) wife of Sherlock Holmes. Stout's tongue was firmly in his cheek, but the idea of a female sidekick for Holmes has occasionally recurred since. The 1971 film *They Might Be Giants* cast George C. Scott as a present-day mental patient convinced he is Holmes and treated by a female Dr. Watson who gradually comes to respect his delusions. Two different TV movies, *The Return of Sherlock Holmes* (1987) and *Sherlock Homes Returns* (1994), featured women in the present day (the first a direct descendant of Watson) who discover a cryogenically frozen Holmes, revive him, and become his assistant. Laurie R. King has written a successful series of mysteries concerning Mary Russell, a young American who meets a retired Holmes in 1915, becomes his apprentice, and eventually marries him. What all these versions have in common with Stout's premise is that the female "Watson" is regarded as being not merely a friend to Holmes, but as (at least potentially) a romantic partner.

For many viewers this possibility apparently remains the central fascination of *Elementary*'s regendered Watson. Halfway through the program's second season, it was still possible for *TV Guide* to ask, on the cover of its October 14, 2013, issue, "Will Holmes & Watson Hook Up?" It is true that the program (again following the conventions of American episodic television, which suggest that creating such a question and then failing to resolve it is one sure way to promote long-term viewership) has, on occasion, hinted at a sexual tension between the two characters. To its credit, however, *Elementary* has primarily treated such a relationship as too easy a road to travel, a possibility to be resisted rather than indulged. The very first meeting between the two raises the prospect, only to immediately dismiss it. When Watson introduces herself to Holmes in the initial moments of the pilot episode, his first speech to her is not the famous "You have been in Afghanistan, I perceive" but rather an extended romantic monologue proclaiming his belief in love at first sight and his earnest certainty that he has never loved as he now loves her. It is immediately revealed, however, that he is merely testing his focus and memory by repeating a speech from a soap opera on one of the several televisions running simultaneously in the room. Watson, who had appeared entranced by Holmes's speech (no doubt in part because he delivers it while shirtless, revealing a fit and heavily tattooed torso), drops her purse and becomes flustered when this truth is revealed; her behavior is the scene's one unfortunate indulgence of conventionally gendered behavior. It does not disguise the fact that the scene is clearly intended to immediately defuse audience expectations of the seemingly obvious development of their relationship.

Of course, there has always been something at least potentially erotic in the relationship between Watson and Holmes, a relationship uneasily developed in stories which operate by "bringing a narrating, observing male into close proximity with another male, the extraordinary object of his gaze" (Bragg 6). Tom Bragg has argued that one of Conan Doyle's primary concerns, once it became clear that the Holmes series would be long-running and profitable, was to undercut the "suspicions of abnormal behavior and transgressive sexuality" which mark Holmes's first appearances in order to recreate him as "masculinity's policeman, the committed (if eccentric) upholder of conventional values" (4, 19). In a similar vein, Jasmine Yong Hall has suggested that the sensational, Gothic nature of many of Holmes's cases is necessary to allow him to maintain his imperiled masculinity and "keep him out of this feminine, marginal area" (301). If Holmes's masculinity is threatened by his eccentricity, Watson's is similarly endangered by his repeated disempowerment, desire and lack. The driving engine of the Conan Doyle stories, as James Krasner has pointed out, is that Watson "takes great pleasure in portraying himself and Holmes as a unit ... and dwells on his personal knowledge of Holmes and his methods" (434). This is despite the fact that the stories frequently reveal Holmes's pleasure precisely in denying knowledge to Watson and that "Watson's convenience, safety or freedom from anxiety come second to Holmes's control over the unfolding of the case" (428). Seen in this light the Conan Doyle stories can be understood as something of a frustrated romance, with Watson forced to continually confront "his combination of mental distance and physical proximity to Holmes's thoughts" (425).

Elementary fundamentally alters almost every aspect of this relationship, but not in the ways we might expect. The most radical change to Watson's character here is not making the character into a woman, but rather removing the traditionally passive defining characteristic of *narrator*. Unlike almost every other Watson, Joan does not write about Holmes (even the Watson of *Sherlock* blogs about Holmes's cases, an act which seems motivated more by the show's desire to seem contemporary than by adherence to the characters' other observed traits); she does not record, but *acts*. In *Elementary*, Watson and Holmes meet not because of a shared need for habitation, but because Joan Watson has been hired by Holmes's (as yet unseen) father to serve as Sherlock's sober companion following his release from rehab, a job which requires her to spend twenty-four hours a day with him to confirm his recovery from addiction is complete. Their relationship is thus immediately defined in professional, rather than domestic, terms, and motivated by Watson's specialized duties—both substantial reversals of the pattern established in virtually every other Holmes text. The three most prominent contemporary reinventions of the Holmes canon all take, as one part of their project, rescuing

Watson from the image of the bumbling, impotent old man who can only trail along, marveling, in Holmes's wake—an image which remains in play largely because of Nigel Bruce's performances alongside Basil Rathbone. The Guy Ritchie films and *Sherlock* have accomplished this by making their Watsons courageous men of action who can be relied upon in moments of physical peril, while still making it clear that they are frequently baffled by the events around them and frustrated at Holmes's jealous guardianship of his privileged knowledge. *Elementary* accomplishes it by making Watson a true partner to Sherlock, a woman who thinks of herself as an investigator, not an investigator's sidekick.

The primary narrative arc of *Elementary*'s first season is dedicated to gradually shifting Watson from her limited, disciplinary role as sober companion to this sense of real partnership with Holmes. Indeed, as we will see, it is Watson who, in the final episode of the first season, engineers the capture of Holmes's great enemy, Moriarty. This marks the culmination of her character arc, but the program's investment in this active version of her character is already evident in the pilot episode. The very first time Watson accompanies Holmes to interrogate a murder suspect—within hours of having learned what Holmes does—she takes note of a potentially incriminating clue, and gestures subtly at it to make sure it has caught Sherlock's notice. He nods to indicate that it has, but then registers surprise when Watson—again, understood here as talking with a murder suspect for the first time in her life—takes over the questioning to ask about his whereabouts at the time of the crime. Later in the pilot episode, when Holmes becomes overly hostile and accusatory in his interrogation of a female victim, Watson sternly sends him outside, apologizes for his actions, and succeeds in getting from her the information Holmes had been unable to obtain. Holmes claims to have manipulated this outcome—a claim he later admits to be false. Indeed, in this initial outing Holmes is frequently desperate and frustrated, acting in counterproductive, antisocial ways; when he identifies the murderer but is unable to produce proof, he simply crashes Watson's car into the criminal's out of no motive other than anger. While he then sits powerless in prison it is Watson who discovers the vital clue leading to the capture of the killer; at the same time she correctly deduces that Holmes's mysterious departure from London involved a woman. By the end of the episode Holmes, while continuing to deny that he needs a sober companion, acknowledges that there is "hope" for Watson as an investigator.

The fulfillment of this hope occupies the remainder of the first season. In the world of *Elementary*, Dr. Joan Watson was a skilled surgeon who resigned from the field after one of her patients unexpectedly died. Her occupation as a sober companion has allowed her to continue to help those in need, but it does not stimulate or interest her as Holmes's work does. When Holmes's father declines to extend her engagement beyond the original six weeks, she pretends that he has done so in order to continue living and working with Holmes. Holmes discovers this ruse almost immediately but, finding her presence useful, allows it to continue. Eventually he simply offers to train Watson as his apprentice/partner, an offer she accepts. Whatever notes of sexual tension exist between the two, nothing in *Elementary* to date contradicts the idea that their relationship is built primarily upon their shared fascination with investigation.

As even this brief summary makes clear, the empowerment of Watson in this new version of the character dynamic mirrors, and is enabled by, a parallel alteration in the character of Holmes himself. J. Madison Davis has pointed out that a survey of stage and screen representations of Holmes over the last century demonstrates a "trajectory ... toward a greater emphasis on Holmes's addiction and neuroses" (12). Such a trajectory certainly accounts for much of both *Sherlock* and the Guy Ritchie films, in which Holmes frequently acts in outlandish, offensive ways, characterized by arrogance, self-absorption and condescension. The Holmes of *Elementary*, as is indicated by the summary of the pilot episode above, is capable of acting in such ways, but with a crucial difference: it is represented, more often than not, as behavior he regrets and often is made, in some way, to pay for. This Holmes is still an addict—but he is an addict in recovery, a concept the show treats with, if anything, excessive earnestness.

While Holmes initially denies his need for a sober companion and claims that dedication to his work is all he needs to resist narcotics, he gradually retreats from this stance over the course of the series. He attends meetings with increasing willingness, takes a sponsor, and in the course of time becomes a sponsor himself. As in the Matthew Scudder mysteries written by Lawrence Block, the language of addiction and recovery is woven into the series at almost every level. It is particularly significant that Holmes is made to acknowledge, multiple times, that even his formidable powers will not allow him to escape addiction unassisted. "Holmes's mastery over the physical world through rational knowledge" (Hall 299) is in and of itself inadequate to the challenges it confronts; the detective no longer stands as the isolated agent of order and reason, but must act as part of a communal whole through the observance of shared rituals and values (the twelve steps of recovery, for example). Of major Holmes texts, perhaps only Nicholas Meyer's 1974 novel

The Seven-per-cent Solution, in which Watson enlists Sigmund Freud to help Holmes break his addiction to cocaine, precedes *Elementary* in using addiction as the means by which Holmes is forced to confront his own limitations and live within societal conventions.

Crucially, *Elementary* represents addiction not merely as a weakness in Holmes but as a mark of his failures. As is gradually revealed over the course of the program's first season, Holmes had been a consulting detective working with Scotland Yard and occasionally dabbling in narcotics to combat boredom or fatigue. In the course of an investigation he met and entered a relationship with a woman named Irene Adler, an art restorer who proved to be his intellectual match. However, Irene was murdered by a mysterious serial killer, known only as "M," whom Holmes had been unable to capture. In the wake of her death Holmes became increasingly erratic and dependent on drugs, to the point that Scotland Yard declined to use his services any further. Holmes was sent, by his father, to a rehab facility in New York, and upon his release began consulting for the NYPD, where he works closely with Captain Tom Gregson and Detective Marcus Bell. This backstory is worth dwelling on because it reveals that the procedural structure is not merely a result of the circumstances of *Elementary*'s production, but more importantly a central facet in an attempted revision of Holmes which is ultimately far more radical than anything attempted by *Sherlock*.

Following the ideas of Robert Ray and Walter Ong, Brendan Riley has argued that the classical detective story (exemplified by the works of Poe and Conan Doyle and featuring a detective who restores order through his absolute understanding of the rational world) and the later hard-boiled variant (exemplified by the works of Hammett and Chandler and featuring a detective who struggles to act meaningfully in an inherently corrupt world) can be understood as responding to the rise of, respectively, photography and film. In this understanding, the detective serves a conservative function, standing against new ways of representing and understanding the world in order "to defend rational thinking ... [and] the relevance of literacy" (913). Riley suggests that if the epic hero was the idealized representative of oral culture, the detective is the corresponding idealized representative of literate culture. He goes on to suggest, through a reading of the television show *Angel*, that we are entering a new mode—"electrate culture"—and that the idealized hero of this phase is not the ruggedly individual detective but rather one who employs "collaborative, database-driven modes of inquiry" and who "relies heavily on his team not just to gather clues, but to solve the mystery" (921, 920). Such a shift is necessitated by "the new paradigms of thought afforded by the new modes of communication common in network culture" (921). To think of this in another way: if the classical detective's world is characterized by rationality, and the hard-boiled detective's world by corruption, the "electrate" detective's world is characterized by complexity.

I would suggest that Riley errs here only in seeing this new detective arising in the twenty-first century, in response to the rise of digital media; what he is in fact describing is the well-established mystery subgenre known as the procedural. If the classical detective corresponds roughly with the rise of photography, and the hard-boiled detective roughly with the rise of film, the procedural corresponds roughly with the rise of television (there are earlier books which can claim to belong to the subgenre, but the towering achievement in procedural fiction is the 87th Precinct series by Ed McBain, begun in 1956 and continuing through more than fifty books). The procedural has no singular, idealized hero; it represents the detective (or, more often, detectives) as merely one moving part within a complex, highly interdependent system, with only limited capacity for autonomous action. The procedural detective is dependent not merely on a partner, but on any number of auxiliary agents (forensic scientists, crime scene technicians, uniformed officers, district attorneys, commanding officers, etc.) and tools (databases, computers, phones, documents, the law itself) to institute order and achieve understanding. As programs from *Hill Street Blues* on have demonstrated, television—with its rigorous schedule, its dedication to routine, and its ability to introduce and maintain large numbers of characters—is particularly well suited to the procedural form. The very opening credits sequence of *Elementary* testifies to its categorization as a procedural; although we see the names of main actors, we do not see their faces. What we see instead is a rolling marble which activates a Rube Goldberg device that simulates various crimes (firing a pistol, smashing a bust with a hammer) and eventually drops a cage over a small figure of a man. Crime here is understood and punished through a mechanistic, industrial process, not through the solitary actions of a single privileged figure. Even the title is significant; *Sherlock* is clearly about an individual, while the word 'elementary' ultimately refers to the process through which justice is achieved.

To transplant Sherlock Holmes—the ultimate embodiment of the classical detective—into the form of the procedural is to radically challenge much that is considered fundamental to the character—his authority, his autonomy, his idiosyncrasy. It is not simply a necessary consequence of the present-day setting; Cumberbatch's character retains the character's traditional sense of isolation and privilege, frequently taunting official figures or taking pleasure in withholding information from Watson. *Sherlock* is not a procedural. By contrast, the Holmes of *Elementary* may occasionally boast of his superiority or mock an officer he considers unfit, but he operates, essentially, as one member of an officially sanctioned team. He depends upon and respects not only Watson, but also Gregson and Bell; he relies upon the information and data provided by autopsies, ballistics reports, and so on. As with his acceptance of the reality and consequences of his addiction, these are behaviors which Holmes resists and must gradually come to accept as the series progresses. Miller's performance captures this eloquently; his Holmes is a picture of repression and containment, fidgety, buttoned-up and vocally clipped until his occasional explosions into action and excitement. He is a man at war with himself, a man struggling to accommodate himself to an unnatural state of being. An effort is being made in this series to rescue Holmes from the "addiction and neuroses" which dominate his recent incarnations, but the effort is frequently a struggle—an attempt to fit a round peg into a square hole—and one made, perhaps, at the cost of also stripping Holmes of his privilege and distinctiveness.

If Miller's performance captures this tension visually, narratively it takes more elusive form in occasional, mysterious references to Holmes's father. In Conan Doyle's stories, of course, almost nothing was revealed about Holmes's family beyond the existence of his older, and smarter, brother Mycroft. In *Elementary*, his father is a wealthy Briton who owns the home where Holmes lives, along with a number of other properties, and provides the income which supports both Holmes and Watson, allowing them to live as unpaid consultants to the NYPD. Despite this apparent largesse, Holmes speaks of his father only with disdain, insisting that the man does not really care about him, but only wishes to avoid the scandal that would result if Holmes, for example, died from an overdose. Holmes senior has yet to actually appear in the series, although his employment of Watson provided the mechanism for its central relationship; his subsequent refusal to continue Watson's employment led to the evolution of that relationship and, on its face, would seem to support Holmes's claim that he has no true love for his son. On a practical level, it is likely that this is simply a way of providing *Elementary* with another long-term plot to be resolved during an appropriate sweeps period. Thematically, however, Holmes senior represents the patriarchal power, knowledge and control which, in his original appearances, belonged to Holmes himself. That power may no longer be visible in the world, but the manipulations of Holmes senior suggest that it is neither completely vanished. It is significant that, despite his resentment, Holmes continues to accept his father's money; in effect, he is licensed and given agency only through his father's countenance. He is thus embedded ever more deeply in the collective, communal logic of the procedural even while remaining indebted to the ultimate authority of a much older, centralized, (literally) patriarchal model of authority. It is this very form of authority which Holmes, in his previous incarnations, represented and wielded; it is now used against him. For all practical purposes, the Holmes senior of *Elementary is* the original Sherlock Holmes, a continual reminder of the authority and autonomy the figure now lacks.

The themes I have been addressing here find their ultimate expression in *Elementary*'s most daring rewriting of the Holmes narrative—not the regendering of Watson, but rather the amalgamation of Irene Adler ("*the woman* ... she eclipses and predominates the whole of her sex") and Moriarty ("the Napoleon of crime") into a single figure. In an episode in the middle of the first season ("M."), Holmes succeeds in capturing the serial killer who had eluded him in London, only to learn that the man, Sebastian Moran, is (here as in the Conan Doyle stories) actually a paid assassin in the employ of a mysterious figure he calls Moriarty. In the last several episodes of the season, Holmes discovers that Irene is alive, and has been held captive and psychologically tortured by Moriarty's agents since her apparent death almost two years previously. He attempts to care for her and guide her recovery, leaving the pursuit of Moriarty to Watson and the police, only to discover, first, that she was in fact not being held against her will, and ultimately that she is in fact Moriarty herself. She had arranged their previous relationship in order to study the detective who had disrupted several of her plans; she had originally intended to kill him, but ultimately decided she could not destroy "a work of art" (and, in fact, she acts to save Holmes when one of her minions defies her orders and attempts to kill him). Holmes fails to prevent Moriarty from carrying out her plan in New York (a complex scheme involving kidnapping, assassination, and currency exchanges, netting Moriarty a billion dollar profit). Watson, however, has correctly perceived that Moriarty truly does love Holmes, and suggests the strategy by which she is apprehended: Holmes fakes a relapse into addiction and near-fatal overdose, drawing Moriarty to his hospital bedside, where she proposes to take him away with her and "show you a different way to live" (*Elementary* "Heroine").

In the Conan Doyle stories, and in most other representations, Moriarty is simply a force of evil to be opposed; he is treated as Holmes's absolute opposite. In *Elementary*, Moriarty is dangerous precisely because Holmes is drawn to her, and to what she represents: the opportunity to act with true autonomy and individual freedom in a world now dominated by the collective logic and conventional values of the procedural. A flashback to Holmes's first meeting with "Irene," when she was posing as an art restorer, shows that he immediately determined that many of the "reproductions" in her London flat were in fact immensely valuable original works of art, which she has obviously replaced with her own forgeries. She defends this as preserving the works from those who do not properly appreciate them; although he is at the time representing one of the very institutions she has defrauded, he says only that he "appreciates your efforts to keep the vulgarities of the modern era at bay" (*Elementary* "The Woman"). Within minutes of meeting Moriarty, and years before learning her true identity, Holmes has conspired with her in an immense theft justified by a shared rejection of the contemporary and a desire to "preserve" the original form of artistic works. This is the first of many moments in which Holmes and Moriarty emphasize, not their difference, but their similarity. Again and again—continuing into the letters they exchange in the second season, once Moriarty has been imprisoned—they tell each other, and others, that only they are capable of truly understanding each other, because of their superiority to those around them. In making Moriarty female—and specifically in making him into "the woman"—*Elementary* allows her to fully embody the seductive force of Holmes's original, privileged self.

It is telling that Holmes perceives that "Irene" has been deceiving him only when he notices, after freeing her from what he believes to have been two years of captivity, that a birthmark on her back has been removed, presumably because it was precancerous. A captor would have no reason to exhibit such care; clearly "Irene" has chosen to have the procedure herself. The symbolism here is so clear as to be almost excessive: the woman is revealed as a threat when she exerts control over her own body by removing an unwanted growth. It is telling, too, that Moriarty is baffled not by Holmes, but by Watson; she cannot understand Holmes's toleration of this "mascot," and assumes that Watson is only interested in Holmes for romantic reasons. When she comes to Holmes's hospital bed, Moriarty tells him that he is the only person in the world capable of surprising her. He tells her that there are two, and that the "mascot" has "solved you" by "diagnosing your condition." Even after being captured by Watson, however, Moriarty, when she eventually reappears in the second-season episode "The Diabolical Kind," cannot understand her, and can only assert again that Holmes will eventually tire of her. Unlike Holmes, Moriarty is incapable of making the transition to a world where the empowerment of a figure like Dr. Joan Watson makes sense.

The Sherlock Holmes of *Elementary* is ultimately a transitional figure, a classical detective in a procedural world; he has been saved from the neurotic excesses of his other recent incarnations at the cost of losing much of the privilege and authority he once enjoyed. Where Irene/Moriarty represents the seductive possibility of reasserting his license to act autonomously, Watson represents his stabilizing commitment to a world of collaboration, responsibility, and convention. This model would suggest that, *TV Guide*'s question notwithstanding, Holmes and Watson cannot "hook up." To do so would be to induce generic hysteria, undercutting the collective model of procedural heroism with the kind of conventional/patriarchal relationship that would not be out of place in one of Conan Doyle's stories. How long *Elementary* can maintain this tension remains to be seen; it is entirely possible that future writers and producers, if the show stays on the air long enough, will take the characters in entirely different directions. At least for the moment, however, *Elementary* has succeeded in demonstrating that truly bringing Sherlock Holmes into the present day involves a great deal more than finding a modern-looking calabash.

Works Cited

Bragg, Tom. "Becoming a 'Mere Appendix': The Rehabilitated Masculinity of Sherlock Holmes." *Victorian Newsletter* 116.3 (Fall 2009): 3–26. Print.
Davis, J. Madison. "Mr. Monk and the Pleasing Paradigm." *World Literature Today* 83.3 (2009): 11–13. Print.
Hall, Jasmine Yong. "Ordering the Sensational: Sherlock Holmes and the Female Gothic." *Studies in Short Fiction* 28 (Summer 1991): 295–304. Print.
"Heroine." *Elementary: Season 1*. Writ. Robert Doherty and Craig Sweeny. Dir. John Poison. CBS, 2013. DVD.
Krasner, James. "Watson Falls Asleep: Narrative Frustration and Sherlock Holmes." *English Literature in Translation* 40.4 (1997): 424–436. Print.
Polasek, Ashley D. "Sherlockian Simulacra: Adaptation and the Postmodern Construction of Reality." *Literature/Film Quarterly* 40.3 (Fall 2012): 191–196. Print.
Riley, Brendan. "From Sherlock to Angel: The Twenty-First Century Detective." *The Journal of Popular Culture* 42.5 (2009): 908–922. Print.
"The Woman." *Elementary: Season 1*. Writ. Robert Doherty and Craig Sweeny. Dir. Seith Mann. CBS, 2013. DVD.

Joan for John
An Elementary Choice
Elizabeth Welch

Time has shown that the most enduring and successful artistic works, whether written, cinematic, or otherwise, are those which continually make profound connections with the people and societies to which they are brought. By definition, in order for a work to be considered classic it should possess an "enduring interest and value" ("Classic"). These texts speak of timeless subject matters which intrinsically bridge generational gaps in their explorations of universal themes. Works deemed "classic" literally stand the test of time. The perpetuated success of the infinitely popular Sherlock Holmes franchise, however, has been due in large part to the entity's virtually seamless ability to adapt and change with its audiences. While other prestigious works have excelled in adapted forms, such as the reimagined Shakespearean plays via *10 Things I Hate About You* or Joss Whedon's *Much Ado About Nothing* they are still very much enjoyed in play forms that mirror the original as well as in films that employ historical settings that primarily reflect that sense of historicity which evokes the original, as would be the case in Kenneth Branaugh's *Henry V*, and Wells' *Macbeth* or *Othello*. The difference between the Conan Doyle and the Shakespearean vehicles is that the Holmsian canon carries a history of films that have constantly adapted both Holmes and Watson to be men of the present, as can be seen throughout the Rathbone serials of the 30's and 40's and in following adaptations. This precedent continues to be adopted by the two current television series in practice and by the current films in spirit. While the Holmes works are undoubtedly classics, they have achieved this prestigious position primarily through this continual transformation via adaptation rather than through the direct conveyance of universal themes. That is, the heart of the stories has remained the same over time, but in order to endure and entice new fans, the numerous Holmesian adaptations have re-imagined the main characters, amongst other comprising elements, to continuously suit the ever-changing populaces.

To the initial readers of Victorian England, Arthur Conan Doyle's Sherlock Holmes stories offered not only relatable characters, but also much needed escapes from the uncertainty that weighed heavily on the readers' minds during this historically dramatic time of change. Needless to say the present world, it being 2015 at this time of this essay, faces vastly different issues. As such, the representations of Holmes and Watson have evolved to reflect this. The tales' foundations have, by and large, held firm. The one and only consulting detective and his companion have always taken on criminal cases which stump even the police. This premise encapsulates the essence of the canon and it could not be altered without sacrificing affiliation with the original writings. The characters within the stories, however, are almost entirely up for subjective interpretation based on Conan Doyle's works. The Sherlock and John which first appeared in 1897 in *A Study in Scarlet* are vastly different creatures from those seen in today's Holmes adaptions. Despite their transformations, the two have always worked to solve crimes. The people of today are different from those of the nineteenth century, but the presence of crime and criminals provides a source of distinct continuity between epochs.

Today, there are those that argue that the latest Holmsian adaptation has taken this transformative practice too far. The pair continue to solve cases with just as much brilliant ingenuity as the original duo, but one particular rendition has provoked many disputes. CBS's 2012 television series *Elementary* has endured heavy scrutinizing dating from well before its original airdate. Despite maintaining the essence of the Sherlock Holmes tales throughout the framework of the show, scholars and fans alike have taken issue. Many claim that its interpretations of Sherlock and John not only work against the integrity of the original, but it also fails to conform to and address the needs and wants of today's society. These claims essentially mark the series as an outright failure in sustaining the spirit of Sherlock Holmes and all that it stands for. Within just the past few years, two feature films, one being a sequel to the other, and two television series, the BBC's *Sherlock* and the American *Elementary* have been brought to audiences. The last in line of this recent slew of new Holmes adaptations, *Elementary* has received more protest and negative criticisms in its depictions of the characters than either of the other two renditions. As per the M.O. of Holmes adaptations, each rendition has drawn from the original tales while placing distinct emphases on specific characteristics of both Sherlock and John in order to highlight certain social relevancies of today (Loock, Kathleen, and Verevis 45). These variations have ranged from simply modernizing the pair's era of existence to vastly altering the relationships the two have with others within the framework of the stories. The peculiar outcry against *Elementary* actually has little to do with the show's selected period or really any choices that would work in opposition to Conan Doyle's oeuvre. It is in the show's portrayal of Dr. John Watson that, critics and fans alike have found issue with. In the case of CBS's *Elementary,* John is now "Joan."

To many Holmes "purists" the choice to rewrite the detective's companion as a woman is "an abomination to all that is canon" (Smith, "Elementary, My Dear Joan Watson: An Egalitarian Sherlock?"). The decision to do so has been met with such fierce hostility that the conflict has gained notoriety. What about this particular decision has warranted such opposition? What should it really matter whether or not Watson is male or female? It is true, there is no arguing that Watson was originally written as a man. As previously stated though, the canon has managed to endure by virtue of its ability to adapt. Holmes and Watson have perpetually evolved with their audiences. Why, in an era that emphasizes the importance of the progressive movement towards fair and equal gender representations has there been such a backlash over this choice? Why should not a woman be invited to stand right alongside the most prolific detective in all of history?

Those averse to "Joan" Watson claim to found their protest in the name of the franchise's purity. Many insist that the 'bromance' between Sherlock and John has actually functioned as the constant force which has enabled the canon to maintain its strength (McLaughlin 6). Others claim that the choice to change Watson's gender fundamentally falls short in upholding the integrity of the original works. While the sentiment of loyalty to such a classically beloved set of works can be appreciated to a certain degree, the level of outright abuse which *Elementary* has received on this count is excessive, to say the least. While many of those who have spoken out will beg to differ, the issue of John being changed to Joan is actually much more of a reflection of societal predispositions towards gender than it is about the intention of staying true to the original works. Certain ideologies pertaining to the expectations of both men and women are so heavily ingrained within cultures that most individuals are unaware of their presence (Thornham 6). Such mentalities are simply acted upon instinctually. The overtly negative reactions to Watson's change of gender is primarily in response to these beliefs. Despite the differences in audience reception, *Elementary* no more or less defies Conan Doyle's works than any of the other adaptations. Holmes is still the astounding detective that solves the cases which stump the police and Watson is his dedicated companion. The show does, however, provide so much more than just another entertaining adaptation. In making the choice to change the character of John Watson to a woman, *Elementary* takes a stance. It takes an active position against passive ideologies which would otherwise continue to permeate misconceptions into the dominant mindset. In changing the gender of the companion to one of the most esteemed and prolific characters in all of the fictional worlds to a woman, *Elementary* challenges society's gender-related fallacies head on. Men and women are, in fact, equal. Dynamics between men and women are not inherently sexual and physical shapes aside, there is nothing innately different between the genders. In making the choice to change John to Joan, *Elementary* sparks the dormant debate necessary in taking the next steps to abolishing these negative mentalities.

Society's reception of the Holmes stories has constantly changed. To the earliest readers, Sherlock provided hope and stability during a tumultuous time. England of 1897 was ripe with uncertainty. Not only were people wary about the state of society, but they were entirely unsure of what was to come next. Industrialization was rapidly revolutionizing the work force. Societal institutions such as marriage and economic classes were being challenged left and right (McLaughlin 5). The very structure of society was in flux and citizens simply did not know where it was all leading. Then along came Sherlock Holmes; he was the man with all the answers. He simply reveled in the unknown and cracked every mystery that came his way, proving that human understanding through sense and logic could overcome any obstacle. Sherlock Holmes thrived in this wholly unpredictable environment. To the readers of Victorian England he represented the strength to conquer everything that life had in store (Wisser 6).

Standing alone, this is what Sherlock's character provided. Alongside his companion Watson though, he offered something else entirely. Together, the pair emphasized the importance of professional camaraderie through a friendship which bridged both the social and working worlds. During the late nineteenth century, men were not generally encouraged to socialize with one another outside of the workplace. This type of bonding was met with the societal anxiety associated with homosexuality (McLaughlin 13). After marriage, it was permissible to associate with other married couples alongside one's wife, but that was the extent. At the time of Conan Doyle's publications, society was beginning to combat this apprehension. Rather than draw from the negative connotation the concept of homosexuality exhumed, it was elected that men should find strength in one another. Strong men made for a stronger society. Sherlock Holmes completely rejected the notion of a "proper" career and marriage. In doing so, he reveled in his companionship with Watson. He even discouraged Watson's decision to conform with expectations, his reaction to Watson's marriage being "I feared as much ... I really cannot congratulate you" (Conan Doyle, "The Sign of the Four" 358). Both he and Watson lived a drastically different style of life, one which was wholly free of expectations and institutions. They developed a friendship through their mutual interests that went beyond simply working together. As Holmes himself would remark to Watson in "The Red-Headed League," "I know ... that you share my love of all that is bizarre and outside the conventions and humdrum routine of everyday life" (Conan Doyle, "The Red-Headed League" 181). It was through this shared love that the two developed a friendship which allowed them each to thrive both personally and professionally. Together they exemplified to readers that one could defy norms and could do so without sacrificing dignity or airs of professionalism. Further, such choices did not make one any more or less a respected member of society. Sherlock Holmes and John Watson showed the world that it was more than perfectly acceptable to be different and, by being so, one could even excel in a chaotic world.

It is now 2013 and society's needs relating to accurate and desired fictional representations have vastly changed. It should go without saying that the public of today does not necessarily demand a male duo within the Holmes adaptations. Society today is nowhere near as sexist as they were at the time of the original writings. The fact that this is how the original stories were written is not wholly relevant to today's society. Women are held significantly higher on the societal spectrum than they were more than a century ago. They presently comprise a significant portion of the work force and there is no reason John Watson, who by profession is a doctor, could not be rewritten as a woman. The stories were originally written for the societies of the time and as such the adaptations are made to accommodate the people of today (McLaughlin 9).

Since they first appeared, Holmes and Watson have been transformed and twisted over and again. All of these interpretations have been received with both praise and criticism in respect to their adherence to Conan Doyle's works, none of which has received such tremendous backlash as *Elementary*'s male and female duo. Joan Watson could hardly be received with any less of an embrace. By sheer virtue of her gender, she had been judged as unfit and has distastefully been begrudged the position as Holmes's companion. Nevermind her characteristics, how she was to interact with Holmes, or how they were to work with each other. None of the facets that might actually be relevant within the framework of the series itself were questioned. Meerly the fact that John was now a Joan was brought into question.

When word of this choice began circulating, Holmes fans were anything but shy about expressing their opinions. Sentiments revolving around the character's gender swap were by and large hostile and many fans were appalled outright at the thought. In summation, Joan Watson's character was perceived as "an abomination of all that [is] canon" (Smith, "Elementary, My Dear Joan Watson: An Egalitarian Sherlock?"). Claims were either seated in outrage on behalf of the integrity of the franchise or they were held on behalf of the famed detective himself. The original works starred two men. Plain and simple. It is also well documented that Sherlock Holmes held virtually no affinity towards the opposite sex. He possessed a well-established "aversion to women" as Watson himself would note in the original writings (Conan Doyle, "The Greek Interpreter" 527). Within the confines of his original character, it is simply not in his nature to be one to work alongside a woman. The detective, in essence, "embodie[d] that very Victorian combination of exquisite manners and deep distrust around all women" (Stagg, "Casting Lucy Liu as Dr. 'Joan' Watson Will Ruin One of the Greatest Bromances of All Time").

In addition to claims that directly address the canon, there are also a number that have been presented based on societal norms and predispositions. It is actually through these sentiments that the first claims were founded. That is, adherence to Holmes fundamentalism aside, all of the criticisms laid against the decision to rewrite John as Joan stem from an ideology which subscribes to the concept that there exists an inherent imbalance between men and women. The two are incapable of working with one another in the same manner as a same sex pair would. A male Holmes and a female Watson will not work for this reason. The attitude has been perpetuated by the media which has long stood firm in its stance that interactions between heterosexual men and women, placed upon equal planes of importance, are inherently sexual. The "climax," as it were, of such relationships is ultimately sex. Fans have utilized this misconception to fuel their position that holds that the "bromance" between the two men has been what has made the tales so enduring. To remove this balance would be detrimental. Rather than being working companions and friends, as two men most certainly would, a man and a woman would become distractions to one another and their work. Holmes' work, specifically, would suffer. As one fan states, "slueths are at their best when they are not trying to seduce their partners" (Stagg, "Casting Lucy Liu as Dr. 'Joan' Watson Will Ruin One of the Greatest Bromances of All Time"). According to these claims then, not only would the male and female dynamic be doomed to fail, but it would ultimately lead to the undoing of the world's greatest and one-and-only consulting detective. All simply because John is now Joan.

To say the least, such assumptions are incredibly sexist and unfounded. Further, they were proposed before *Elementary* even aired. These issues had nothing to do with who this new Watson was or who she was meant to represent. She was judged solely on the basis of gender. Now, nevermind Sherlock; nevermind John; nevermind the whole of the franchise. Is it acceptable, in the twenty-first century, to make assumptions on a person's abilities and their potential based solely on their gender? The simple answer is no. Yet, Joan is an "abomination" for the sake of being a woman (Smith, "Elementary, My Dear Joan Watson: An Egalitarian Sherlock?"). The sentiments revolving around her negative reception go beyond stereotypical notions. Audiences at least tend to generally acknowledge stereotypes and their inaccuracies, recognizing that preconceived categorization may not be considered reliable. Yet, the assumptions which afflict *Elementary* are so instinctively reactionary that the majority of the populous is unable to recognize the perpetuating patriarchal ideologies which have fueled them.

As part of the replicative pattern of enculturation which may change our understanding of these ideologies, the canon of Holmes may play a part of no small significance. The malleable adaptability of the works has historically proven how it may represent something wholly different to the readers and audiences of different times. What the canon has proven again and again is that it relishes in embracing the culture and society to which it is being presented and it does not shy away from liberally playing with the stories' characters to suit its audiences. Changing John to Joan is simply the next in the long line of liberties artists have taken in reimagining Conan Doyle's world. Today, in an age of progressing gender equality, via actuality and representation, there is no reason that Sherlock Holmes would not be capable of standing right alongside a woman in his work. The Sherlock of today does not "need" a male companion. While the prevalent patriarchal ideologies make it difficult to do so, the people of today need to be shown this. Joan is more than worthy and entirely capable of standing next to Sherlock Holmes. In fact, she should be invited to do so.

This first step towards uncovering the roots of these contentious and overtly assumptive mentalities towards Joan is in questioning them. On this front, there have been those who have acknowledged the rather abrasive opposition against the female Watson. In working through many of their own feelings, some have found that their predispositions have been, in most cases, baseless. Gaby Dunn wrote a rather astute introspective blog entry on the issue. In a conversation with another individual, Dunn, a self-proclaimed Holmes "purist," came to the conclusion that through her instinctual defense of the original works, she had failed to look at the big picture of what *Elementary* stood for ("Dr. Joan Watson, Racism, and the Sherlock Vs. Elementary Backlash"). A section of her discussion in question reads:

> THEM: Don't you complain all the time about the degrading hooker or victim or nagging wife parts for women on dramas?
> ME: But ...
> THEM: Don't you think it's nice that there's a big network show with a strong, complex female lead—a female lead of color—on par with her male co-star? Given equal credit and equal footing?
> ME: ...
> THEM: Yeah.

In being called out on her own reluctance, Dunn recognizes that it is not necessarily about staying fundamentally true to the original works, but rather about what this new adaptation, at large, means. At the end of her entry, Dunn concludes that "this change could be a really good, necessary thing—bigger than Sherlock Holmes, and more important, interesting and exciting than sticking to the way the story's been told before" ("Dr. Joan Watson, Racism, and the Sherlock Vs. Elementary Backlash"). In one fell swoop, Dunn manages to crack the transparent sheath of conditioned ideologies to allot her readers, who are likely to be fans themselves, the ability so simply ask why. Why is Dr. Joan Watson a bad thing?

Once this active questioning is initiated, it is then necessary to deconstruct the various claims which have been presented against *Elementary*'s choice. The foremost of which is that along with losing John as a man, the works also loses that "bromance" which fans have come to love so much. The somewhat more clinical and original term for which is "homosocial bonds." The attitudes surrounding the necessity of these kinds of relationships stem from archaic mores that revolved around masculinity. Strong men constituted a strong society. In the late nineteenth century, when Sherlock first appeared, men dominated the professional sphere, but were not held in as high regards in the domestic and social scopes. Despite tensions about homosexuality, homosocial bonds were encouraged in order to ensure that men were in charge in all aspects of life. The push was deemed the "flight from domesticity." In expanding their eminent domain to reach out beyond their own households and professional endeavors "not only could professional men better society by contributing to the nation's industry and economy, but also, through friendship and bonding, they could positively influence other men in society" (McLaughlin 15–6).

The societal goals of this notion gradually evolved and the term "bromance" came into play. While the original sentiment holds little to no relevancy in today's society, it is important to understand how it correlates with today's Holmes and Watson and the dynamic they share. The label of "bromance" is allotted to them simply for the sake of ruling out a homosexual relationship. Simply put, they are friends. They rely on each other for both personal and professional support. They frequently argue and do not get along, but that is all well because they are friends and at the end of the day; they will always be so. This relationship works, many claim, because they are both men. This brings in the next most prominent issue laid against changing John to Joan. Men and women, according to many, are incapable of sustaining a friendship such as theirs. As Dunn so politely surmised earlier—why?

This mentality is driven behind the media-perpetuated vehicle that the genders are inherently different. Within the frameworks of both films and television shows, dynamics between men and women are constantly propelled by sexual tension. Inevitably, a male and female pair will end up in bed together. This is even more so the case with crime-based series (Byerly and Ross 23–4). This is a myth, however. Gender is a fluid construct (Ross 368). What the media deems to be true, as far as its exclusivity in defining the characteristics of each gender, is based on a yet another archaic notion. Men go out and provide for their families while women stay at home and tend to the house. As such, both men and women, despite the gradual progression to move away from such role-based representations, are still predominately shown in fulfilling their assigned gender expectations.

This binary divider between the genders only functions to perpetuate the idea that men and women are incapable of sustaining platonic friendships. The media dictates this myth as truth. In the case of CBS's *Elementary*, due to the Holmes stories' intrinsic subject matter, it is even more susceptible to this bias. As S.E. Smith states in his Global Comment article "television seems obligated to make male/female crime duos both heterosexual and in love with each other" (Smith, "Elementary, My Dear Joan Watson: An Egalitarian Sherlock?"). While this is not a written rule, it is a concept which has sustained numerous television series and films alike. Those behind the production of such pieces have simply neglected to deter from the theory-driven notion because it works. It is this passive negligence that encourages the naïve mentality whose stance is "if it's not broken, don't fix it."

Passivity has been and continues to be the fundamental facet which has allowed these negative mentalities to exist for as long as they have. While broken may not necessarily be the right descriptor for the concept of a crime-based show featuring a romantic male and female dynamic, it is detrimentally narrow-minded for the media to present this as the only viable option, especially in regards to the romantic aspect. Unfortunately, the lack of interest in bringing about change is due, by and large, to the fact that the number of men working in prominent positions within the media industry greatly outweigh the number of women working in similar positions. That is not to say that men should be blamed, by any means. The policy of fair and equal representation of the genders is simply not a prominent issue for men en masse (Thornham 39). That being said though, the showrunner for *Elementary* is a man. Rob Doherty elected to take a stance in writing John Watson as a woman. It is thanks to choices such as his that society can more readily move towards understanding that there is nothing inherently different between the genders.

When passivity is what stands between stagnation and change, the only way forward is through challenging. The well-known feminist film theorist, Theresa de Lauretis readily embraces the need for a "revolution" in transforming the ways in which women are depicted and viewed in the media. She declares that it is the "depiction of reality" which needs to be challenged (Thornham 37). It is not enough, de Lauretis says, to simply examine the depictions and discuss them. That too, is passive. Works need to be produced which counter the established norms presented by the media in order for attention to be brought to the issue. *Elementary* succeeds in doing just that. Through its predominately negative reception, sexist ideologies and societal predispositions pertaining to the "novel" decision to make John Watson a woman are brought to the foreground and become a subject for debate. In the particular case of *Elementary's* revolutionary choice, the deep roots of loyalty for the Holmes canon have been cultivated for more than a century. Over time, *The Adventures of Sherlock Holmes* have earned their place as a staple in so many childhoods spanning over multiple generations and across the world that the concept of bringing about change to this beloved series is approached with utmost sincerity. While the hostile reactions towards John being changed to Joan were predominately the result of long-standing patriarchal ideologies, the level of devotion for Conan Doyle's works heightened anxiety over the change. This added tension further ensured that the issues of gender representation would be front and center for questioning. For this reason, *Elementary* stands as an exemplary catalyst to aid in the progression of overcoming this toxic passivity and ultimately moving towards fair and equal gender representation in the media.

What many fans and scholars fail to acknowledge in their judgments over a female Watson is that the original works fought against norms as well. Sherlock and John were not "normal." Their lives were anything but ordinary. *Elementary*, along with taking a stance against unfair gender representation, actually holds truer to the sentiments of the original works than a number of the other adaptations. The heart of adaptation theory itself states that

> in many ways, adaptations reflect the society in which they are created. The principles that are embraced, charged, or rejected are indicative of the society and culture that make those choices. Just as the original texts are reactionary to their contemporary society, so too are the adaptations [McLaughlin 9].

Just as the original works took a stance against norms, giving hope and pride to many of its readers, so does this stance of switching John for Joan. This is what the society of today strives for: equal representation of the genders in the media. It maintains that men and women are not inherently different. The sentiment that this affirmation counters stems from a residual notion where popular culture is clutched with a convulsed fist, oozing patriarchal bias over all productions. It only makes sense that the most classic stories then, be implemented in taking this stance against this notion. Even better that this change be laid upon a figure, John Watson, who is perceived as the equal to the greatest, most prolific figure in all of cinema.

While the stance itself is a strong one in and of itself, the choice to change John to Joan would fall terribly short should it not follow through with the adequate, if not complex, characterization of Dr. Joan Watson within the series, as well as convey the nature of her dynamic with Sherlock. *Elementary* does its part to more than just deliver in this matter. Not only does Dr. Joan Watson work alongside Holmes in stride, but she also maintains her independence. Unlike the original Watson, Joan has a life outside of her work with Holmes (Smith, "Elementary, My Dear Joan Watson: An Egalitarian Sherlock?"). She has a family and she socializes. While readers caught glimpses of Watson's life beyond the cases in the original works, remarks of such activities were more or less met with snips of disdain from Sherlock. Such would not be the case with the pair as depicted in *Elementary*. Sherlock frequently encourages Joan in her activities outside of cases. He respects that her life does not revolve around him, nor would he ever anticipate it to.

Overall, Joan is a real woman in a real role. Her position as Sherlock Holmes's companion aside, this is a rarity. The media constantly "frame[s] (in every sense of the word) women within a narrow repetoire of types that bear little or no relation to how real women live real lives" (Byerly and Ross 18). *Elementary*'s choice not only draws attention to the perpetuated ideology that dictates the inherent differences between men and women, but through Joan it also offers an example of what a real woman looks like. While it can be argued that the roles of women today have expanded to include more than just the house-wife, there still exists a bias that places women within very specific roles in both films and televisions. These claims can be countered with the sentiment that if this tendency were not true, Joan's reception would not have been anywhere near as negative. A female Watson would have been taken with the same level of criticims as other adaptations if women were more fairly represented. As far as *Elementary* is concerned, "while one show cannot be expected to carry the burden of all women's expectations, it is precisely the scarcity of positive images of women that makes many women viewers continue to want exactly such a representation" (Byerly and Ross 28). As Sherlock came along just when he was needed in 1897, so did Joan in 2013.

CBS's *Elementary* is not the latest in a long line of "buddy" crime shows. For that matter, nor was the source from which it was derived. Sherlock Holmes and John Watson first offered their audiences a reality that brought them a sense of solace. In both the characters and their adventures, people found relatability and hope. As another respectable adaptation of Conan Doyle's works, *Elementary* does the same. By igniting a storm of criticims via the decision to change Holmes's companion to a woman, the series sheds light on the passivity which has enabled the perpetuation of gender-roles in the media. Amidst the waves of backlash the show has received, many have come to question this passivity and have thereby actively broken the stagnation, allowing for further change to take place. Not only has the show inspired this progression, but it has also provided audiences with a complex female character who stands on her own two feet, completely separate from the famed detective himself. Further, he respects her for it. The pair's dynamic breaks the societal expectations of sexual tension with a wholly relatable platonic relationship between the two. The show manages to shatter so many predispositions by making such a seemingly innocuous decision. Its timing in doing so could not be more appropriately placed either. In just the past few years, society has experienced waves of progression in the ways of acceptance. Now is the time people are calling for change. Now is the time to push forward. In an age where the possible benefits far outweigh the potential consequences, the choice to change John Watson to Joan Watson was quite simply *Elementary*.

Works Cited

"Classic." *OED Online*. June 2013. Oxford University Press. Web. 27 Aug. 2013.
Byerly, Carolyn M., and Karen Ross. *Women & Media: A Critical Introduction*. Oxford: Blackwell, 2006. Print.
Conan Doyle, Arthur. "The Greek Interpreter." *The Adventures and Memoirs of Sherlock Holmes*. New York: Modern Library, 1946. Print. 527–48.
_____. "The Red-Headed League." *Tales of Sherlock Holmes*. New York: Grosset, 1915. 181–206. Print.
_____. "The Sign of the Four." *Tales of Sherlock Holmes*. New York: Grosset, 1915. 235–359. Print.
_____. "A Study In Scarlet." *Tales of Sherlock Holmes*. New York: Grosset, 1915. 1–131. Print.
Dunn, Gabby. "Dr. Joan Watson, Racism, and the Sherlock Vs. Elementary Backlash." *The Thought Catalog*. The Thought Catalog, 31 Aug. 2012. Web. 17 July 2013.
Loock, Kathleen, and Constantine Verevis. *Film Remakes, Adaptations, and Fan Productions*. London: Palgrave, 2012. Web. 17 July 2013.
McLaughlin, Rebecca. *A Study in Sherlock: Revisiting the Relationship between Sherlock Holmes and Dr. John Watson*. Honors thesis. Bridgewater State, 2013. Web. 17 July 2013.
Ross, Karen, ed. *Handbooks in Communication and Media, Volume 18: Handbook of Gender, Sex, and Media*. Hoboken: Wiley-Blackwell, 2011. Web. 2 Aug. 2013.
Smith, S.E. "Elementary, My Dear Joan Watson: An Egalitarian Sherlock?" *Global Comment*. Global Comment, 21 Feb. 2013. Web. 19 July 2013.
Stagg, Guy. "Casting Lucy Liu as Dr. 'Joan' Watson will Ruin One of the Greatest Bromances of All Time." *The Telegraph*. The Telegraph Blogs, 29 Feb. 2012. Web. 19 July 2013.
Thornham, Sue, ed. *Feminist Film Theory: A Reader*. New York: New York University Press, 1999. Print.
Wisser, Katherine Mary. *The Creation, Reception, and Perpetuation of the Sherlock Holmes Phenomenon, 1887–1930*. MA thesis. University of North Carolina at Chapel Hill, 2009. Ann Arbor: *Proquest*. Web. 5 Aug 2013.

Joan Watson
Mascot, Companion and Investigator
Lucy Baker

The history of Holmesean fanworks go back to the era of the original itself, and Sir Conan Doyle's permissive "Marry him, murder him, do what you will to him" directed to a playwright seeking to marry off Holmes in his own fanplay (Eyles 34). From there on Sherlock Holmes, in various guises, has appeared in hundreds of interpretations. Occasionally a mouse, a robot, cryogenically frozen, reincarnated or reinterpreted entirely into a new "successor," Holmes-the-character provides a colorful canvas to echo and work with. Modernizing the series has again had an illustrious history, including the contemporaneous modernizations of the early parts of last century such as the Rathbone films. *Elementary* (2012) is one of the more recent adaptations enjoying a measure of commercial and critical success, albeit one that has taken the rare path of regendering. In *Elementary*, the character of Dr. John Watson is reworked from the male, white, British veteran of the originals and so many remakes to Dr. *Joan* Watson, a Chinese-American ex-surgeon played by Lucy Liu. Also reworked and regendered is Moriarty, which shifts their rivalry from the masculine homoerotic (as per some adaptations) to a regendered homosocial relationship, positioning Joan not as simply an amanuensis but as an agent in her own right. Joan's position as an iteration within the Archontic Sherlock, that intricate collection of texts, paratexts, metatexts and mind palaces that make up modern understandings of the works (Black, Leveque, and Stewart 1–5; Derecho 65) allows for her character to simultaneously reinterpret and critique other iterations and media itself, particularly through her relationship with Jamie.

In search of clarity, given the prevalence of Holmsean adaptations, references to the characters will be as follows: Joan, Jamie and Sherlock refer to the *Elementary* characters of the same name, Watson, Moriarty and Holmes refer to the original characters and other Archontic versions will be marked as Series Name Character. The Archontic iterations as a whole will be identified as "Archontic Character." This method owes a debt of gratitude to fannish naming conventions dealing with the endless numbers of character variations.

Current adaptations of the Holmes mythos that dominate media fandom are the BBC television series *Sherlock*, the Guy Ritchie film series with Robert Downey, Jr., and Jude Law, and CBS' *Elementary*, with Jeremy Brett and Basil Rathbone holding spaces almost as "Holmes' Emeritus." Literary adaptations, pastiches, and continuations (legitimate or not) are less apparent in the landscape, even including the original stories.[1] The focus of both fandom and the media is often on the character of Sherlock Holmes, and secondarily on the relationship with Watson. Other named characters, such as Irene Adler, Professor Moriarty, Mrs. Hudson and various victims, perpetrators and police officers, weave in and around that dyad of Holmes and Watson. In *Elementary*, Watson is regendered; unlike other (uncommon) adaptations where the female Watson is a descendant or reincarnation, Joan Watson is an even rarer occurrence; she is simply a woman, without explanation as to why she has come to take this place in the work. Moriarty is also similarly regendered, in that the characters of Irene Adler and Professor Moriarty are combined into Jamie Moriarty.

The central conceit of the stories is not simply the relationship between Watson and Holmes, as integral as it is. Rather, what the pair *does* is what boundaries, defines and separates their relationship. They are agents of change and action; they save people and solve crimes while maintaining and developing a relationship that has become renowned, if not entirely understood or codified. The variables and variations in the dyad are a result not only of differing interrogations of the texts (are they queer, are they straight, are they *really* men, is this a triumph of the rational over the emotional, Imperialism and colonialism and the death of the British empire going stiff-lipped and righteous into the sea) but of the text itself (Kestner 39; Porter 115). A mass of continuity errors and the effects of authorial intent gone skewed and bitter, the Holmes stories have had an effect out of all proportion to the texts and it is that dyad of Holmes and Watson and what they *do*, that is often claimed as the reason for the success. The real crux of the success is this: the fans. Call them Sherlockians, Holmeseans, whatever you may, their devotion to the text and manipulation of it and expansion from it has kept the story going.

One of the famous pastimes of the Holmseans is The Great Game, the (im)polite fiction that the stories are just as they are told, the diaries and writings of Dr. John Watson passed through Conan Doyle as some sort of amanuensis. The Great Game, as it is played, remains a problem for adaptations—not for their place as a retelling of the works, but for their own internal structure that avoids the way the canon has become part of the weave of media, with adaptations and retellings and costumes and even idioms. Which gives rise to something like the Good Game, in that each adaptation induces the audience to pretend, to treat seriously, that this manifestation of Holmes and Watson is either a continuation of the original (via cryogenics or reincarnation or possession) or the birth of it within a new environment; one must use the metaknowledge of canonical representation while also accepting the absence or erasure of the original. This lack of the varied history within the text is often earmarked by deliberate references to it—for instance, at a not entirely serious level, *Elementary* refers to *The Great Mouse Detective* in its opening credits by mimicking in live action the Rube-Goldenberg like contraptions from the cartoon. This connection was spotted by fans but not referred to by the credit designer in an interview about his work at the blog *The Art of the Title* (2013) (Taylor). More seriously the adaptation also references canon in titles, in the cases themselves. The aptness, the skill, with which this intertextuality is played out becomes a mark of distinction and taste within the Archontic.

It also provides a significant playground for the audience and fandom to examine and analyze, and is a tool being used by many media producers (adaptations or otherwise) to prompt that play. The intertextuality, between media properties and canon and paratextual elements, can give rise to problematic concerns about representation and understanding; the neutral masculine (white) default allows for a kind of freedom that a female, or non-white, character cannot claim. Similarly aspects of the original which remain unsettling but contemporaneously understandable within the canon (particularly racial and gender stereotypes) are almost magnified in adaptations and the decision to include or erase those aspects loom large. In addition, characteristics, qualities and values that are praised or even overlooked in the canonical Holmes stories become ugly stereotypes in adaptations that change the gender/race of the original characters. Each adaptation must in some way interact not only with the original stories, but in the myriad ways those characters can be read as an artifact of literary history and contemporary politics (including the ongoing effects of historical racism, colonialism and sexism). This has resulted in what several online commentators call a kind of Trojan horse of updating—characters and situations which are moved into modern imaginations with a hasty paintjob of emancipation and equality, without changing the underlying structure (Loving; McDougall; Valentine).

The place of the female Watson, of Joan-the-character, cannot be decontextualized from the media landscape she inhabits. The essences of the male Watson—emotionally astute, caretaker, protector, secondary to Holmes, traumatized, devoted (Porter 10, 2012)—must find an equal representation in the female but those essences and characteristics are performed and read within the gender boundaries. Queer readings of the relationship become heterosexualized in this characterization, echoing the "straightwashing" of historical figures. However that reading remains coded in the original and in most Archontic iterations (to varying degrees of "coded" [Porter 186]) and the heterosexualization operates only as a sort of reaction to a palimpsest not to the text itself. Instead, in this adaptation, the sexual tension remains at an intellectual level and lampshaded from the moment the characters meet: Sherlock says to Joan, "Do you believe in love at first sight?" and is revealed to be quoting from the TV show in the background (*Elementary* "Pilot"). Joan's reaction is not represented romantically—there are no lingering shots of her eyes or her face, no auditory cues such as breathing—but is a far more realistic shock and confusion. The reluctance to sexualize the relationship has been expressed by the show runners in interviews online from the beginning of the series; audiences, however, are well aware of the ways in which series will use sexual tension within the works (Bennett). Detective shows and police procedurals have a history of their own use and abuse of sexual tension (*Moonlighting*, *The X-Files*, or in adaptations, *Miss Fisher's Murder Mysteries*) as do other genres, and this overarching theme is what fans are reacting to—a kind of metatext that *Elementary* is (thus far) subverting.

Joan is portrayed as being traumatized by the medical incident that prompted her career change, yet comfortable with her medical expertise when assisting Sherlock; similar to the canonical and Archontic Watson as a damaged yet functioning hero (through his military or medical prowess). Her emotional intelligence is an echo of Watson's, the seemingly innate understanding of people's feelings and how they interact with the more intellectual observations made by Holmes; an innate understanding filtered through and subverted by Joan's race and gender. The specters of the Dragon Lady, or Exotic Orchid, or other racialized sexist stereotypes, are subverted or absent in the text. Joan's family is not the familiarly exotic Chinese stereotype headed by a brutally feminine matriarch; instead they are loving, if not understanding their daughter's work. Similarly Joan's martial prowess is not linked to the mystic or innate but to tutelage and work. She is neither hypersexualized nor desexualized and maintains both dating and a sexual relationship outside the relationship she has with Sherlock. Those stereotypes are instead worked around; at one point Sherlock infers that Joan, of course, knows an unnamed martial art and would use it at his command, and in another instance Joan drinks Chinese herbal tea and prepares it for Sherlock, defending it both as a cultural artifact from her family and as a medically proven remedy.

> WATSON: Well, you asked for coffee, but you got tea.
> HOLMES: No, I'm British, this is not tea.
> WATSON: There's some traditional Chinese herbs in there. I poked around the stalls in Chinatown while I was waiting for you. I found the ingredients for the same tea my mom used to make me when I was sick.
> HOLMES: Well, all due respect to your mother, I would prefer something proven by a scientific method.
> WATSON: The herbs in that tea have been proven scientifically to inhibit the movement of neutrophils, improve the function of protective cilia, and contribute to longer-lasting, more vasodilated erections [*Elementary* "You Do It to Yourself"].

Her race and gender inform her characterization without relying on the reproduction of stereotypes in order to perform the canonically appropriate level of Watson-ness.

The absence of fully realized female and non-white characters of the Holmesean Archives is occupied and restructured by Joan, as a deliberate act of both differentiation by the creators of the show to address both nascent copyright concerns associated with the BBC's *Sherlock* and to address the imbalance of the original, as reported by several news outlets online (Sherwin). The reinterpretation of Holmes and Watson as a male-female duo raises numerous specters based in fannish experiences of media. There is suspicion around the heterosexualizing of queer subtexts and fan metanarratives, and also the depowering and sexualizing of the female version thus replicating gender roles and norms within a fictive piece, and also romanticizing a platonic heterosexual relationship as a commercial rather than creative choice. This has variously been expressed by critics and fans online as a kind of "infection" of femininity and politics into the presumed purity of the original (Coren). A purity that necessitates the rejection and othering of the feminine and female and anything other than the good men of the British empire; again, an Archontic variation on the series rather than a nuanced attendance to the canon itself. Theirs is not a relationship that holds up the weight of the empire, rather it exemplifies the tensions of the era and the limitations of masculinity (Kestner 48).

The relationship between Joan and Sherlock develops continually through the series, moving from sober companion to partner, with various missteps and detours along the way. The changes are often characterized by serious discussions and radical honesty, mimicking the values Joan carried with her as a sober companion. Her initial appearance in the series is marked by a passivity marked only by reaction to Sherlock, almost akin to inscrutability but rather than being situated as a racial performance or characteristic, it is professional boundary setting and decision making within the context of the addict-companion relationship. This has been remarked on by some part of the audience and critics online as evidence of female passivity, of Joan's inability to match Sherlock's intellectuality, "a mere scold and literal babysitter"—problematic as a gendered interaction, in spite of the Archontic Watsonian emotionality (Ryan). When read as part of the entire series, her actions and passivity at the beginning are manifestations of professional and personal strength. Also, reactions to those aspects of the series are examples of the ways in which canonical characterization is read differently in adaptations due to gender, and the way personal values and characteristics are weighted according to gender. The emotional intelligence of the Archontic Watson is subversion within Joan, due both to race and gender; she still inhabits that space of the emotional conduit for Sherlock but without the canonical sex, the canonical masculinity and whiteness, the meaning of the support and translation of his intellect is different. This characterization was noted in the infamous "Watson Is a Woman" essay (Stout 163), yet when the character is regendered the meanings of Watson the woman are remarkably different.

Post-sober companion Joan is depicted as not only lying (albeit uncomfortably) to Sherlock about her continued employment, but also willing to assist in several criminal activities. The familiar Archontic relationship where Watson is the helpmeet to Holmes, and willing to compromise certain values in pursuit of support, is well trod including in contemporary adaptations. In this case however, her willingness comes from a desire to extend her own self, her position as partner to Sherlock. A selfishness that resonates differently, again, due to her femaleness. An extension of her caring capacities, or an endangerment of her own self, in pursuit and protection of Holmes offers little subversion and simply reduced to a convenient plot point and support token. By changing the motivation behind the actions, *Elementary* retains the structure of the relationship, including the actions and the provocations, while developing a kind of truthfulness to the depiction of Joan as a woman who is ruthless, loyal, and competent. The relationship remains valuable without being weakened by the use of those tropes that fans and critics alike were wary of.

Joan's elevation to full partner, handling cases without the overview of

Sherlock and assisting Sherlock, is less a feature of the stories and more a conceit of the genre the canon has been adapted into—police procedurals. This creative decision, to adapt into a genre rather than to "purely" adapt (for a given value of "pure") is part of many critical responses to the work and inextricable from the representation of the female characters. The common tropes and scriptwriting limitations of commercial TV present boundaries around *Elementary*, including the absence of queer representation in recurring characters, the methods used by detectives. The presence of multiple characters of non-white backgrounds (main, recurring and bit parts) and the lone trans character push at those boundaries, particularly in the case of Joan, but they are still bound by the medium. This medium comes with expectations about female detectives and thus far *Elementary* has shied away from many of them. This representation echoes the canon, somewhat, and undermines much of the metatextually situated criticism aimed at the heterosexualizing of a "queer" narrative. Sherlock's sexual activity is not focused on Joan, or even Jamie for all that they were romantically involved, but is instead represented through a series of non-standard relationships; a sex worker, regular casual partners, an older woman he maintains a sexually explicit penpal-type relationship with, occasionally an important figure in a case. Joan's responses to the "other women" contain no jealousy, and none is implied, further moving their relationship from the medium-driven expectations and into the more canonically implied (intense) platonic bond. The scene where she throws him out of an interview with a victim encapsulates not only his manipulation but her understanding of him as a manipulator and as an investigator; he manipulates her and the victim in order to create a situation for them to bond and for Joan's interrogation to become more astute but she is aware of this confronts Sherlock for his unnecessary interference.

> SHERLOCK: "I knew it, I knew if I started a row in there you'd come to her defence, and if you came to her defence she might very well tell you the truth."
> JOAN: "You're so full of it" [*Elementary* "Pilot"].

The arc of character development in *Elementary* is necessarily bound with genre (procedural) and format (American television series format of twenty-two, 45-minute episodes); this restriction on the characterization and plot development is highlighted in critiques which address the "ease" of the crime solving, or the metatextual reading into the meaning of the "guest star" as "spoiling" the mystery. The restrictions of the form do not apply to many other adaptations, although they are prevalent in the Holmes-inspired *House* or *Psyche*. Indeed, much of the criticism of *Elementary* holds those loose

Archontic versions as preferable ways of dealing with the restrictions of the format and distancing the expansive genius of the canon from the closed in cases of the television series format. This format however affects the flow of character development and the introduction of Archontic elements by placing them within the existing rhythm and heavily codified television series format. This allows for readings within and against both the format restrictions and expectations, particularly around romance, and within and against the canon/Archive. Australian TV network Channel 10 produced a promo for the first season of *Elementary* which used the tools and techniques most often seen in fanvids to create a romantic subplot. They used scenes from the first five episodes intercut to create the illusion of sexual tension. This, while not from the creators of Elementary, shows clearly how the resistant non-romantic narrative of the series is in conflict with dominant readings of the format, not the work itself.

The biggest variation in the actual relationships in *Elementary* is not the sexual and romantic relationship between Joan and Mycroft, in spite of its on-screen oddness and awkwardness, or even that between Jamie (Adler/Moriarty) and Sherlock. Rather, it is the relationship between Joan and Jamie. The Mycroft/Joan relationship is signposted with misinformation and the kind of incredibly realistic yet cringe-inducingly awkward conversations that mark a relationship that has a lot more to do with plot and the classical homosocial covenant than characterization and canonical referencing. The position of the two Holmes brothers in conflict over Watson is not unique to *Elementary* and neither is it changed overmuch by the introduction of the sexual relationship. It replicates Sedgwick's homosocial triangle—where two men act out a relationship through the sexualized means of a female third party—but without the intensity of focus otherwise offered to that kind of imagery which negates the importance of the woman in order to place a greater focus on the men (Sedgwick 22, 1985). The Irene Adler and Sherlock relationship is a sexualization of the canonical "The Woman," albeit with the added obstacle of Adler being Moriarty and Holmes' soul mate nemesis. That relationship forms one arm of the new homosocial triangle—a lesbian homosocial triangle (Castle 70), between Joan and Jamie and Sherlock.

Jamie is introduced as the dead Irene Adler, whose murder is revealed to have prompted Sherlock's drug addiction and "rock bottom." Moriarty is the shadowy figure who paid the serial assassin "M" to murder her, and who orchestrates a number of criminal enterprises. Further along in the series she is found to have survived, to have been held captive by Moriarty. Then, via a small scar left by mole removal surgery she is unmasked as Moriarty by Sherlock.

However, it eventually is *Joan* who organizes and coordinates the operation which captures her. Until this, the relationship between Jamie and Sherlock is foregrounded and Joan is orbiting the pair at a distance. At one point Jamie calls Joan a "mascot," a manifestation of the gendered underestimation that Jamie herself notes as the impetus for the creation of the false male front of Moriarty. After the denouement, Moriarty's focus is turned to Joan. Her introduction in series two is heralded by an enormous portrait of Joan, painted by Moriarty in prison. She is also revealed to be a mother, and her maternal interest behind not only an escape, but her cooperation with Sherlock, Joan and the police. The revelation of her parental status does not lessen her criminal activities or nature, adding another layer atop an already complex character and one which undermines much of the gendered rhetoric around parenting and reproduction as a professional (albeit criminal) woman.

Joan and Jamie remain locked in a kind of homosocial bond, acted out and through their individual relationships with Sherlock. Castle identifies the erasure of lesbianism from Sedgwick's homosocial framework as erasing the lesbian entirely (Castle 70) and that method and means of erasing aligns with Gaten's critiques of the way neutralizing gender serves to erase the woman, rather than to expand the categories and representation of women (Gatens 25, 1996). Yet in the case of Jamie and Joan, their femininity is not neutralized—they present femininely without being bound to only femininity and their relationship is a deeply intimate, if antagonistic, one. The portrait Jamie paints of Joan anchors and dominates her cell; not only a reminder of her own internalized sexism causing defeat but an enormous space, physical and intellectual and creative, being taken up by another woman (*Elementary* "The Diabolical Kind," 2014). The biggest fan of Joan is Jamie, and that devotion is imbued with femininity and femaleness; Castle refers to lesbian homosociality as being a fan of women and Jamie's initial misanthropy grounding itself as misogyny towards Joan is transformed. The foregrounding of this, even as the cases resolve and revolve around Sherlock, form a kind of palimpsest well within the bounds of a queer celluloid closet, much like the vaunted queer Holmes and Watson of the Archives. And, manifesting Castle's arguments about the idea that the homosocial has no use to the female-female relationship as it "denominates the continuum" (Castle 70; Sedgwick 3), the relationship between Joan and Jamie is not boundarized by what could be considered friendship, or even antagonism, but a deeply intimate bond acted out and through their male point of contact, Sherlock (*Elementary* "The Diabolical Kind," 2014). While the relationship is non-platonic and previously sexual for Sherlock and Jamie, it is no longer so, and the other lines of the triangle remain non-sexual and platonic. Thus, queer subtext does find a place within *Elementary* but rather than involving any Archontic Holmes it focuses on the relationship between Joan and Jamie. The portrait is one of the most obvious examples of a queer kind of attention between the pair, and the position of Joan as the only person, other than Jamie's "soulmate" Sherlock, who can "surprise" the all-knowing, all-understanding genius of the criminal mastermind. This elevation of Joan to the same investigative level as Sherlock and Moriarty, yet still maintaining the nurturing conduit of the Archontic Watson.

Joan's inhabitation of the Watsonian body is a lengthy process that requires the watcher to perceive the characteristics of the Canonical Watson, and those Archontic ideations, and parse them through the body of Joan. Joan's embodiment as a woman is one moderated through the actress, Lucy Liu. A fannishly lauded aspect of that embodiment is her wardrobe—as stereotypically feminine as that may be as a facet of characterization and critical concern, it is a fruitful and deliberate one. The transition of the canonical and Archontic Watson's sartorial choices, constrained by masculinity and race and class, into the similarly constrained but highly performative arena of women's fashion touches on the ways in which presentation in general is read differently. The waistcoat, the jumper, the cardigan, all read differently on the female body. Even if the body is B(b)utch, the transgression is occurring (Halberstam 267). Avoiding this transgression, *Elementary* instead feminizes the female body, through clothing and action. However, Joan is introduced while wearing winter jogging gear, a scarf, hat, hooded sweatshirt, and leggings, that reveal her bodily femininity but her outfit does not perform it, instead situating her character in the realms of action (*Elementary* "Pilot," 2012). Her outfits do not denote a specific internal character, the way menswear would have, but instead have a kind of verisimilitude. Numerous fannish blogs, primarily on Tumblr, focus on her outfits, her accessories, and have critiqued the same, such as Joan's Fashion Show, What Would Joan Watson Wear, and Joan Watson's Closet, and posts on blogs like *Oh No They Didn't* that not only go into the clothing, but interview the costume designer. Most notoriously the episode where Joan walks through snow in four-inch stacked boot heels has been criticized as "nonsensical," while recognizing it as a factor of the form given the height differences between the two leads and the need to frame the shots. The kind of hyper-attention to women's sartorial choices, critiquing and consuming, has its roots in capitalism and can often manifest in an excessive weight placed unfairly on the female and the feminine (Elam 32). Sherlock's shirts, socks and tattoos come under similar levels of scrutiny but the way those affectations are read by fans, by critics, is steeped in the character.[2] The masculinity of checked socks and tight, transparent character t-shirts are unremarked upon, or the entirely realistic but anti-designed tattoo collection, remain static under the masculinity of the character, the encompassing manliness of Holmes. Yet, in an uncritically reproduced example of Butlerian gender performativity, Joan's embodiment and femininity is an unstable and perpetually "lacking" characteristic necessitating constant oversight and critical engagement lest it spill into too much or not enough (Butler 33, 2011).

The importance of Joan is not only contained within the story of her as Watson but also within her Archontic effects and the media landscape that she acts within. The roles available for women, for minorities, remain minimal and the success of an adaptation that changes those aspects of a character echoes out beyond the work as a kind of meme (Smith and Cook 1). Regendering is not a new adaptational technique, not even within the Holmes Archive (a Russian adaptation regenders both Watson and Holmes for example) but the ways in which *Elementary* changes the character and the ways in which it doesn't are integral. Importantly, the regendering was not only a "fresh look" at a character, or a new way of telling the story, but a concretely political act by the showrunners to reject the homogenous nature of the original works and the idea that as an adaptation, reinscribing and reinforcing that homogeneity is acceptable even when it presents an unrealistic version of reality. Fans have, when the political natures of regendering (or racebending) have been targeted, renamed the male white default as a political statement of its own. The reformation and bending of the political and social field of engagement is, at its core, the wider impact of regendering. Joan's characterization is not simply a part of the Archontic Watson, or even the Holmesean Archives, but she becomes part of a greater creative and feminist praxis which destabilizes the foundations of the works and critically addresses the shortcoming of the originals and the readings.

So while the regendering is important, and exposes the character and the Holmsean Archive, to great roles and characterization of women, it relies heavily on the maleness and implied masculine power of the original for its impact. From that foundation it works towards a fully realized and complex characterization that touches on the points necessary for an iteration of Watson (and thus Holmes), that is sensitive to and inclusive of the effects gender and race have on not just character and audience reception, but on the development and rationale for that characterization. Nonetheless the reception of Liu's Joan Watson has included both racial and gendered stereotypes and has included critiques heavily invested in various Archontic iterations. The place of the Sherlock Holmes mythos cannot be understated in this reaction and the investment fans have in Archontic iterations such as BBC's *Sherlock*, or Jeremy Brett's series, or more rarely the Guy Ritchie franchise. A certain kind of class consciousness is embedded in some of those critiques, in that an American version is necessarily "low class" and appealing to the lowest common denominator; this is probably why very few fans claim Robert Downey Junior as *the* Sherlock, but many are happy to claim Benedict Cumberpatch or Jeremy Brett, in spite of all three being non-historically accurate depictions that necessarily focus on parts of the canonical descriptions. Similarly fans will allow a certain enjoyment of *Elementary* with the hastily applied coda that they do not consider it a *Holmes* story, not really, it's just by accident they share some names. Almost as if they were purposefully invoking Russ and the spirit of how to suppress women's writing, in this case, women Watsons; yes it is a woman Watson but it doesn't actually count because she shouldn't be a Watson at all, she is badly adapted, she isn't masculine enough, she isn't enough, she doesn't *count* (Russ 4). If she did count as a Watson, then the audience must confront how they read the maleness of the Watson, how they read and operate under the male default and what that means to their consumption practices (and creative ones).

Ultimately, however, Joan is a foil to Sherlock, and a companion, just as Watson is the foil and companion to Holmes. Her importance is evident through him, and through the connection to the Archontic. Joan invites and insists the audience confront the masculinity of not only Watson, but the Archontic Watson, and indeed the entire concept of the 'every man' character that Watson is lauded as an archetype of. Her relationships, with Sherlock and Jamie and Mycroft, offer a representation of the ways in which a female character, without the force and power of the male original behind her, becomes less realized, less real, through the common tropes of narrative function. Regendering can only go so far, as feminist and creative praxis, and Joan's importance can only be maintained for so long until she is again brought back to the fold, as both Watson-the-helpmeet and as a female character, unable to deconstruct the ways in which she in constructed.

Notes

1. These broad statements are based on the raw numbers of works available on fannish sites.
2. Sherlock's tattoos particularly are objects of something like a fetish, in and out of the show, but are remarkably embodied textually and are in fact Miller's own collection of ink.

Works Cited

Bennett, Alanna. "Elementary Creator Defends Decision to Make Watson a Woman." *The Mary Sue*. N.p., 13 July 2012. Web.
Black, Suzanne, James Leveque, and Lizzie Stewart. "The Archontic Holmes: Understanding Adaptations of Arthur Conan Doyle's Sherlock Holmes Stories in the Context of Jacques Derrida's 'Archive.'" *FORUM: University of Edinburgh Postgraduate Journal of Culture and the Arts*. N.p., 2012. Google Scholar. Web. 27 Nov. 2013.
Butler, Judith. *Gender Trouble: Feminism and the Subversion of Identity*. New York: Routledge, 2011. Print.
Castle, Terry. *The Apparitional Lesbian: Female Homosexuality and Modern Culture*. New York: Columbia University Press, 1993. Print.
Coren, Victoria. "Lucy Liu Playing Dr Watson: Put That in Your Pipe and Smoke It." *The Guardian*. N.p., 14 Oct. 2012. Web. 14 Aug. 2014.
Derecho, Abigail. "Archontic Literature: A Definition, a History, and Several Theories of Fan Fiction." *Fan Fiction and Fan Communities in the Age of the Internet: New Essays*. Ed. Karen Hellekson and Kristina Busse. Jefferson, NC: McFarland, 2006. Print.
"The Diabolical Kind." *Elementary*. Hill of Beans Productions, Timberman-Beverly Productions, CBS Television Studios, 2 Jan. 2014. Television.
Doherty, Robert, creator. *Elementary*. Hill of Beans Productions, Timberman-Beverly Productions, CBS Television Studios, 2012–2015. Television.
Elam, Diane. *Feminism and Deconstruction: Ms. En Abyme*. London: Routledge, 1994. Print.
Eyles, Allen. *Sherlock Holmes: A Centenary Celebration*, 1st U.S. ed. New York: Harper & Row, 1986. Print.
Gatens, Moira. *Imaginary Bodies Ethics, Power, and Corporeality*. London: Routledge, 1996. Open WorldCat. Web. 25 Feb. 2014.
Gracie. "Watson's Wardrobe." N.p., n.d. Web. 2 Feb. 2015.
Halberstam, Judith. *Female Masculinity*. Durham: Duke University Press, 1998. Print.
"Joan Watson's Closet." N.p., n.d. Web. 2 Feb. 2015.
"Joan's Fashion Show." N.p., n.d. Web. 2 Feb. 2015.
Kestner, Joseph A. *Sherlock's Men: Masculinity, Conan Doyle, and Cultural History*. Aldershot: Ashgate, 1997. Print.
Loving, Olivia. "Creativity (or Lack of It) in Hollywood: Adapted Scripts Take Over." *NYU Local*. N.p., 2 Mar. 2012. Web. 12 Jan. 2014.
McDougall, Sophia. "I Hate Strong Female Characters." *New Statesman*. N.p., 15 Aug. 2013. Web.
"Oh No They Didn't!—Elementary: A Joan Watson Fashion Post." N.p., n.d. Web. 2 Feb. 2015.
"Pilot." *Elementary*. Hill of Beans Productions, Timberman-Beverly Productions, CBS Television Studios, 27 Sept. 2012. Television.
Porter, Lynnette. *Sherlock Holmes for the 21st Century: Essays on New Adaptations*. Jefferson, NC: McFarland, 2012. Print.
Russ, Joanna. *How to Suppress Women's Writing*, 1st ed. Austin: University of Texas Press, 1983. Print.
Ryan, Maureen. "'Elementary' Review, 'Vegas' Review and 'Made in Jersey' Review: The Pleasures and Pains of CBS' New Dramas." *Huffington Post*. N.p., 25 Sept. 2012. Web. 14 Aug. 2014.
Sedgwick, Eve Kosofsky. *Between Men: English Literature and Male Homosocial Desire*. New York: Columbia University Press, 1985. Print.
Sherwin, Adam. "Legal Thriller Looms as Sherlock Takes His Caseload to New York." *The Independent*. N.p., 21 Jan. 2012. Web. 14 Aug. 2014.
Smith, Stacy L., and Crystal Allene Cook. "Gender Stereotypes: An Analysis of Popular Films and TV." Report prepared for the Geena Davis Institute for Gender and Media, Los Angeles, 2008. Print.
Stout, Rex. "Watson Was a Woman." *The Saturday Review of Literature* 23.19 (1941): N.p. Print.

Taylor, Noah. "The Art of the Title: Elementary." *The Art of the Title*. N.p., 21 May 2013. Web. 15 Aug. 2014.
Valentine, Genevieve. "Elementary Demonstrates the Right Way to Update a Classic Hero." *io9*. N.p., 21 May 2013. Web. 20 Mar. 2014.
"You Do It to Yourself." *Elementary*. Hill of Beans Productions, Timberman-Beverly Productions, CBS Television Studios, 6 Dec. 2012. Television.

Conflations of "Queerness" in 21st Century Adaptations
Ayaan Agane

Recent adaptations of Arthur Conan Doyle's Sherlock Holmes stories have engendered the phenomenon of a gay Sherlock Holmes. While the notion of a sexual and/or romantic relationship between Holmes and his devoted assistant, Doctor Watson, is far from new—slash fan fiction abounds on the internet portraying the famous couple as lovers, and Graham Robb convincingly argues Conan Doyle's Sherlock is gay—the BBC's *Sherlock* series (2010–) and the Warner Brothers' *Sherlock Holmes* film franchise (2009 and 2011) both present strong homoerotic themes surrounding Sherlock characters who are not, beyond superficial and comedic subtext, actually gay. In contrast with slash fan fiction, Holmes and Watson never consummate their erotic tension on screen in either of these adaptations. Nevertheless, rumor and innuendo abound: Robert Downey, Jr., who plays Holmes in the Warner Brothers' franchise directed by Guy Ritchie, salaciously rejected labeling the film a bromance—"I think the word bromance is so passé. We are two men who happen to be roommates who wrestle a lot and share a bed" (Carroll para. 9); A.O. Scott describes Ritchie's Irene Adler as a "beard" meant to "dispel a few hints of homoerotic subtext" (Thomas 41); paratexts that sensationalized Ritchie's Holmes as gay prompted threats from the Sherlock Holmes copyright owner to withhold permission for the film's sequel; Holmes and Watson in the BBC's *Sherlock* series must constantly endure assumptions and accusations they are a couple (in nearly every episode); and the South Korean channel OCN's trailer promotions for the *Sherlock* series suggest romance with "moody close-up shots of both Holmes and Watson" and "on-screen written statements such as 'Love of the Loveless'" (Lavigne 20).

Both series and film franchise revel in implying that Watson brushes up against more than Holmes's genius. In this essay, I will show how the persistent suggestion of a gay Holmes/Watson relationship, coupled with the adaptations' refusal to commit to portraying these characters as actually gay, stems from a twenty-first century tendency on behalf of both adaptors and audiences to conflate different queer identities.

Arthur Conan Doyle dismissed suggestions of his iconic sleuth as either romantic or erotic, writing in a letter to Joseph Bell, "Holmes is as inhuman as a Babbage's Calculating Machine, and just about as likely to fall in love" (Graham and Garlen 24). Writer/co-creator of the BBC's *Sherlock* series Steven Moffat likewise rejects Holmes as a lover: "The fact is, people say he shows no interest in women, therefore he must be gay. He shows no interest in men, either. That's just not what he does" (Lavigne 15). Moffat demonstrates an acute awareness of his audience's cultural perceptions and assumptions. Sherlock Holmes's asexuality may offer a queer reading of Holmes's character, but twenty-first century audiences often have difficulty imagining any nonheteronormative identity other than gay.

David Halperin denies "queer" as a synonym for "gay," proposing that "'queer' does not name some natural kind or refer to some determinate object; it acquires its meaning from its oppositional relation to the norm.... It is an identity without an essence" (Thomas 45). Halperin's useful definition positions queerness as opposite to the cultural norm, an interpretation that allows for unlimited gender and sexual identities. I argue that the queer potential of Sherlock Holmes in the adaptations under discussion is more a question of gender politics, and how those gender politics inform twenty-first century perceptions of sexuality, than a question of Sherlock Holmes's homosexuality. For the purposes of this discussion, I will focus on the gender politics of Holmes and Watson's domesticity, demonstrating how postmodern adaptors and audiences who have updated their impressions of gender identities and relations within the home nevertheless affirm and desire to see their traditional counterparts.

The mainstream, wide-release adaptations of the Sherlock Holmes stories look at Victorian gender politics through a postmodern lens, and these portraits must answer to large audiences and large studios, each with equally large aesthetic and financial expectations. As Ashley Polasek reasons, "The financial demands of modern big-budget films dictate that they must be made to appeal to an audience far beyond those who are fans of, indeed, who are aware of Conan Doyle and, as such, offer a Sherlock Holmes more linked to the historical moments in which the adaptations are made and consumed than the moments in which the source was written or the film set" (387). Sherlock Holmes adaptations, whether set in the nineteenth or twenty-first centuries, seek mass appeal by connecting the source text with our own historical moment, in which questions and confusions about queer identity are perfectly apt. When Moffat explains his audience's tendency to set up a binary between straight/gay (i.e., if Holmes is not straight, he must be gay), he tacitly acknowledges *Sherlock*'s engagement with such assumptions; after all, even if the series' writers do not imagine a gay Holmes, they consistently and explicitly point to this potential interpretation. From the moment that Mrs. Hudson genially inquires if Watson will need the second bedroom at 221B Baker Street in the *Sherlock's* "A Study in Pink," Holmes and Watson's sharing of domestic space raises the question of whether they are lovers. This cultural assumption, alien to nineteenth-century readers, is nevertheless rooted in the Victorian domestic ideal.

Holmes and Watson's home, 221B Baker Street, is perhaps the most well-known fictional address. Despite wide divergences from Conan Doyle's stories in various adaptations over the last century, this domicile serves as an enduring feature of the Holmes universe, tying any adaptation to the original series. Sherlockian Ronald B. De Waal emphasizes the home's importance in the Holmes mythos: "That magical 221B Baker Street and all the canonical characters who inhabit our minds and hearts are a world in themselves" (Taylor 93). The apartment on Baker Street shapes the world of the canonical Holmes and Watson, and its legacy lives on in Sherlock societies (Baker Street Irregulars), board games ("221B Baker Street: The Master Detective Game" and "221B Baker Street Detective Game"), and historical recreations.

The prominence of 221B Baker Street in the original Holmes stories merits a discussion of the Victorian definition of "home." An 1851 English census notes that it is "so much in the order of nature that a family should live in a separate house that 'house' is often used for family in many languages" (Chase and Levenson 4). If a house connotes a family, Holmes and Watson share not only a professional partnership but also an intimate relationship, and attempts to qualify that intimacy have a long history in both scholarship and creative adaptation. In *In the Company of Strangers: Family and Narrative in Dickens, Conan Doyle, Joyce, and Proust* (2011), Barry McCrea argues Holmes and 221B Baker Street "function ... as symbolic queer contrasts to genealogy and the rule of family" (77), as 221B Baker Street houses a "biologically infertile" couple (69). The mere adjacency of Holmes and Watson in the domestic sphere, however, does not fully justify queer interpretations of their relationship (and hence does not fully explain gay interpretations, either); rather, the queerness of the Holmes/Watson pairing lies in the domestic feminization of Watson, an activity well enjoyed by Holmes adaptors.

Ideal Victorian domesticity positioned the home as a safe shelter and the home's mistress as the guarantor, proponent, and protector of that space. John Ruskin provides an archetypal definition of the ideal Victorian home:

> This is the true nature of home—it is the place of Peace; the shelter, not only from all injury, but from all terror, doubt, and division. In so far as it is not this, it is not home: so far as the anxieties of the outer life penetrate into it, and the inconsistently minded, unknown, unloved, or hostile society of the outer world is allowed by either husband or wife to cross the threshold, it ceases to be home; it is then only a part of that outer world which you have roofed over, and lighted fire in. But so far as it is a sacred space, a vestal temple, a temple of the hearth watched over by Household Gods, before whose faces none may come but those whom they can receive with love,—so far as it is this, and roof and fire are types only of a nobler shade and light,—shade as of the rock in a weary land, and light as of the Pharos in the stormy sea; so far it vindicates the name and fulfills the praise of Home [Archibald 5–6].

Ruskin's concept of home is neither space nor sentiment singly but a combination—the container and that which is contained. Ruskin's definition centers on the security of home (shelter from injury) and presence of love, but it also strongly emphasizes the absence of doubt, the unknown, and division. The Victorian home therefore depends on its cohesive, rigid regularity, in which everything is known, understood, and relegated to its proper place, and in which any aberration is summarily rejected without objection. The ideal Victorian mistress guarantees such regularity.

Coventry Patmore's 1854 poem "The Angel in the House" realizes this ideal mistress. Patmore's "angel" "is a domestic saint, a priestess whose moral purity and fine sensibilities preserve the sanctity of the middle-class space from the corruption of the outside world" (Archibald 5). The "angel in the house"'s virtue closely aligns to Ruskin's definition of home, for her moral fortitude and "fine sensibilities" keep corruption at bay and fill the home with its due sentiment. Patmore's "angel"—whether a figure criticized or affirmed—has deeply informed cultural perceptions of femininity for the last one hundred and sixty years. Sixty-seven years after Patmore first published his poem, Virginia Woolf declared, "Killing the Angel in the House was part of the occupation of a woman writer" ("Professions for Women"). Sixty-two years after Woolf's assertion, folk rock musician Jonatha Brooke sang, "I thought I was by myself, but I cannot kill the angel in the house" (The Story). Diana C. Archibald asserts that the "domestic 'angel' is so pervasive an ideal that even when no female character fitting her description appears in a novel, the angel's presence is felt" (5). As I will later demonstrate, adaptors and audience's feel the angel's presence when regarding John Watson.

Iterations of Patmore's "angel" live on in postmodern popular culture, which continually embraces wives as ideal homemakers who manage and protect hearth and home. Magdalena Zawisza and Marco Cinnirella's 2010 study on gender stereotypes in television advertisements measured the effectiveness of traditional and nontraditional gender roles in commercials. Zawisza and Cinnirella describe traditional gender roles as "associated with work for men ... and home for women" (1768). Their experiments yielded unexpected results: traditional gender roles for women in advertisements proved more effective than nontraditional ones *regardless of the participants' attitudes toward gender roles* (1767). In other words, the results of Zawisza and Cinnirella's experiments suggest that the participants (79 percent of whom were British) responded more positively to traditional female gender roles in ads even if those participants didn't condone such roles. Paul Bloom, professor of psychology at Yale University, confirms this phenomenon: "there's so many social psychology experiments showing ... that even in cases where we know a stereotype doesn't apply, and we know it's mistaken, we're guided by it anyway. And these are done for the most part I think by well-intentioned people" (Raz). As Diana Archibald suggests, the Victorian angel's presence persists even when she is out of context. Twenty-first century viewers look for and even possibly desire, perhaps unconsciously, to see women as representatives of the home. Although the BBC's twenty-first century adaptation *Sherlock* may not involve a Victorian setting, nineteenth-century British values leech into the series from the source material—just as characters, plots, and dialogue do—and current adaptors and viewers stand ready to apply traditional gender roles to any domestic couple, even if that requires feminizing an otherwise masculine character.

The BBC's *Sherlock* (2010) series, which aired the same year as Zawisza and Cinnirella's study, initializes the feminization of John Watson by associating him with home while associating Holmes with work. Watson moves to 221B Baker Street in episode one, "A Study in Pink," jobless and in desperate financial straits, and episode two, "The Blind Banker," opens with a split scene of the domestic roles the pair will play. As Sherlock fights a masked assailant, presumably in connection with a case, John conducts the household shopping (and has to borrow money from Sherlock later to complete the task). Sherlock further states, "All that matters to me is the work. Without that my brain rots" (*Sherlock* "The Great Game"). Sherlock proves the head of the household, who, as the aforementioned 1851 census claims, "supports and rules the family" (Chase and Levenson 4). While living with Sherlock, John's only official job at a clinic is short-lived, and his main source of income becomes assisting Sherlock. In addition to supporting John, Sherlock's "rule" over him is unquestionable, as he continually manipulates John throughout the series. For example, when John storms off angrily in "The Hounds of Baskerville," Sherlock's text messages recruit the doctor without resolving their dispute. When John petulantly texts Sherlock asking why he should interview someone, Sherlock sends him a picture of the attractive woman. "Oh, you're a bad man," John says, but John's next scene shows him interviewing her (*Sherlock* "The Hounds of Baskerville"). Moriarty sums up the pair's power dynamic when he calls John Sherlock's "pet," "so touching and loyal" ("The Great Game").

Beyond grocery shopping, John demonstrates how badly 221B Baker Street needs a "woman's touch." Upon seeing the apartment for the first time, John remarks, "This could be very nice, very nice indeed ... soon as we get all this rubbish cleaned out" (*Sherlock* "A Study in Pink"). John must continually show the "managerial competence" (Archibald 11) required of the angel in the house, because otherwise their refrigerator would only contain human heads ("The Great Game"), and their microwave and dishes would be filled with eyeballs ("A Study in Pink" and "The Sign of Three"). Not surprisingly, the only housekeeping Sherlock offers to do (buying milk and beans) only serves to pacify John so Sherlock can secretly meet Moriarty—another manipulation ("The Great Game").

John also serves as the moral center of the household, thus fulfilling the angel in the house's ethical obligation. Virginia Woolf described the angel thus: "Above all—I need not say it—she was pure" ("Professions for Women"). In addition to the juxtaposition of John's concern for Moriarty's victims and Sherlock's apathy toward them in "The Great Game," the series perpetually depicts John as the honorable soldier and Sherlock as the self-proclaimed, unfeeling sociopath. In "A Study in Pink," Sherlock describes the cabbie's shooter as having "a strong moral principle"—a deduction that makes the sleuth realize the shooter is John. Furthermore, in "A Study in Pink," John refuses to accept what Mycroft implies is a vast sum of money in return for information on Sherlock—a person he barely knows at this point—despite John's dire financial situation. John thus serves as a "moral and social counterweight to Holmes" who must "smooth over social situations" that the decidedly amoral Holmes has difficulty navigating (Toadvine 57).

Sherlock's sociopathy not only precludes him from understanding or caring about morality; it also robs him of experiencing sentiment. When Sherlock shocks the detectives into reproachful silence after wondering why a woman would still grieve a daughter who died "ages ago," he looks to John to analyze the social situation. "Not good?" he asks. "A bit not good, yeah,"

John replies ("A Study in Pink"). "The Hounds of Baskerville" echoes this exchange:

HOLMES: So they didn't have it put down then. The dog.
WATSON: Obviously. Suppose they just couldn't bring themselves to do it.
HOLMES: I see.
WATSON: No, you don't.
HOLMES: No, I don't. Sentiment?
WATSON: Sentiment [*Sherlock* "The Hounds of Baskerville"].

Holmes cannot comprehend why the proprietors of a strictly vegetarian restaurant would have ethical and sentimental reservations about euthanizing a vicious dog. Here, as always, John analyzes data and deduces in the only manner of which the great Sherlock Holmes is incapable, pacifying tense social situations when necessary.

As the moral center of their home, John acts as a civilizing force for Sherlock. Sherlock's sociopathy alienates him from the society he analyzes with a cold and distant eye, and John, in moments like those listed above, teaches Sherlock how to understand—and eventually experience—emotion. Chase and Levenson argue that the Victorian home is "the figure for social redemption" (9). Viewers may easily see John as this figure through Sherlock's wedding speech:

I am dismissive of the virtuous, unaware of the beautiful, and uncomprehending in the face of the happy ... John, I am a ridiculous man, redeemed only by the warmth and constancy of your friendship.... Today you sit between the woman you have made your wife and the man you've saved—in short the two people who love you most in all this world. And I know I speak for Mary as well when I say we will never let you down, and we have a lifetime ahead to prove that [*Sherlock* "The Sign of Three"].

Sherlock's assertion that John has "saved" him, along with his strong declaration of love for John, illustrates the extent to which John has served as a civilizing force for the self-declared sociopath.

"His Last Vow" showcases the redemption Sherlock describes in his speech. Although the show introduces viewers to a cold, sociopathic Sherlock in the series' open, *Sherlock* later reveals that the consulting detective did not always have this affliction. Mycroft clues the audience into Sherlock's first love—a dog named Redbeard. When Sherlock insists he has not become attached to John, asserting his emotional distance, Mycroft quips, "Do you remember Redbeard?" to which Sherlock responds, "I'm not a child anymore, Mycroft" ("The Sign of Three"). In a flashback during "His Last Vow," viewers learn of Redbeard's euthanasia during Sherlock's childhood and are left to assume Sherlock's grief motivated his antisocial behavior, which developed into complete emotional detachment. Sherlock therefore equates sentiment with immaturity.

The vow to which the episode's title alludes—that Sherlock will never let John down—takes the form of Sherlock's redemption. In killing Magnusson, thus protecting Mary, Sherlock demonstrates selfless and self-sacrificing sentiment for John, illustrated by the scene's cinematography. The scene shifts between showing Sherlock (surrounded by English secret service after having killed Magnusson) and Mycroft in a helicopter above. Mycroft utters, "Oh Sherlock, what have you done?" ("His Last Vow"). The scene cuts back to Sherlock, now portrayed by a crying child, still surrounded by gun-wielding agents. This visible vulnerability of Sherlock provides an answer to Mycroft's question—Sherlock has redeemed himself through sentiment, having reverted back to his childhood self in order to fulfill his vow for John. As a vehicle for Sherlock's redemption, John is further associated with the home.

The domestic, feminine role John undertakes in *Sherlock* motivates viewers' perceptions of the couple as gay. Viewers and adaptors, despite their postmodern sensibilities, ascribe gendered domestic roles to romantic couples only, which forces a gay connotation of queer gender identities. The creators' awareness of these cultural assumptions incite their comic playfulness with the couple's perceived homosexuality. That is why Mrs. Hudson inquires if John and Sherlock "had a little domestic" after they argue ("The Great Game"); why a restaurant proprietor brings a candle to their table because it's "more romantic" ("A Study in Pink"); why when Mrs. Hudson learns of John's engagement to Mary she remarks, "What's his name?" and later, "A woman? ... You *have* moved on, haven't you?" (*Sherlock* "The Empty Hearse"); why Irene Adler refers to them as a couple (*Sherlock* "A Scandal in Belgravia"); why the proprietor of an inn apologizes for not being able to get them a double room ("The Hounds of Baskerville"); and finally why one of John's girlfriends says, after John cancels a date to stay at Baker Street in case Sherlock relapses (ever the domestic angel keeping the corruption of the world at bay), that John is a "great boyfriend, and Sherlock Holmes is a very lucky man" (*Sherlock* "A Scandal in Belgravia"). The comedic potential of toying with viewers' interpretations of queer gender and sexuality seems limitless.

Guy Ritchie's two Sherlock Holmes film adaptations, *Sherlock Holmes* (2009) and *Sherlock Holmes: A Game of Shadows* (2011), in many ways present a more mature Holmes and Watson pairing (played by Robert Downey, Jr., and Jude Law, respectively). The couple is older, they have lived together for many years, and they have solved more cases together. *Sherlock Holmes* illustrates their seasoned domestic harmony in their first scene together. As Watson strangles an assailant, his banter with Holmes reveals Holmes has both forgotten his pistol at home and left the stove on. Their domesticity looms large even in the very midst of danger, and Watson's retrieval of the pistol and admonishment about the stove demonstrates his competent management of the domestic sphere, a characteristic of Patmore's angel. After asphyxiating the assailant, Watson and Holmes shake hands, remove their hats, and regard the body in perfect harmony. When Holmes and Watson later learn their last case has indeed not yet ended (inciting Holmes's iconic "The game's afoot"), the scene echoes this harmony as they together recite a passage from *Henry V*. The couple demonstrates synchronicity achieved by years of friendship in which the couple has shared not only a profession but a home.

Unlike the BBC's *Sherlock* series, which commences with the beginning of John and Sherlock's domestic relationship, Guy Ritchie's adaptation opens with the waning of this domiciliary arrangement. The audience's first glimpse of 221B Baker Street shows the doctor will soon exchange his feminine domestic role for a masculine one. As he discusses his upcoming move to a new home with a patient, Watson informs that "there will be a woman's touch too" (*Sherlock Holmes*). His patient suggests the appropriateness of this change after hearing Holmes's gunshots from another room: "Your colleague won't be moving with you, will he?" and, a few minutes later, "I smell gunpowder. It's not right, you know. Not in a domestic environment" (*Sherlock Holmes*). In Watson's final days at Baker Street he showcases his feminine governance of the home (all the more saliently in the film's Victorian setting) as he makes excuses for Holmes's indoor shooting to his patient and assures a frightened Mrs. Hudson she does not have to go into Holmes's room by taking the morning paper in himself.

Ritchie's first Holmes film presents a John Watson pulled between two domestic spheres—his long-shared home with Holmes and his imminent living arrangements with Mary. Watson mirrors his literary counterpart, who finds himself "sporadically drawn back to 221B and to Holmes in some 'dark business' or other. And conversely, while he is living with Holmes, he always keeps one eye fixed on the domestic, heterosexual world he left behind" (McCrea 83–84). Conan Doyle's Watson, after meeting Mary in *The Sign of Four* (1890), feels drawn to the more traditional Victorian household that his relationship with Holmes has precluded: "As we drove away I stole a glance back, and I still seem to see that little group on the step—the two graceful, clinging figures, the half-opened door, the hall-light shining through stained glass, the barometer, and the bright stair-rods. It was soothing to catch even that passing glimpse of a tranquil English home in the midst of the wild, dark business which had absorbed us" (qtd. in McCrea 84).

At the film's inception, Ritchie's Watson has decided to give up the 'wild, dark business' that composes his domestic life with Holmes for a "tranquil English home" with Mary. In this new arrangement, Watson will rely on Mary to take the role he has long played with Holmes, that is, the angel in the house, whose purview is domestic tranquility and regularity, as described by John Ruskin. Watson reveals this intention while discussing his marriage with Holmes in *A Game of Shadows*:

> HOLMES: Marriage. It's the end, I tell you.
> WATSON: I think of it as the beginning.
> HOLMES: Armageddon.
> WATSON: Rebirth.
> HOLMES: Restriction.
> WATSON: Structure.
> HOLMES: Answering to a woman!
> WATSON: Being in a relationship, a life in matrimony, the possibility of a family [*Sherlock Holmes: A Game of Shadows*].

Watson has thus far provided for Holmes what he now desires Mary to give him—structure. Such a drastic move for Watson—switching from his feminized, queer gender identity in the home to a traditional masculine one—constitutes 'rebirth.'

Ritchie's first Holmes movie depicts Watson employing the same civilizing role as his BBC counterpart. His intercession between Holmes and Mrs. Hudson, his encouragement of Holmes taking on another case, his reproachfulness in the face of Holmes's wild ways depicts him as Holmes's civil mediator. Guy Ritchie aptly summarizes this role in his description of Jude Law's Watson as "the alkaline to Robert's [Holmes's] acid" (Polasek 388). Mrs. Hudson therefore shows concern about Watson's impending nuptials: "What will I do when you leave, Doctor? He'll have the whole house down" (*Sherlock Holmes*). Mrs. Hudson points to Watson's management of Holmes, the absence of which threatens to herald the domestic sphere's ruin.

Mrs. Hudson's remarks prove prophetic, as Watson's separation from 221B Baker Street in *A Game of Shadows* demonstrates. Watson returns to find a disheveled Holmes strung out on coca leaves, drinking embalming fluid, and frenetically harassing his landlady to feed his snake and worm his goat. The effects of Watson's absence are prominently displayed in the pair's now ruptured synchronicity:

WATSON: You do seem—
HOLMES: Excited? I—
WATSON: —manic
HOLMES: —am!
WATSON: Verging on—
HOLMES: Ecstatic.
WATSON: —psychotic. I should have brought you a sedative [*A Game of Shadows*].

Watson and Holmes no longer share the harmony once afforded them by their shared living. Their cacophonous conversation showcases Watson's concern for Holmes, but his lack of foresight of Holmes's condition (registered in his surprise and his not having brought the sedative) coupled with the weight he's gained eating Mary's muffins—which Holmes cannot help point out—demonstrate how Watson has become accustomed to being one who is managed instead of one who manages. As Mrs. Hudson implores Watson to intervene, she highlights the civilizing role Watson has played in his domestic relationship with Holmes.

In addition to having a civilizing role, Watson is feminized by Holmes in a variety of stereotypical ways, generally after Holmes has incensed the doctor. In an argument, Holmes tells his friend, "You're overtired.... You're feeling a bit sensitive," a dismissive remark Watson deplores (*A Game of Shadows*). In *A Game of Shadows*, Holmes similarly tells Watson, "There's no need for hysterics," and when Watson claims he's never visited Brighton before, Holmes replies, "Or you're just too fragile to remember" (*A Game of Shadows*). Holmes's treatment of Watson as a hysterical figure echoes chauvinistic utterances long employed by the patriarchy. The gaslighting to which Holmes subjects Watson about his memories additionally provides a window into their gender dynamic at 221B Baker Street.

Watson's engagement to Mary offers him a chance at heteronormative masculinity, an opportunity Holmes desperately wants to thwart. Holmes's dissatisfaction with Watson's engagement manifests in a number of ways: his refusal to meet Mary, his insinuation she is a gold digger, and his explicit disapproval as illustrated in his assessment of marriage as "Armageddon." Holmes furthermore manipulates Watson, similar to his BBC counterpart, when he brings a dead body into Watson's office, clearly hoping to elicit Watson's interest in the case. When Holmes once again leaves his revolver as he undertakes more "dark business," Watson shows his awareness of Holmes's manipulation: "He left it there on purpose" (*Sherlock Holmes*). Regardless, Holmes's machinations work, and Watson voyages again into the fray. Even as Watson prepares to leave 221B Baker Street, Holmes displays his masculine control over him in this scene, to which Watson submits begrudgingly but with a smile.

The film franchise's most salient queer innuendo occurs during Watson's interrupted honeymoon in *A Game of Shadows*. Despite Holmes's varied efforts to convince Watson of his error, the wedding proceeds on schedule, which foments Holmes's desperate attempt at keeping Watson at 221B Baker Street—the reversal of the pair's gender roles. Holmes's clumsy drag disguise emphasizes his desperation: "I agree it's not my best disguise, but I had to make do" (*A Game of Shadows*). Holmes "makes do" in his plan to preserve Watson as a companion, playing the happy bride as he throws Watson's real wife off the train, breaking the connubial image of the bridge over which the train passes. The rife sexual innuendo in Holmes and Watson's ensuing fight parodies marital consummation in what becomes Watson's honeymoon with Holmes rather than with his wife. Watson mounts Holmes, who wraps his legs around Watson's neck and removes his skirt, followed by his directive for Watson to lie down with him in the spooning position. Holmes confirms the honeymoon plot when he informs Watson of their new destination: "Paris. The most sensible honeymoon destination of all."

The shifting (yet still queer) gender dynamic between Holmes and Watson provides comic gay subtext, but Holmes schemes to restore the duo's former, nonsexual relationship rather than introduce an erotic component to it. The consummation scene is subtext, after all, buried within what is actually physical violence, the motivation of which is hardly sexual. While gay readings of Holmes in this scene could certainly bear fruit, I argue that the literal context of this scene (a fight about throwing Mary off the train) subverts such interpretations. Furthermore, as Holmes's desire for a return to their normal dynamic soon emerges, I view the scene as Ritchie's acknowledgment that the pair *acts* like a romantic couple (via queer gender politics) but in no way exhibits desire or potential to become one. Holmes's primary objective in this scene is to save Watson's (and Mary's) life, hopefully preserving his partnership with the doctor in the process. In a moment of dramatic suspense on their mission, Holmes asks Watson, "At this moment, are you as happy as you would be on your honeymoon in Brighton?" (*A Game of Shadows*). Holmes beckons Watson with adventure, showing how his work persists as a strong motivator for him, which requires Watson's original feminine helper role—a role Holmes feels confident Watson enjoys. Put simply, though Holmes clearly desires Watson's companionship, evidence of any erotic or romantic desire is lacking. The decidedly nonsexual concurrent dialogue, tone, and body language of the fight/consummation scene suggests a jocose moment that does not hint at any closeted erotic desires of its participants.

Holmes's attempt to secure Watson's fellowship ironically produces the opposite outcome, as Holmes fails to recognize the balancing and soothing effect of their domesticity. If Watson experiences any enjoyment during their exploits, it soon wanes as the stakes raise and danger increases. The home first and foremost provides safety and security, and as Holmes drags Watson around the globe—France, Germany, Switzerland, a gypsy camp of dubious location—Watson pines for the tranquil domestic life he has left behind, whether at Baker Street or his new home with Mary. After Watson revives a nearly dead Holmes, he displays the strain caused by the dangerous game they play with Moriarty:

> HOLMES: I'm sorry you didn't get to Brighton.
> WATSON: Me too ... I think we should go home.
> HOLMES: I concur. We're going home ... via Switzerland [*A Game of Shadows*].

Watson's tired plea to go home, choked out after a weighty silence, demonstrates childlike desperation. Holmes at first appears to understand the urgency with which Watson needs his domestic life back, but his love of adventure (and his belief in Watson's equal love of it) spurs him on, and the game's locations multiply until London feels like an impossible destination; indeed, the couple never make it back to London together. Despite its humorous elements, Holmes's plan backfires, and the film closes with Watson restored to heteronormative masculinity in his life with Mary.

The gender dynamics of the BBC's *Sherlock* series and Guy Ritchie's *Sherlock Holmes* films elicit compelling questions about how twenty-first century people—whether artistically or scholarly inclined or not—interpret queerness. Though this study does not focus on CBS's *Elementary*, another recent Holmes adaptation, this show could perhaps continue the work with gender politics exhibited by the adaptations under discussion, especially considering John Watson's transmutation into Joan Watson, a woman literally employed as Sherlock Holmes's caretaker, a "sober companion." My analysis of the BBC and Warner Brothers adaptations' conflation of queer identities does not suggest prejudice on the part of the adaptors; on the contrary, I argue that these adaptors knowingly play with their audiences' expectations, which could enlighten more it than conceals about interpretations of queerness. Nevertheless, this study merits the question, When does our conflation of all non-gender-normative/nonheteronormative identities with homosexuality become pernicious? Conflict occurs within queer communities about who belongs, and who has the right to claim queerness—conflict transgender communities often confront in queer rallies and allegiances in the United States. As tolerance for being gay increases, and legal battles legitimize lifestyles and identities long considered perverted, continuing dialogue about queerness has never been more necessary for both civil rights and individual dignity.

Works Cited

Archibald, Diana C. *Domesticity, Imperialism, and Emigration in the Victorian Novel.* Columbia: University of Missouri Press, 2002. Print.
Carroll, Larry. "Robert Downey Jr., Jude Law Explore 'Bromance' on 'Sherlock Holmes' Set." *MTV News.* Viacom International, Inc., 11 Feb. 2009. Web. 11 Aug. 2014.
Chase, Karen, and Michael H. Levenson. *The Spectacle of Intimacy: A Public Life.* Princeton: Princeton University Press, 2000. Print.
Graham, Anissa M., and Jennifer C. Garlen. "Sex and the Single Sleuth." *Sherlock Holmes for the 21st Century: Essays on New Adaptations.* Jefferson, NC: McFarland, 2012. Print.
Lavigne, Carlen. "The Noble Bachelor and the Crooked Man: Subtext and Sexuality in the BBC's *Sherlock.*" *Sherlock Holmes for the 21st Century: Essays on New Adaptations.* Jefferson, NC: McFarland, 2012. Print.
McCrea, Barry. *In the Company of Strangers: Family and Narrative in Dickens, Conan Doyle, Joyce, and Proust.* New York: Columbia University Press, 2011. Print.
Polasek, Amy. 2013. "Surveying the Post-Millennial Sherlock Holmes: A Case for the Great Detective as a Man of Our Times." *Adaptation* 6.3 (2013): 384–393. Print.
Raz, Guy. "Playing with Perceptions." *TED Radio Hour.* 14 Nov. 2014. *NPR.org.* Web. 5 Mar. 2015.
The Story. "The Angel in the House." *The Angel in the House.* Elektra, 1993. CD.
Taylor, Rhonda Harris. "A Singular Case of Identity: Holmesian Shapeshifting." *Sherlock Holmes for the 21st Century: Essays on New Adaptations.* Jefferson, NC: McFarland, 2012. Print.
Thomas, Kayley. 2012. "'Bromance Is So Passé': Robert Downey, Jr.'s Queer Paratexts." *Sherlock Holmes for the 21st Century: Essays on New Adaptations.* Jefferson, NC: McFarland, 2012. Print.
Toadvine, April. "The Watson Effect: Civilizing the Sociopath." *Sherlock Holmes for the 21st Century: Essays on New Adaptations.* Jefferson, NC: McFarland, 2012. Print.
Woolf, Virginia. "Professions for Women." *The Death of the Moth and Other Essays.* Orlando: Harcourt Brace, 1942. Digital File.
Zawisza, Magdalena, and Marco Cinnirella. "What Matters More—Breaking Tradition or Stereotype Content? Envious and Paternalistic Gender Stereotypes and Advertising Effectiveness." *Journal of Applied Social Psychology* 40.7 (2010): 1767–1797. Print.

A Questionable Bromance
Queer Subtext, Fan Service and the Dangers of Queerbaiting in Guy Ritchie's Sherlock Holmes *and* A Game of Shadows

Hannah Mueller

"Who taught you how to dance?" An Introduction

"I thought you'd never ask," John Watson remarks dryly when Sherlock Holmes holds out his hand in a silent request to join him for a dance, and they take off, waltzing with other couples on the dance floor at the peace summit in Reichenbach, Switzerland. Of course, their dancing actually serves the purpose of searching for the assassin among the attending diplomats, and thus preventing a war between France and Germany, but that doesn't stop Holmes from asking afterward: "By the way, *who* taught you how to dance?" It is a rhetorical question, but Watson doesn't point that out. "You did," he replies instead, with a fondly exasperated smile that only widens when Holmes responds, suddenly almost embarrassed: "Well, I've done a fine job" (Ritchie, *Game of Shadows*).

It is their last conversation before Watson has to watch helplessly as Holmes drags his nemesis James Moriarty with him over the rail of the balcony into the deadly Reichenbach Falls, sharing a last meaningful glance with his friend before disappearing into the abyss.

Scenes like this, seemingly full of wistful flirtatiousness and romantic complications, explain why so many reviews of Guy Ritchie's 2011 movie *Sherlock Holmes: A Game of Shadows* (2011) referred to the on-screen relationship between Sherlock Holmes and John Watson as a thinly-veiled gay love story. "*Sherlock Holmes: A Game of Shadows* is Gayer, Steamier, and Explodier Than

Before" wrote the online media journal *i09* (Newitz), while other critics jokingly changed the movie title into "Sherlock Homo: A Game of Eyeshadow" (Ayers) and "Sherlock Holmes: Out of the Closet" (Whitty).

The obvious presence of homoeroticism in *Sherlock Holmes* (2009) and its sequel *A Game of Shadows* (2011) notwithstanding, this essay argues that Ritchie's movie adaptations should not be seen so much as a queer interpretation of Arthur Conan Doyle's famous stories; instead, the numerous hints at a romantic relationship between Robert Downey, Jr.'s Holmes and Jude Law's Watson should be understood as an intentional form of fan service directed at LGBT audiences and slash fans in media fandom.

As such, *Sherlock Holmes* and *A Game of Shadows* can serve as examples for the effect the entertainment industry's awareness of fan culture has on the representation of sexuality in contemporary popular culture. In particular, the practice of "queerbaiting" in *A Game of Shadows* demonstrates that the increasing familiarity of producers with the interests of fan communities does not necessarily lead to a change in representation, but instead may lead to the containment and control of fans' resistant readings and transformative practices. Under the pretense of fan- and queer-friendliness, then, these adaptations end up reiterating the sexism and homophobia inherent in the homosocial culture in which the original texts are rooted.

"Five very happy years": The History of a Fandom

Scholars and movie critics have pointed out that the PR campaign for Ritchie's first Sherlock Holmes movie in 2009 relied heavily on its association with the popular neologism "bromance" (Thomas). The interpretation of the movie as bromance—that is, a saga of male friendship and homosocial bonding—was supported in particular by the two male leads, Robert Downey, Jr., and Jude Law, who kept hinting at romantic feelings between the super detective and his partner. During a press conference at San Diego Comic Con 2009, Downey, Jr. described their relationship as "circumstantial homosexuality" (Huver), and Law made similar, if somewhat less explicit statements:

> LAW: It was pitched to me, before we even met, that there was this uncharted territory between them, this kind of Butch and Sundance vibe. And we took that and ran with it. And I think we embraced slightly more the domestic ... the domesticity of this couple. And if you go to the books and you realize that they are living with each other...
>
> DOWNEY JR.: It would be weird if it wasn't dysfunctional.

LAW: Right. [Pauses, puts his hand on RDJ's arm, leaves it there] Or overly formal ["Robert Downey, Jr., y Jude Law"].

The idea of a romantic relationship between Holmes and Watson was invoked not only in statements about the movie, but also by the actors' behavior towards each other. Interviewed together, both Law and Downey, Jr. frequently initiated physical contact, as in the abovementioned interview; during their appearance on the Graham Norton Show they made a point of staring lovingly into each other's eyes, and on different occasions, they admitted to "crushing" on each other: "It has to be Downey [Robert Downey, Jr.]!" Law told *MTV News* in 2013 when asked about his "mancrush." "Has to be! Only because he'd be devastated if I said anyone else!" ("Exclusive!").

Fans were delighted at these public displays of affection: "How are they so adorable??? HOW? Robert petting Jude on the head like a kitten, I am SO CHARMED :D," one fan wrote online (the-randomist), and another went even further in their (not necessarily serious) speculations: "totally fucking each other. y/y?" (TW-31988).

While Downey and Law's statements during public appearances certainly drew a lot of attention from fans and media alike, Ritchie's was not the only or first published adaptation of Arthur Conan Doyle's characters that toyed with the idea of a romantic relationship between the protagonists. Billy Wilder's 1970 movie *The Private Life of Sherlock Holmes*, for example, invokes a romance between Holmes and Watson when Holmes, in an attempt to let down a very ardent female admirer, suggests that he and Watson are more than just friends: "You see, I am not a free man.... A bachelor living with another bachelor, for the last five years. Five very happy years" (*The Private Life*). And while Wilder merely hints at the idea of a relationship between Holmes and Watson, a number of published Sherlock Holmes pastiches[1] are much more explicit in their exploration of the romantic tension between the two characters.[2]

Still, although speculations about the nature of Holmes' and Watson's relationship have a long tradition, they tended to remain on the fringes of the fan community, a consequence of the discourse that dominated Sherlock Holmes fandom throughout the 20th century. The fannish practices of the "Sherlockians" or "Holmesians," who traditionally reject the label "fan" for themselves, claiming a place among the aficionados of high culture rather than the fans of pop culture (Pearson 106–7), are guided first and foremost by the ideal of preserving the spirit of the original texts, and the extremely prolific body of writing brought forth by this fan community has been characterized by its loyalty to the "canon"—that is, the oeuvre produced by Arthur Conan Doyle himself. A big part of "Sherlockian scholarship" is even based on the assumption (and the suspension of disbelief) that Holmes and Watson are actual historical figures, not fictional characters; and the fan scholars treating Conan Doyle's writings as fiction share the focus on textual hermeneutics and historical research. Likewise, the most famous form of fictional Sherlock Holmes fan writing, the pastiche, is traditionally judged by its proximity to Conan Doyle's own writing style (Pearson, *Always* 149–150; Polasek 429). This fidelity to canon and the general suspicion toward non-canonical writings and adaptations is probably one of the main reasons for the relative marginality of speculations about the sexual preferences of Holmes and Watson: "there is a strong affirmational tradition within the Sherlock Holmes fan community" (Polasek 44).[3]

The promotional efforts for Guy Ritchie's movie in 2009, however, were not just directed at the established Sherlockian community. In fact, the advertising for the movie aimed to attract other groups of fans that were at home not (only) in the literary tradition of Arthur Conan Doyle's writings, but in the world of contemporary geek culture, sci-fi and fantasy, and cult cinema. The official trailer for the movie did not linger on the promise of murder mysteries and methods of logical deduction—instead, it teased with action scenes, a steampunk[4] setting, Rachel McAdams in Victorian lingerie, and bromantic banter between Holmes and Watson (Ritchie, *The Official Trailer*). The cast, crew and setting of *Sherlock Holmes* represented an accumulation of "fan credit" that the movie was bound to cash in at the box office. Director Guy Ritchie had already somewhat of a cult film director status for shooting gritty movies such as *Lock, Stock and Two Smoking Barrels* (1998) and *Snatch* (2000), main actor Robert Downey, Jr., had gained overwhelming popularity with different divisions of the comic and sci-fi fandom for his role as *Iron Man* in 2008, the decidedly steampunk-y twist to the Victorian setting was meant to appeal to other parts of fantasy and sci-fi fandom—and the advertising of the movie as bromance was directed at yet another very specific group of fans: "[T]hat homoerotic aspect of the film was pretty canny, and a big part of its advance marketing. It no doubt drew a lot of people into theaters who might otherwise have skipped out on a Guy Ritchie film. And count me in that camp. I mean, give me queer subtext over *Lock Stock and Two Smoking Barrels*—or *Snatch*—any day!" (Ayers).

The fans that Ayers, writer for the gay online media journal *The Backlot*, referred to in his review, are an audience group that has only come into the focus of the entertainment industry's marketing efforts in the last decade:

LGBT audiences, and queer and female media fans, in particular those with an interest in what fan terminology calls "slash": the concept of imagining two (often canonically straight) fictional characters of the same sex to be involved in a romantic or sexual relationship. Known for their interest in the queer subtexts they find in popular texts (particularly in male-oriented genres like science fiction, western, action, crime and horror), slash fans are a subcategory of transformative media fandom—a diverse and loosely connected global community that is characterized by its practices of media criticism and creative appropriation of pop culture in fan works like fan fiction, art, or videos.[5] Once a more or less secretive underground subculture, media fans and their practices have moved to the foreground of the industry's awareness as fan works have become easily accessible online, and producers, writers and actors openly admit to reading fan discussion forums and fan fiction sites. As Henry Jenkins elaborates in his book *Convergence Culture*, companies have begun to understand the importance of fan support for commercial success: "the media industry is increasingly dependent on active and committed consumers to spread the word about valued properties in an overcrowded marketplace, and in some cases they are seeking ways to channel the creative output of media fans to lower their production costs" (Jenkins, *Convergence* 138). The industry has reacted to these changes by developing a new attitude towards grassroots fandom and fan works, which mostly oscillated between gentle encouragement and purposeful ignorance before. Now producers are keen on improving their relationship with the fans by actively encouraging fan participation, in order to increase mouth-to-mouth publicity, gain valuable feedback, ensure viewer loyalty or create new markets for merchandise.

The advertising of *Sherlock Holmes* as a bromance with homoerotic undertones should be seen as part of this new strategy, aimed at winning new audience groups for a product that in the past would have been mostly advertised to male straight audiences. Of course, in the case of *Sherlock Holmes*, this was a somewhat obvious choice. The promotional efforts could fall back on the (marginal, but existent) tradition of Holmes/Watson romance in the established Sherlockian/Holmesian community, and several people involved in the movie had already worked on projects that held a certain significance for both the LGBT and the slash community, guaranteeing their interest in this film. Ritchie was known by slash fans for the gay subplot in his 2008 gangster movie *Rock'n'Rolla,* Downey, Jr. had starred as gay editor Terry in *WonderBoys* (2000) and next to Val Kilmer's queer PI in *Kiss Kiss Bang Bang* (2005), and Jude Law was still remembered for his early role in the homoerotic thriller *The Talented Mr. Ripley* (1999), as well as, at least by loyal Holmes fans, for his small role in an episode of the TV show *The Casebook of Sherlock Holmes*, in which his character wore a dress and posed as a woman (Cox).

"Gladstone is our *dog!"*
Bromance in Sherlock Holmes *(2009)*

The movie itself fulfilled the promises of its promotion, presenting all the "elements common to the bromance...: back-and-forth banter, a love-hate dynamic, codependency, masculine physicality and action, male camaraderie and loyalty, and potential homoeroticism" (Thomas 38). In Ritchie's *Sherlock Holmes*, Holmes and Watson fight side by side, not bothering to wait for their backup: "Where's the Inspector?"—"He's getting his troops lined up."—"That could be all day." They bicker and banter like the proverbial old married couple: "Get that out of my face."—"It's not in your face; it's in my hand."—"Get what's in your hand out my face." Most importantly, they actively discourage each other from pursuing relationships with anyone else, and Holmes in particular refuses to face the reality of Watson's engagement and meet his fiancée, as can be seen in the following conversation:

> WATSON: Mary's coming.
> HOLMES: Not available.
> WATSON: You're meeting her, Holmes!
> HOLMES: Have you proposed yet?
> WATSON: No, I haven't found the right ring.
> HOLMES: Then it's not official.
> WATSON: It's happening, whether you like it or not! 8:30, The Royale. Wear a jacket.
> HOLMES: *You* wear a jacket.

Of course, while Holmes is clearly jealous of Watson's relationship with Mary Morstan (Kelly Reilly), he is equally fascinated with super-spy Irene Adler (Rachel McAdams), who keeps getting the better of him, despite his prowess as thinker and fighter. Regardless of the overt bromance motif, the movie is still fairly ambiguous in its representation of Holmes' sexuality: "In the first film, Ritchie and his screenwriters develop Holmes' sexuality in several directions simultaneously" (Graham/Garlen 30).

In fact, the constellation of Holmes being desperate for both Watson and Adler's attention, combined with allusions to masochistic physical desires (like the pleasure he takes from getting beaten up in boxing matches), opens the text to an interpretation of Holmes as (sexually) submissive, rather than ambiguously queer: Watson's description of the relationship between Holmes and Adler fairly explicitly spells out the dynamic of domination and submission that drives it:

> WATSON: Look at you! Why is the only woman you've ever cared about a world class criminal? Are you a masochist?
> HOLMES: Allow me to explain.
> WATSON: Allow *me*. She's the only adversary who ever outsmarted you ... twice. Made a proper idiot out of you.
> HOLMES: Right, you've had your fun.
> WATSON: What's she after, anyway?
> HOLMES: It's time to press on.
> WATSON: What could she possibly need?
> HOLMES: Doesn't matter.
> WATSON: Alibi? A beard. A human canoe. She could sit on your back and paddle you up the Thames.

On the other hand, most of the scenes alluding to a relationship between Holmes and Watson focus on the domestic nature of their relationship, rather than imply sexual tension. The argument between Holmes and Watson, after Holmes' investigations earn them a night in prison, exemplifies this:

> HOLMES: You've never complained about my methods before.
> WATSON: I'm not complaining.
> HOLMES: You're not? What do you call this?
> WATSON: I never complain! How am I complaining? When do I ever complain about you practicing the violin at three in the morning, or your mess, your general lack of hygiene, or the fact that you steal my clothes?
> HOLMES: Uh, we have a barter system...
> WATSON: When have I ever complained about you setting fire to my rooms?
> HOLMES: *Our* rooms...
> WATSON: The rooms! Or, or, the fact that you experiment on my dog?
> HOLMES: *Our* dog...
> WATSON: The dog!
> HOLMES: Gladstone is *our* dog!

Like in the cliché of the long-married couple, shared habits seem to play a more important role for Holmes and Watson than sexual attraction, a portrayal that tones down the homoerotic undercurrents of their friendship: "But for all the homo hoohaw, that Holmes and Watson bromance in the first film was fairly tame" (Ayers).

The current was strong enough to be detected by fans, however, who saw the movie for what they had hoped it to be: "I'm sorry," one fan wrote, "but if you didn't see the subtext in this one, you weren't watching it right. It was thisclose [sic] to being canon" (amelia-17). The proliferation of fan works inspired by *Sherlock Holmes*—including reviews, videos, artworks, and fan fiction—reflect the impact this movie had on the slash community. The fairly young, but established fan fiction archive *Archive Of Our Own*, for example, hosts an impressive number of fan stories in a large variety of fandoms, among them a category named "Sherlock Holmes & Related Fandoms." In the two years between the archive's foundation in 2007 and the premiere of *Sherlock Holmes* in late 2009, only 115 Sherlock Holmes-related stories were posted on the site (some of them dated back to the years 1993–2006, indicating that they had been written before 2007), and this number included stories about various adaptations, like Laurie R. King's pastiche *The Beekeeper's Apprentice* (2002) or the Disney movie *The Great Mouse Detective* (1986). Out of those stories, about 62 percent were tagged as slash, and 54 percent featured Holmes/Watson as a couple,[6] suggesting that even before the movie premiere, the idea of a Holmes/Watson romance was a fairly established concept in media fandom, despite the marginality of Sherlock Holmes-related fan fiction in general.

With the premiere of *Sherlock Holmes* in 2009, the number of posts drastically increased. In the six months between the movie premiere and the premiere of the BBC television show *Sherlock* in late July 2010 alone, a good 500 stories were posted on the archive, the majority tagged for the movie "Sherlock Holmes 2009," although some stories were tagged for "Arthur Conan Doyle—Sherlock Holmes," implying that the movie also sparked a renewed interest in the original stories. Out of these 500 stories, which appear to be more or less directly inspired by the first movie, an overwhelming 70 percent have a Holmes/Watson pairing (354 stories, among those 337 Holmes/Watson stories and 17 stories with three- or foursomes including Holmes/Watson). An additional 8 percent (42 stories) are other slash (m/m) or femslash (f/f) pairings, and only 20 percent are not slash (104 stories with a heterosexual pairing, or no romantic/sexual pairing).[7]

This development (combined with the success of the BBC show *Sherlock*, which premiered half a year after Ritchie's first movie[8]), set the stage for what should have been an enthusiastic reception of the sequel: By the time *Sherlock Holmes: A Game of Shadows* came into the theaters in December 2011, Sherlock Holmes was an established media fandom with a large fan base awaiting Ritchie's second movie.

"You know what happens when you dance?" Raising the Stakes in A Game of Shadows *(2011)*

It seemed unavoidable that the sequel would return to the subtextual homoeroticism and bromantic banter of the first movie, and in fact, the second movie demonstratively upped the ante in regard to the Holmes/Watson bromance: not without reason, Newitz described the movie as "gayer" and "steamier" than its predecessor. Most noticeably, the sequel almost completely ignored the heterosexual romance plots for the sake of male bonding. While Adler appeared to have a certain fondness for Holmes in the 2009 movie, she still managed to outsmart him most of the time. Using his attraction to her as a weapon against him, she drugs his wine and then leaves him naked and tied to the bed in one memorable scene that invokes BDSM practices and sexualizes their relationship, but also shows her superior abilities. In *A Game of Shadows*, however, Holmes has the upper hand, and his attitude towards her is decidedly more confident and snarky. Even more importantly, their interaction is brief, because Adler is killed by Moriarty (Jared Harris) only ten minutes into the movie, even before the opening credits. Her absence sets up the dynamic between Holmes, Watson and Watson's wife Mary Morstan as a love triangle. The movie highlights Holmes' dependence on Watson, implying that Watson's absence following his engagement with Mary has left Holmes increasingly unstable because he is not capable of functioning without his friend. "You do seem ... manic ... bordering on psychotic," Watson states when he visits Holmes, who is drinking formaldehyde and has, according to the housekeeper, been living "on a diet of coffee, tobacco and coca leaves" (Ritchie, *Game of Shadows*). Holmes then proceeds to boycott Watson's stag night and almost makes him miss his wedding, only to pull him away again from his wife on the way to their honeymoon. While Watson and Holmes go on an adrenaline-fueled honeymoon of their own, the newly-wed Mary Watson is forced to spend the rest of the movie in the company of Holmes' brother Mycroft (Stephen Fry).

Of course, Watson really seems just as little prepared to live without Holmes, as becomes apparent in the scene in which Watson frantically attempts to revive a dying Holmes and finally saves his life by injecting (penetrating) him with Holmes' own wedding gift, an adrenaline-filled syringe, in a strange Victorian reenactment of the iconic scene from Quentin Tarantino's *Pulp Fiction* (1994).

But not only do Holmes and Watson basically elope together in *A Game of Shadows*, their relationship is also noticeably more sexualized and physical than in the first movie. This becomes most obvious in the infamous scene in which a cross-dressing Holmes pushes Morstan out of a moving train, right before engaging Watson in a wrestling match that bears strong resemblance to an act of sexual intercourse: "The furious Law tackles Downey, ripping off his drag costume in a comic wrestling match that looks as if they are rolling down Brokeback Mountain" (Covert).

Other allusions are more subtle, like Holmes' side comment to Watson while they are staying with the Romani people: "For God's sake, don't dance!" he warns. "It'll be the death of you! You know what happens when you dance?" (Ritchie, *Game of Shadows*). It never becomes quite clear what Holmes is referring to here. Watson dances with abandon, Holmes watches him intensely, and nothing terrible happens. But his remark makes the final interaction between Holmes and Watson—the aforementioned waltz and the following flirtatious interaction—even more meaningful, considering that it was Holmes who taught Watson how to dance. The movie is careful to point out that clearly, there is history between these two men, a history that includes dance lessons and subsequent events that seem to be better left unmentioned.

As shown above, the movie critics picked up on the heavy-handed implications of homoeroticism. The majority of reviews at least made mention of it, although many of them did so in a rather critical way. However, the target of their criticism was not the fact that the movie allowed the audience to imagine a romantic relationship between Holmes and Watson, quite the contrary: Critics resented that the implication was at once too demonstrative, and not explicit enough. On the one hand, *A Game of Shadows* seemed to cross the line that other bromance stories at most toe—the line that separates subtext and text, and allows slash fans to see a gay romance where most other people see mere friendship. "Given Robert Downey, Jr.'s queeny, hilarious, cranked-to-11 performance as the titular genius, you might actually not want to call that subtext," *The Salon* wrote, and didn't seem to mean it as a compliment: "It's more like supertext, if that's a word" (O'Hehir). *Empire* similarly stated that the homoeroticism in the movie was "less a subtext than extended routine" (Nathan). On the other hand, critics pointed out that for a movie that so demonstratively toyed with the idea of a same-sex romance, it seemed surprisingly reluctant to seriously consider the reality of a queer relationship: "*A Game of Shadows* is so overt in its insinuations that it becomes a distraction, begging one to imagine what an honestly homosexual retelling of the Sherlock Holmes character might look like" (Mercer). The the movie seemed to mock the idea it had put into its audience's heads in the first place: "The sad thing is that Downey's instincts aren't necessarily wrong—

Holmes' affection for Watson runs deep. But Downey disrespects his own idea, covering it up with wink-wink references and not-so-subtle innuendos. Neither provocative nor proud, it's merely a simpering satire" (Whitty).

Surprisingly, slash fans had similar reservations, but where the journalists still carefully tried to explain what exactly was wrong with Ritchie's portrayal of Holmes' and Watson's relationship, the fan community already had a term for it. *A Game of Shadows*, the fans decided, was guilty of queerbaiting: "I really liked noomi rapace's character, i really liked the silly gags, i really liked the music and the ridiculous steampunk feel," one fan wrote. "i did not like the honestly highly offensive stereotypes of romani folks and i resented the queerbaiting" (iambickilometer, lowercase spelling in original).

"Wink wink nudge nudge": Queerbaiting and Misogyny in A Game of Shadows

Queerbaiting, at least in its contemporary form, is a fairly new phenomenon[9]: It describes the tendency of creators to purposefully write queer subtext into a movie or show, in order to draw the attention of a queer and female fannish audience—much to the same audiences' despair.

For LGBT and female fans who take pleasure in reimagining texts predominantly written for straight male audiences, queer subtext in male-oriented texts of popular culture has for a long time been an important source of imagination. The homoerotic undertones of male friendship portrayed in popular culture were so appealing to LGBT audiences and media fans in the past because representation of actual queer characters had been rare, and the representation of functional queer relationships even rarer.[10] "When I started writing for AfterEllen," media journalist Heather Hogan writes in 2013, "there was barely enough lesbian pop culture news to fill a weekly column. We went an entire year without a major lesbian character on broadcast TV. I'm talking like five years ago, that was the reality. Not one single major lesbian character. And gay guys weren't all that present on broadcast TV either" (Hogan).

In this hostile climate, slash fan fiction was one way of transgressing the experience of overwhelming heteronormativity in (popular) culture: by bridging the enforced gap between homosociality and homosexuality at the foundation of patriarchal heteronormativity (Sedgwick 1–27), by sexualizing straight male bodies, or simply by undermining authorial authority.[11] But the concept of transgression becomes more complicated if the subtexts slash fans zoom in on are purposefully included precisely for their sake, now that the industry has started to pay attention to the practices and interests of fans. When Jenkins first discussed this development in *Convergence Culture*, he was hopeful that the industry's awareness for fan interests would lead to a more harmonious relationship between producers and consumers. But since then, scholars like Matt Hills and Suzanne Scott have pointed out that the industry's newfound knowledge also bears the risk of a containment and restriction of fans' readings strategies (Hills, *Torchwood*; Scott).

What fans call queerbaiting is one of the more problematic consequences of the industry's reaction to fan culture. While the intentional inclusion of queer subtext acknowledges and seemingly rewards slash fans' interest in queer storylines, it also takes away their pleasures of transgression, becoming instead a marketing strategy: now, when slash fans see queer subtext in a bromance movie, they don't subvert its heteronormativity, but read the movie exactly the way it was intended. Maybe even more dangerously, queerbaiting excludes the possibility of representing actual queer relationships. Queer subtext can function as a stand-in when queer representation, for one reason or another, is impossible; but it is not an adequate replacement. In the case of queerbaiting, the text invokes homosexuality, but contains it by turning it into an inside joke, as fans themselves point out: "throughout sherlock holmes adaptations, to my knowledge not one has been explicitly queer. the closest we have gotten is queer baiting which adaptations such as guy ritchie's and moffat's sherlock holmes has [sic] done to an offensive degree. it is giving us the potential for a queer relationship through a wink wink nudge nudge, but ultimately playing it up as [sic] laughs or as a means of titillating the audience" (icicleman, lowercase spelling in original).

Eve Sedgwick, in her work on the homoerotic undercurrents in homosocial bonds between men, showed that what distinguishes homosexual from homosocial relationships is the homophobia that functions to suppress the homoerotic desire in homosocial relationships and thus secures heteronormative patriarchy (Sedgwick 1–27). Similarly, LGBT and slash fans are aware that the difference between queerbaiting and queer representation is the way in which the former limits the possibility of actual homosexuality by using the idea for comic relief. Queerbaiting, then, is not just a marketing strategy to win over certain audience groups, but a strategy that makes for texts with homophobic undertones.

> ORBITINGASUPERNOVA: It is NOT okay to promote queerbaiting as actual lgbtq representation. Many shows with dude/dude relationships queer bait because most audiences accept it as being totally ~gay friendly~ without being actually ...

you know, gay. And then the writers get credit for being super ~gay friendly~ without actually writing critical, real and honest queer stories. If you get offended by the phrase, 'no homo,' then you should be offended by queerbaiting.

MYMINDTARDIS: *Sherlock Holmes: Game of Shadows*, I'm looking at you [Orbitingsupernova].

But the avoidance of queer representation by means of subtext was not the only problem fans and film critics had with *A Game of Shadows*' employment of the bromance trope: "Bromance is rarely achieved in modern cinema without a side helping of misogyny, and *A Game of Shadows* is no different in that it mostly associates women with domesticity, and domesticity itself with the constraining of male self-expression" (Roz T).

Sedgwick showed how homosocial culture works to systematically exclude women from male-dominated communities, and the same is true for many stories of male friendship in popular culture: When male friendship takes the place of romance in cinematic narratives, there is no room for women anymore—after all, romance is often the only purpose of female characters in male-oriented movies. The representation of Holmes and Watson's friendship in *A Game of Shadows* works in a similar way, as movie critics have pointed out:

> But as the story races across Europe, and Holmes and Watson don goofy costumes and engage in all manner of misdirection, it becomes embarrassingly clear that this movie has little interest in inviting women into its boys' club. (Rachel McAdams, who was a game foil in the first movie, appears briefly here, but not long enough to balance the scales.) Fun and fleet as *Sherlock Holmes: A Game of Shadows* often is, it leaves the sour taste of misogyny in your mouth [Kelly].

The reviewer for the *Star Tribune* agrees: "There's an undercurrent of misogyny in the way women are dismissed or knocked around here" (Covert). The increase of bromantic tension between Holmes and Watson in the movie sequel is inversely proportional to the importance of the female characters: In *Sherlock Holmes*, Irene Adler and Mary Morstan get to pursue their own interests, and for the most part they manage to keep up with Holmes' attempts to outrun them. Adler is Holmes' equal, if not superior when it comes to their professional activities, and she gets to be part of the action-fueled finale. Morstan wins, despite Holmes' best attempts, the battle over Watson's attention, and gets Holmes back for trying to break them up: She throws a glass of wine in his face for insulting her, and leaves him at the jail when she comes to bail out Watson. While the movie clearly fails the Bechdel Test, it does present two female characters with minds of their own—two characters that the sequel seems to try hard to get rid of as quickly as possible. Adler's affection towards Holmes is turned into the weakness that gets her killed, while Morstan is pushed out of a moving train into a lake, a merely symbolic death that takes her out of the action nevertheless—and leaves the floor open for more scenes between the two male protagonists: "Did you just kill my new wife?" Watson yells at Holmes, seconds before literally jumping him and ripping off his clothes in the following wrestling match (Ritchie, *Game of Shadows*).

Furthermore, much of the humor provided by the bickering between the men unfolds at the expense of women. Especially in Holmes' derisive comments about Watson's engagement and marriage, meant to expose his jealousy and abandonment issues, bromance functions as an excuse for sexism. When he comments on Watson's "heinous handmade scarf ... clearly one of your fiancée's early efforts," he reduces Mary to the domestic sphere and simultaneously questions her domestic talents. Holmes' insults towards housekeeper Mrs. Hudson, whom he likes to call "dear sickly sweet nanny," are similarly gendered and played up for laughs (Ritchie, *Game of Shadows*).

His brother Mycroft's backhanded compliment to Mary, on the other hand, serves more than one function. One the one hand, he expresses the sentiment that male companionship is always preferable to female company, echoing the stereotypical misogyny of homosocial societies when he says: "You know, although our time together has been but a brief interlude, I'm beginning to understand how a man of a particular disposition, under certain circumstances—extreme ones, perhaps—might grow to enjoy the company of a person of your gender" (Ritchie, *Game of Shadows*). But his comment also suggests a possible homosexual preference, labeling him, the celibate eccentric nudist, as queer, and thus reaffirming Holmes' and Watson' heterosexuality in comparison: if Mycroft is identified as gay, surely that means Sherlock and John Watson are not.

This constant lacing of queer subtext with misogyny is particularly problematic for the slash fans targeted by bromance marketing, who are, after all, to a large part female. The constant unkind treatment of female characters in bromance stories creates the sense among female fans that not only do producers not understand or respect their demand for actual queer representation, they also do not understand or respect them as female fans. "Add to that fridging[12] Irene and the really misogynistic treatment of Mary Morstan and I was spitting," one fan (legionseagle) writes furiously, and another comments: "I will gladly dance with you in the field of wonderful homoeroticism, but let's not forget that far, far too often, 'subtracting ALL the hetero' comes at the price of gross narrative misogyny. Is it too much to ask for a movie that, yes, is *that* gay, and doesn't throw its women under the bus in the process?" (autoluminescence).

"I wouldn't blink": An Outlook

Of course, this remark by a Holmes fan shows the double-edged nature of the problem that plagues *Sherlock Holmes* and *A Game of Shadows*. On the one hand, LGBT and media fans' concerns about the homophobic and misogynist implications of the bromance hype are an immensely valuable form of media criticism and absolutely should be taken seriously as such. On the other hand, fans' protests do not mean that they will necessarily stop watching the texts they criticize, if only because of a lack of alternatives, or because the theme of romantic male friendship is still appealing to them, despite their concerns. Ultimately, the box office as well as secondary and tertiary sales still have more influence on studio decisions than fannish complaints.

At the time of this essay's publication (2015), a third *Sherlock Holmes* movie is in pre-production, and main actor Jude Law already announced that it is going "to be better than the other two" (de Semlyen). What this means for the development of the Holmes/Watson relationship remains speculation for now, although one critic already made predictions: "Where the Holmes and Watson partnership goes from here is a tossup, but I wouldn't blink if they ultimately reprise the finale of 'Some Like It Hot'" (Covert). This is probably a guess as good as any regarding the question what the third of Ritchie's Holmes movies is going to bring, but as entertaining as a scene like this would undoubtedly be, the difference between the original and a potential reenactment is obvious: Billy Wilder's (in)famous movie finale used comedy as a means to propose the possibility of a functioning long-term queer relationship during a time when Hollywood's production code still restricted the representation of any kind of alternative sexuality. In the 21st century, when high school musical dramedies like *Glee* (2009–2015) show love, sex and marriage proposals between same-sex couples on U.S. network television without teenaged viewers even blinking an eye, the same kind of joke has to fall short, and instead leaves the audience to wonder what Hollywood could do with a serious queer imagining of Holmes and Watson's relationship, and whether it is ever going to happen.

Notes

1. Pastiches are, in the Sherlockian community, derivative fictional texts by different authors that are not just based on Arthur Conan Doyle's writings, but try to imitate the writer's style.
2. Among others: Piercy Rohase, *My Dearest Holmes*, 1988; Larry Townsend, *The Sexual Adventures of Sherlock Holmes*, 1993; T.D. McKinney and Terry Wylis, *Kissing Sherlock Holmes*, 2011; Joseph deMarco, *A Study in Lavender: Queering Sherlock Holmes*, 2011; L.A. Fields, *My Dear Watson*, 2013.
3. Sherlock Holmes fandom in its traditional form did, until very recently, not come into the focus of fan studies scholarship, despite dating back as far as the early 20th century. In an article from 2007, Sherlockians expert Roberta Pearson still commented: "Sherlockians have so far (with the exception of a previous article of mine: see Pearson, "It's always 1895") escaped academic scrutiny, despite being probably the oldest established fandom" (Pearson, "Bachies" 105). Because much of early fan studies scholarship in the 1990s was driven by the desire to make the subversive or feminist potential of fan culture visible, scholars focused heavily on transformative and/or female-dominated fan practices, and therefore the mostly affirmational and male-dominated community of the Sherlockians and Holmsians most likely did not register immediately as a relevant subject (Pearson, "Always 1895"; "Bachies"; "Good").
4. Steampunk refers to a subgenre of science fiction that does not rely on futuristic settings, but instead depicts an alternate history. Most commonly, steampunk fiction features an alternate version of the Victorian age or the Wild West that includes anachronistic technology, in particular the (steam engine-driven) technology envisioned in futuristic/utopian texts at the time.
5. Unfortunately, this is not the place to delve into a detailed account of the history and practices of media fandom; for a brief history of this community, see Coppa.
6. Forty-four percent (51 stories) were Holmes/Watson stories, an additional 10 percent (12 stories) featured threesomes with Holmes/Watson and another character, and 7 percent (8 stories) had other slash (m/m) or femslash (f/f) pairings.
7. Of course statistical data can only give limited insight into the transformation of a community, but as Polasek has demonstrated in her study of the reception of BBC's *Sherlock*, numbers can certainly be helpful in demonstrating the impact of particular texts on fandom.
8. Hills and Polasek have both discussed how the BBC TV show *Sherlock* (2010) managed to bring together different groups of fans, thus causing "a fragmentation in the traditional fan discourse" (Polasek 41) by "drawing together established Sherlockians, fans of the other work of executive producers Steven Moffat and Mark Gatiss (especially *Doctor Who*), readers passionately focused on the relationship between Sherlock (Benedict Cumberbatch) and John (Martin Freeman), and fan audiences drawn to Cumberbatch-as-Holmes, as well as to the show's use of contemporary styling such as its Belstaff coats or Spencer Hart suits, and its highly stylized televisuality, attributable to the directorial input of Paul McGuigan" (Hills, *Epistemological* 29). But while it is true that the BBC show ended up outdoing previous Sherlock Holmes adaptations in its popularity with media fans, it was Ritchie's *Sherlock Holmes* that first stimulated the interest of transformative fandom in *Sherlock Holmes*, in particular regarding the Holmes/Watson relationship.
9. It could be argued that the entertainment industry has employed similar strategies in the past: When homosexuality was somewhat "en vogue" in the early 1930s, Hollywood "responded to this development by including homosexual characters and themes in film, and also by allowing some of its stars to project an ambiguous sexual and gender image" (Gregg 140).
10. Media fans have been invested in changing this situation for decades, as documented for example by Jenkins's study *Out of the Closet and Into the Universe: Queers and Star Trek* (Jenkins, "Out"), an account of the battle *Star Trek* fans have been fighting for the inclusion of a queer character into the *Star Trek* universe.
11. Scholars have provided a number of explanations for the slash phenomenon: some consider slash a radical subversion of heteronormative texts (Penley), others see it as the act of uncovering already existent homoerotic subtext (Gwenllian Jones). Green, Jenkins and Jenkins manage to show that fans themselves often provide the most insightful and differentiated analysis of their own practices (Green/Jenkins/Jenkins).

12. "Fridging" is a fannish term originating from comics fandom, where it refers to the constant negligent and violent treatment of female characters in superhero comics. For more information, see the website *Women in Refrigerators* (Simone).

Works Cited

Amelia-17. *Sherlock Holmes: Ignore the Homoerotic Subtext Behind the Curtain*. LJ, 7 Jan. 2010. Web.
Autoluminescence. *Untitled*. Tumblr, 2012. Web.
Ayers, Dennis. "Sherlock Homo: A Game of Eyeshadows." TheBacklot.com, 2 Jan. 2012. Web.
Conan Doyle, Arthur. *The Adventures of Sherlock Holmes*. Oxford: Oxford University Press, 1993. Print.
Coppa, Francesca. "A Brief History of Media Fandom." *Fan Fiction and Fan Communities in the Age of the Internet*. Eds. Kristina Busse and Karen Hellekson. Jefferson, NC: McFarland, 2006. 41–59. Print.
Covert, Colin. "'Sherlock' II Fights Crime with Panache." *The Star Tribune*, 15 Dec. 2011. Web.
Cox, Michael, dir. "Shoscombe Old Place." *The Casebook of Sherlock Holmes*, Episode 3. Granada Television. Manchester. 7 March 1991. Television.
De Semlyen, Phil. "Jude Law Talks Sherlock Holmes 3. 'It's going to be better and smarter than the others.'" *Empire*, 26 Sept. 2013. Web.
deMarco, Joseph. *A Study in Lavender: Queering Sherlock Holmes*. Maple Shade, NJ: Lethe Press, 2011. Print.
"Exclusive! Side Effects star talks Channing Tatum's feelings for him..." *MTV News*. MTV, 8 Mar. 2013. Television.
Fanlore. *Timeline of Slashed Sources*. Web.
Fields, L.A. *My Dear Watson*. Maple Shade, NJ: Lethe Press, 2013. Print.
Graham, Anissa M., and Jennifer C. Garlen. "Sex and the Single Sleuth." *Sherlock Holmes for the 21st Century: Essays on New Adaptations*. Ed. Lynette Porter. Jefferson, NC: McFarland, 2012. 24–34. Print.
Green, Shoshanna, Cynthia Jenkins, and Henry Jenkins. "Normal Female Interest in Men Bonking: Selections from the Terra Nostra Underground and Strange Bedfellows." *Theorizing Fandom: Fans, Subculture and Identity*. Eds. Cheryl Harris and Alison Alexander. Cresskill, NJ: Hampton Press, 1998. 9–38. Print.
Gregg, Ronald. "Queering Brad Pitt: The Struggle between Gay Fans and the Hollywood Machine to control Star Discourse and Image on the Web." *LGBT Identity and Online New Media*. Eds. Christopher Pullen and Margaret Cooper. New York: Routledge, 2010. 139–146. Print.
Gwenllian-Jones, Sara. "The Sex Lives of Cult Television Characters." *Screen* 43 (2002): 79–90. Print.
Hills, Matt. "Sherlock's Epistemological Economy and the Value of 'Fan' Knowledge. How Producer-Fans Play the (Great) Game of Fandom." *Sherlock and Transmedia Fandom: Essays on the BBC Series*. Eds. Louisa Ellen Stein and Kristina Busse. Jefferson, NC: McFarland, 2012. 27–40. Print.
_____. "Torchwood's Trans-Transmedia: Media Tie-ins and Brand 'Fanagement.'" *Participations: Journal of Audience and Reception Studies* 9, no. 2 (2012): 409–428. Web.
Hogan, Heather. "'Glee' Recap 4.13: A Hummel is a Homo Version of a Hustla." *AfterElton* (now *The Backlot*), 8 Feb. 2013. Web.
Huver, Scott. "Robert Downey Jr.'s Man Crush." *People*, 27 July 2009. Web.
Iambickilometer. *Untitled*. Tumblr, 19 Feb. 2013. Web.
Icicleman. *Untitled*. Tumblr, 2012. Web.
Jenkins, Henry. *Convergence Culture: Where Old and New Media Collide*. New York: New York University Press, 2006. Print.
_____. "'Out of the Closet and Into the Universe': Queers and Star Trek." *Science Fiction Audiences:*

Doctor Who, Star Trek, and Their Fans. Eds. John Tulloch and Henry Jenkins. New York: Routledge, 1995. 237–265. Print.
Kelly, Christopher. "Second 'Sherlock Holmes' Movie a Fast-Moving Charmer." Dfw.com, 17 Dec. 2011. Web.
Legionseagle. Untitled. Dreamwidth, 11 Aug. 2012. Web.
McKinney, T.D., and Terry Wylis. Kissing Sherlock Holmes. Amber Quill Press, 2011. Print.
Mercer, Benjamin. "A Homoerotic, Bullet-Time Cash Grab." CinemaSoldier, 2011. Web.
Nathan, Ian. "The Swinging Detective." Empire Online, December 2011. Web.
Newitz, Annalee. "Sherlock Holmes: A Game of Shadows Is Gayer, Steamier, and Explodier Than Before." io9.com, 16 Dec. 2011. Web.
O'Hehir, Andrew. "'Sherlock Holmes: A Game of Shadows': Guy Ritchie's Cheerful, Idiotic Sequel." Salon, 15 Dec. 2011. Web.
Orbitingsupernova. But If I Can Expand on That Slash Shipping Post Going Around. Tumblr, 2012. Web.
Pearson, Roberta. "'Good Old Index,' or, The Mystery of the Infinite Archive." Sherlock and Transmedia Fandom: Essays on the BBC Series. Eds. Louisa Ellen Stein and Kristina Busse. Jefferson, NC: McFarland, 2012. 150–164. Print.
Pearson, Roberta. "Bachies, Bardies, Trekkies, and Sherlockians." Fandom: Identities and Communities in a Mediated World. Eds. Jonathan Gray, et al. New York: New York University Press, 2007. 98–109. Print.
_____. "'It's always 1895': Sherlock Holmes in Cyberspace." Trash Aesthetics: Popular Culture and Its Audience. Eds. Deborah Cartmell, et al. London: Pluto Press, 1997. 143–161. Print.
Penley, Constance. Nasa/Trek: Popular Science and Sex in America. London: Verso, 1997. Print.
Polasek, Ashley D. "Winning 'The Grand Game': Sherlock and the Fragmentation of Fan Discourse." Sherlock and Transmedia Fandom: Essays on the BBC Series. Eds. Louisa Ellen Stein and Kristina Busse. Jefferson, NC: McFarland, 2012. 41–53. Print.
Ritchie, Guy, dir. Sherlock Holmes. Warner Bros./Village Roadshow Pictures/Silver Pictures, 2009. Film.
_____. Sherlock Holmes—The Official Trailer. Warner Bros., 2009. Film trailer.
_____. Sherlock Holmes: A Game of Shadows. Warner Bros./Village Roadshow Pictures/Silver Pictures, 2011. Film.
"Robert Downey Jr. y Jude Law." Interview in Madrid on occasion of movie premiere, January 2010. Yahoo!Cine. Yahoo Espana, Nd. Web.
Rohase, Piercy. My Dearest Holmes. Charleston: BookSurge, 1988. Print.
Roz T. "Film Review: Sherlock Holmes—A Game of Shadows." The Flaneur, 26 June 2012. Web.
Scott, Suzanne. Revenge of the Fanboy: Convergence Culture and the Politics of Incorporation. Dissertation, University of Southern California, 2011. Web.
Sedgwick, Eve. Between Men: English Literature and Male Homosocial Desire. New York: Columbia University Press, 1985. Print.
Simone, Gail, et al. Women in Refrigerators. 1999. Web.
The Graham Norton Show, Season 10, Episode 8. BBC One. London. 16 Dec. 2011. Television.
The-randomist. GIFS v 2.0—Jude Law and Robert Downey Jr. LJ, 3 Feb. 2010. Web.
Thomas, Kayley. "'Bromance Is so Passé': Robert Downey, Jr.'s Queer Paratexts." Sherlock Holmes for the 21st Century: Essays on New Adaptations. Ed. Porter, Lynette. Jefferson, NC: McFarland, 2012. 35–47. Print.
Townsend, Larry. The Sexual Adventures of Sherlock Holmes. New York: Masquerade Books, 1993. Print.
TW_319988. Robert Downey Jesus and Hobo Law Acting All Married on Graham Norton + Bonus Eddie Izzard! LJ, 17 Dec. 2011. Web.
Whitty, Stephen. "'Sherlock Holmes: A Game of Shadows': A Loud, if Handsomely Produced, Adventure." The Star Ledger/NJ.com, 16 Dec. 2011. Web.
Wilder, Billy, dir. Some Like It Hot. Ashton Productions/The Mirisch Corporation, 1959. Film.
_____. The Private Life of Sherlock Holmes. Mirisch Production Company, 1970. Film.

Sherlocked
Homosociality and (A)Sexuality
Karma Waltonen

"You don't have a girlfriend, then?"—*Sherlock* "A Study in Pink"

In one of his famous "New Rules" segments, Bill Maher recently noted, "[Sir Arthur Conan Doyle] was a surgeon, and he created Sherlock Holmes and Dr. Watson. So he was not only smart, he was way ahead of his time on gay marriage" (*Real Time with Bill Maher* 2013).

The relationship between Holmes and Watson is sometimes imagined as superhero to sidekick, sometimes as brilliant mind to mere assistant, but in contemporary imagination, usually as a joining of two best friends. One of our newest iterations of the characters, BBC's *Sherlock*, emphasizes the romance in this bromance for comic effect. The characters often end up on what seem like dates, deal with the discomfort of wanting to deny assumptions of their homosexuality while not coming off as homophobic, and depend on each other, domestically, as partners do.

The series contrasts playful allusions to the characters' possible homosexuality with clearly homosexual characters and establishes that both men can and do attract women, and that Watson evidently can return those feelings. While the series rejects a homosexual reading, numerous moments invite an *asexual* reading for Holmes, which this essay will explore in some detail, as it is the most likely classification for the BBC Sherlock Holmes. However, our detective's true yearnings remain one of the great mysteries of the series—all we know for sure is that his code name (given by a decidedly biased Moriarty) is The Virgin. This uncertainty allows for the series to play with Holmes and Watson, and this play always stresses their extraordinary (if nonsexual) attachment to each other. The strong attachment actually counters Eve Sedgwick's traditional notion of homosociality (which states that in heteronormative societies, like Western countries in the Victorian era, women are used to reinforce the bonds between men, both strengthening the male relationship and refuting any assumption of impropriety).[1] As demonstrated by the following analysis of the major characters, in *Sherlock*, *every* relationship, with men or women, family or strangers, friends or foes, strengthens the homosocial (and asexual) link between our heroes.

A Little Bit of History

An analysis of homosociality or non-normative sexuality on television should consider TV history. (I will not repeat the whole history of the gay movement on TV here, though I will say that both Ron Becker [2006] and Matthew A. Henry [2012] do wonderful jobs with just that in their respective books.) In *Gay TV and Straight America*, Becker characterizes the 1990s as "a period in which America became increasingly preoccupied by debates over diversity, social fragmentation, and cultural relativism" (4). This period, according to Becker, led to what he calls *straight panic*:

> In the early 1990s, however, multiculturalism helped intensify fears that such developments were undermining faith in the value and/or possibility of a unified American identity. More broadly, then, *straight panic* refers to the anxiety felt by mainstream America and Americans confronting a social landscape where monoculturalism seemed maligned and difference prized. Members of a naïve mainstream ... struggled to make sense of their newly exposed social positions and tried to navigate a culture where racial and gender as well as sexual identities mattered [4 original emphasis].

The anxiety Becker discusses might best be understood in one of the great catchphrases of the 1990s, from the GLAAD winning episode of *Seinfeld*, "The Outing" (1993). The comedy situation in the episode is predicated on two potential misunderstandings—the male characters' fears that they might be read as gay and the fear that, if they protest too strongly, they will be read as homophobic. Thus, their protestations end with "not that there's anything wrong with that."

Sherlock premiered nearly twenty years later. There are still some texts on TV whose comedy is based on the 'they might think I'm gay' anxiety, but these tend to be aimed at less sophisticated audiences. Their "not that there's anything wrong with that" moments are often perfunctory—done merely as a nod to political correctness—to avoid letters—rather than as in the original, which satirized both homophobia and political correctness.

Becker notes, concerning straight panic: "Sedgwick, of course, argues that the inherently unstable boundary [between heterosexual and homosexual] is exploited by a patriarchal social system, generating an ever-present fear of being labeled homosexual[,] which structures and disciplines normative gender and sexual identities" (22). As we watch Holmes and Watson react to being labeled gay by various members of their community, we might well ask if this is true any longer. Do the characters *fear* this gay label?

Holmes and Watson, like many other characters on prime time TV, live in a metropolitan world with homosexual neighbors, coworkers, and so on. However, it is rare to have a non-heterosexual character in a leading role on prime time. Additionally, the *physical* expression of same-sex desire, especially between men, is usually absent.[2] That is, our gay characters, especially if they are men, are gay in name only, at least on the visible screen.[3]

John Watson

"You're a great boyfriend. And Sherlock Holmes is a very lucky man."
—*Sherlock* "A Scandal in Belgravia"

John Watson must contend with many observations on his relationship with Sherlock. People are either commenting on his friendship—remarking that Sherlock is incapable of having friends and warning Watson away (or, in Mycroft's case, trying to exploit the friendship)—or assuming that the friendship is in fact more. Mrs. Hudson first makes the mistake when showing them what will be their apartment, wondering "if [they'll] be needing two bedrooms"; John's answer is to say that of course they will (*Sherlock* "Study"). Mrs. Hudson then only seeks to reassure him that she understands the modern world—that he need not fear being out to her. He does not correct her then or when, a bit later, she compares her marriage to his relationship with Sherlock: "My husband was just the same" (*Sherlock* "Study"). It is only two years after Sherlock's death, when John thinks he is ready to move on, that he attempts to correct her again (*Sherlock* "The Empty Hearse"). John also does not correct when (a) Mycroft asks, "Might we expect a happy announcement by the end of the week?" (*Sherlock* "Study"); (b) Mrs. Hudson asks if the roommates have "had a little domestic" (*Sherlock* "The Great Game"); and (c) when Mycroft snottily refers to them being "*pals*," when noting that John slept on his date's couch instead of in her bed the night before (*Sherlock* "Game").

When Sherlock and John are investigating the Hound, the barman apologizes for not being able to provide them with a double room. Watson starts to say, "we're not..." but gives up. When asked if his partner is a "snorer," he does not bother adjusting the misapprehension (*Sherlock* "The Hounds of Baskerville"). By this point, being mistaken for gay is a running gag, but John's discomfort does not seem all that uncomfortable. Here, does he begin a correction because he does not want to be seen as gay or because he wants to reassure the barman that they have not been inconvenienced? (Or both?)

In this same episode, John flirts with a woman to get information for Sherlock. The woman's horror at being used is compounded when she learns that John is Sherlock's "live-in PA"—"live-in" is the part of the revelation she repeats aloud before telling John to talk to (read: flirt with) the *man* who has just revealed the information (*Sherlock* "Hounds").

In the first episode, John is mistaken as Sherlock's partner several times; it is only after being scared by Sherlock's enemy (Mycroft) and being abandoned by Sherlock at the crime scene that John finally corrects someone firmly, stating, "I'm not his date" twice to the restaurant owner, who wants to bring them a romantic candle. This moment could be read as John being scared of being seen as gay, but it might be that John is merely acting out of fear about his relationship with Sherlock overall—their friendship is not yet solidified. In this scene, John is still relying on his cane rather than on Sherlock (*Sherlock* "Study").

Right after this denial, John tries to establish whether Sherlock is gay, straight, or other. He is unable to do so. A few episodes later, when confronted with Sherlock's confusing response to The Woman, he asks Mrs. Hudson if Sherlock has ever even had a relationship; he wonders how those who are closest to him do not know (*Sherlock* "Scandal").

John is just not worried enough about being labeled gay to consistently deny it. (Sherlock never troubles himself to.) When John takes exception to being given the nickname "confirmed bachelor" in the papers, we laugh at the running joke, but this might be less evidence of gay panic and more evidence that John would rather have a better nickname or one that would not give him trouble when trying to "get off" with women (*Sherlock* "The Reichenbach Fall").

Perhaps John does not succumb to straight panic because society has changed in the last two decades or because he is still able to get dates. Alternatively, perhaps it is because John's heterosexuality is confirmed in the show both by his occasional verbal denials and by his dates, culminating in his marriage.

This confirmation reminds me of the 2000 film *The Contender*. A female politician is accused of having a sexual escapade in her youth. She refuses to comment, as she maintains that a male politician would not be subjected to having to answer questions about whether he had adventures during his college years. The public never learns whether the allegation is true. This lesson on the sexual double standard is somewhat undercut, however, by the revelation of her innocence *to the audience* at the end of the movie (Lurie).

John's dates serve in much the same way—they reassure the audience—if not the other characters[4]—that John is a confirmed heterosexual. They also function as women often do in homosocial relationships. Sedgwick posits that women cement the bonds between men, allowing them to be close without being read as gay. When Sherlock wants to "get some air" with John, but John puts him off for a date, Sherlock crashes it. It is difficult to tell, as the night goes on, whether Sarah or Sherlock is the third wheel. It is clear, though, that, in Sherlock's mind, Sarah is a pretense that allows Sherlock to go to the circus with John (*Sherlock* "The Blind Banker").

Molly is similarly used by Moriarty to get closer to Sherlock. Moriarty pretends to date her, but the twist is that he also pretends (perhaps pretends) to be gay. Thus, Moriarty uses Molly as his beard *in a performance as a beard* to get Sherlock's attention and to deflect it at the same time (*Sherlock* "Game").

Molly might be used as a figurative beard, but Mary is introduced to us in conjunction with John's literal mustache. While one might expect Mary to serve as a wedge between the men (the series emphasizes the danger with the repetition of "the end of an era" in the wedding episode), she and Sherlock bond over their antipathy to John's facial hair (*Sherlock* "Hearse"). Unlike other women John has been with, Mary actively encourages the bond between the men rather than resenting their closeness, even though Sherlock spoils her marriage proposal from John (*Sherlock* "Hearse").

Surprisingly, Sherlock serves much the same purpose for Mary and John's relationship, as he seeks to keep them together when Mary's lies are revealed. His forcing them to confront the problem, his telling John that Mary can indeed be trusted, and his later sacrifice for Mary's secrets, along with his earlier intervention with Mary's suitor/friend, show that he keeps his "first and last vow"—to "always be there" for both of them and their baby (*Sherlock* "The Sign of Three"). A friend and best man's support of a heterosexual relationship is considered so common that it does not have a 'homosocial'-esque moniker. However, Sherlock does not participate in common interpersonal relationships. The viewers expect him to be threatened by Mary and to attempt to subvert this relationship as he had subverted the others.

However, Mary and Sherlock are alike—both of them will scheme to keep John happy, which means "[keeping] him in trouble" (*Sherlock* "The Last Vow"). They are, much to John's initial dismay, both psychopaths—John is "abnormally attracted to dangerous situations and people" (*Sherlock* "Vow"). The relationship between the three is abnormal as well, and the show mines it for both comedic and emotional effect. At the wedding, when Sherlock tells the couple that they are to be parents, he asserts himself as their child in a joke. His continual hints that John should name the baby Sherlock (which, we are told, is a girl's name) further solidify his position within the family unit. At the wedding, though, the hint of potential polyamory is cut short when they decide not to dance together: "There are limits." Mary learns, though, that Sherlock taught John how to waltz "behind closed curtains" (*Sherlock* "Sign").

The world of John and Sherlock is not completely without evidence of straight panic, however. Kitty Reilly, when cornering Sherlock, thinks his relationship with John is newsworthy: "You and John Watson, just platonic? Can I put you down for a 'no' there...?" Sherlock, true to form, does not answer. Her next line reveals that being labeled gay is still considered non-normative—she is threatening the men: "There's all sorts of gossip in the press about you. Sooner or later, you're going to need someone on your side. Someone to set the record *straight*." Sherlock is not worried about this—it is Kitty's other story—the one about him being a fraud—that finally gets his attention and causes some panic (*Sherlock* "Reichenbach").

Still, the way the characters and the series play with the line between homosocial and homosexual allows us to think about both our society and their relationship.[5] For example, there is John's joke at the end of "The Great Game": "I'm glad no one saw that.... You—ripping my clothes off in a darkened swimming pool. People might talk." This moment reveals a lot about where we are in terms of gay acceptance. The men laugh about anxiety over being read as gay, although we know they do not feel this anxiety very keenly. Moreover, the laughter is necessary to cut an emotional moment for them, as Sherlock was thanking John for being willing to sacrifice himself. Heartfelt moments are difficult for Sherlock, and thus, the safety of a joke—even a "gay" one—allows both men to feel comfortable.

Sherlock Holmes

"Sex doesn't alarm me."
"How would you know?"
—*Sherlock* "Scandal"

It seems fitting that the original Sherlock Holmes appeared at around the same time the word "asexual" began to be applied to human sexuality.[6]

However, it is only recently that "asexuality" has been seen as an identity. In fact, the OED still refers to this word as a condition of abstinence, not yet as an identity. Asexuality is a sexual orientation in which the subject does not experience sexual desire for other people. The subject can, however, develop the same emotional attachments to other people as non-asexuals do. That is, friendships and love relationships can arise, but the asexual individual does not experience sexual attraction to strangers or partners.

At first, one might disqualify BBC's Sherlock as an asexual because of the claim of emotional "normalcy" inherent in the definition—Sherlock, as we know, has problems knowing or caring when he is being insensitive; he has problems making and maintaining familial relationships and friendships. However, we should remember that Sherlock could be both socially inept/narcissistic *and* asexual. That is, Sherlock would be capable of *his* usual emotional attachments, but without the desire to have sex with another person.

Asexuality would explain why Sherlock is a virgin.[7] After all, Sherlock is not above giving into temptation, especially when bored (as evidenced by his drug addiction). However, if sex has never been a temptation, then we would understand exactly why he has not had it. Why would Sherlock do something he does not want to? While Sherlock might romantically love "The Woman," there is no evidence that he is sexually attracted to her. *Her* pulse races; *her* pupils dilate. We have no proof of any such passion from him; we only know that he seems emotionally or intellectually drawn to her (*Sherlock* "Scandal"). This asexuality might explain why girlfriends (and boyfriends) are not "[his] area" and why he is "married to" his work (*Sherlock* "Study").

The asexuality theory is supported by various statements made by the show's creators, who use the word. As Carlen Lavigne, in "The Noble Bachelor and the Crooked Man: Subtext and Sexuality in the BBC's *Sherlock*," argues, "the writers on the series all agreed on Holmes' asexuality as overtly established within the narratives" (15). However, as asexuality is still not very well understood in culture, it is possible that the creators are using the word in a vernacular sense—meaning not quite hetero—not quite homo—too off the scale of human normal human relationships to fit. (It is also likely that the creators know exactly what the word means, but that some members of the public are likely to misunderstand it—thus, they might assume that the vernacular definition is what the creators intended. As the following analysis argues for a more nuanced understanding of Sherlock's asexuality, I hope the creators intended the non-vernacular definition.)

The vernacular obscures two central facts—one about Sherlock and one about asexuals. Sherlock is assumed to be outside the realm of normal human relationships by some people because he is strange. It is assumed that he does not have feelings, morals, or friends. In his darker moments, he gives into those assumptions too. When he is frightened, in "The Hounds of Baskerville," for example, he tells John, "I don't have any friends." The next day, in an attempt to make up, he says, "Listen, what I said before, John, I meant it. I don't have friends. I've just got one" (*Sherlock* "Hounds").

This moment illustrates not only his close relationship to John, but also a modicum of emotional intelligence. Although Sherlock's friends often have to tell him how to behave in public, he does realize when he hurts those who care about him, and, without prompting, he will try to put things right.[8]

The other issue that is often misunderstood concerns a central fact about asexuality. Asexuality is not mutually exclusive with being hetero-, homo-, or bi-. That is, many asexuals still form romantic feelings and partnerships and still have preferences for the type of people they partner with. Because sexuality is not part of the relationship, however, a hetero-preference, for example, is described as being hetero-romantic, hetero-asexual, and so on. Thus, even if we decide that Sherlock is asexual, we are still left to ponder whether he is hetero-romantic, homo-romantic, or bi-romantic.

As previously noted, Sherlock, unlike John, never corrects people when they presume that the Watson/Holmes relationship is romantic. This could be read as Sherlock not caring what other people think, although Sherlock loves correcting people. One conversation between Holmes and Watson, however, deserves a close look:

> WATSON: You don't have a girlfriend, then?
> HOLMES: Girlfriend? No, not really my area.
> WATSON: All right ... Do you have a boyfriend? Which is fine, by the way.
> HOLMES: I know it's fine.
> WATSON: So you got a boyfriend?
> HOLMES: No.
> WATSON: Right. Okay. You're unattached. Like me. Fine. Good.
> HOLMES: John, erm ... I think you should know that I consider myself married to my work, and while I'm flattered by your interest, I'm really not looking for any...
> WATSON: No. I'm ... not asking. No. I'm just saying, it's all fine.
> HOLMES: Good. Thank you [*Sherlock* "Study"].

Here, in the very beginning of the friendship, Sherlock misreads John's questions as a come-on. His attempt at deflection is one of the traditional codes for non-normative sexuality—"I'm married to my work"—an old explanation for why one might not be in a heterosexual marriage/relationship is now code for why one might not be in a sexual one.

The discussion also includes a variant of the "not that there's anything wrong with that" statement on both their parts, although it is not used for comic effect. Both men are serious in their assertions that there is not anything wrong with it—both men, after all, have gay siblings. Yet as we parse Sherlock's words, we want to tease out further meaning. Is he saying that women are not his area, but a homo-romantic relationship might be? Is he saying that relationships, since they presume sexuality, simply are not his area? Whatever the case, Sherlock and John and the show are signaling that all possibilities are fine.

It is also possible in this moment that Sherlock is not aware of his identity as asexual. People come to understand their sexual identities at various points in their lives. As asexuality is almost completely ignored by the culture,[9] it's possible that it is not on the radar for him—that he actually sees himself as wedded to his work—and has not established an identity for himself yet, especially if he considers the need to do so inconsequential.

Social scientists and psychologists working on asexuality have difficulty with asexuality as well. One recent article, "Theoretical Issues in the Studies of Asexuality" (2011), by CJ DeLuzio Chasin, discusses, for example, the problem researchers have with asexuals who do not consider asexuality to be mutually exclusive with other identifications (though researchers' questionnaires often do). As DeLuzio Chasin notes,

> This distinction between the sexual and the romantic appears to be featured prominently in the self-produced asexual materials, discourses, and discussions that self-identified asexual people are likely to have encountered. It is in this context where identity labels such as demisexual, hyposexual, romantic, and aromantic asexual, hyporomantic, straight -A, gay -A, bi -A, gray -A, etc. take on meanings, as people attempt to position themselves not only according to the genders of people to whom they experience attraction, but also according to the degrees to which (and the ways in which) they do so [715].

Sherlock is nothing if not scientific. Since science is lagging behind how actual asexuals see themselves, Sherlock might have some catching up to do, especially since he is hardly likely to be part of a consciousness-raising asexual community due to his asocial nature (one senses that Sherlock has never been part of a group due to his independence, social awkwardness, and disdain for lower intellects).

It is significant, though, that Sherlock misreads John in this moment.

Sherlock's talent is reading clues and reading people, though he tends to read them based on assumptions of typical behavior rather than based on an actual understanding of individual psychology. Sherlock is rarely wrong. The fact that his mistakes all involve issues of sexuality certainly point toward this being a problem for him—is this because he has a blind spot in this area? An inability to empathize based on his asexuality (acknowledged or otherwise)? This lack of empathy could certainly be explained by asexuality—if Sherlock does not experience desire as the majority of the population does, then he would naturally have problems truly understanding it in all of its complexity.

In addition to misreading John's inquiry about a boyfriend, Sherlock's mistake in his initial reading of John is not knowing that John's estranged sibling is a woman (*Sherlock* "Study"). He does not notice Moriarty for what he is on first meeting. Moriarty seems only to be another example of Molly's poor choices in men. Here, Sherlock is able to catch that Moriarty is gay, but not that Moriarty has put on an over the top gay act *for him* (*Sherlock* "Game"). Sherlock is also unable to read The Woman when she presents herself to him in the nude (although certainly that decision should tell him a great deal about her). When she comes to him later, as the damsel in distress, he falls completely for her act and puts himself in the role of her prince without a second thought. Perhaps this is because she manages to wrap herself in his bed, his clothes, thus literally throwing him off the scent (*Sherlock* "Scandal").

Arguably, his other mistakes are due to his complicated feelings for John. Although there are clues, including the perfume he later uses to tell John about Mary's duplicity, he does not put them together until he finds her in Magnussen's office. Nor does he believe that she will fire her weapon. There is also a significant miscalculation with Magnussen. Sherlock believes he has provided Magnussen with a pressure point—his drug addiction—while Magnussen knows Sherlock's real pressure point—John—the whole time (*Sherlock* "Vow").

The Woman and Moriarty

"Suddenly, I'm Mr. Sex."
—*Sherlock* "Reichenbach"

No analysis of Sherlock's sexuality could be complete without considering Irene Adler, The Woman. As previously mentioned, Irene throws Sherlock off his game, proving herself to be as capable of fooling him as Moriarty is—both are able to deceive Sherlock, to outmaneuver him almost into checkmate.

Sherlock is clearly not bored in Irene's presence, making her special among both women and men. In addition, even though she aligns herself with Moriarty, proving herself a threat to both him and the empire, he still saves her. This could be because he knows she could never destroy him—he has both beaten her and she is too attached to really hurt him. Yet his saving her is evidence that he is sentimentally attached too.

While Sherlock may not be *sexually* attracted to Irene, it is entirely possible that he is *romantically* drawn to her, that he sees her as a kindred spirit—smart, controlling, etc. His pupils do not dilate when she asks him to dinner, but that does not mean he does not want to spend time with her. The problem, besides her desire for sex, would be his inability to trust her (*Sherlock* "Scandal").

Evidence of this being a hetero-romantic relationship is also found in the bonus feature on the DVD. Benedict Cumberbatch, in an interview, says that Sherlock meets "one of his deadliest enemies—in the shape of love." The director, Paul McGuigan, says of the scene where Sherlock describes the boomerang accident: it's "part of the love story" ("Sherlock Uncovered").

Of course, Sherlock is derisive of romance when he chides Irene for having feelings for him: "I've always assumed that love is a dangerous disadvantage. *Thank* you for the final proof" (*Sherlock* "Scandal").[10] However, his decision to keep her ring tone and her phone, along with his last telling utterance to himself of her moniker, with the emphasis on the definite article ("*The* Woman"), certainly provides evidence of his sentimental—and romantic—attachment to her (*Sherlock* "Scandal").

It is worth noting that The Woman is paralleled to Moriarty in several ways. Both evidence attraction to Sherlock, though Moriarty might claim that slipping Sherlock his number was a gay ruse (pun intended).[11] They evidently discuss Sherlock and his sexuality, as Irene tells Sherlock that Moriarty calls him The Virgin (*Sherlock* "Scandal"). As mentioned previously, they are both able to thwart Sherlock and are both able to perform in front of him without being detected. They are both admired by Sherlock for their intelligence. They both give Sherlock codes with their bodies. They both interest him. They are both fun to play with, even if they do not play fairly.

They are both Sherlock's equals—both made for him.[12] John makes this clear when, after listening to Sherlock and Irene banter for a while, he gives them suggestions for baby names (*Sherlock* "Scandal"). Moriarty is Sherlock's arch criminal. Jim's lie—that Sherlock created a master criminal—a consulting criminal to match a master sleuth—a consulting detective—is believable because of the idea of balance. Jim wants Sherlock to be his equal and seems genuinely disappointed when he has beaten him. Jim wants them to be equally intelligent. He is also upset that Sherlock might be "on the side of the angels." At the end of Jim's life, when Sherlock is able to convince him that they are the same, that while he is not a criminal, he is also not an angel, and that they are equal, Jim is happy to have found his match (*Sherlock* "Reichenbach").

Our criminals are also matched with each other—and with Sherlock—in that their sexualities are in question.[13] Moriarty asks Sherlock if he enjoyed his gay act, but we are never certain if his performance *was* an act. His only visible moment of possible heterosexuality is when he subjects a guard to having to put her hand in his pocket, yet this is likely just a power play (*Sherlock* "Reichenbach"). Perhaps it is only because we only see Moriarty working, but he also seems to be married to his work—and his work here is Sherlock. After their initial meeting, when he slips him his number, Moriarty calls Sherlock—through a kidnapped woman. The first words we have with Moriarty being Moriarty are "Hello, sexy." Moreover, the last body that Moriarty takes in this fashion before revealing himself is notably John's (*Sherlock* "Game").

The Woman is also outside the realm of normative sexuality due to her profession. She is a dominatrix, but we do not actually know if that is what turns her on since what she might do for money might not be what gives her pleasure in intimacy. That is, while she knows what other people like (as she consistently reminds us), we can never be certain about her.

And while she has an attraction to Sherlock—she is sherlocked—she is also a professed lesbian. This is revealed to John as they discuss the love triangle they find themselves in:

> IRENE: Are you jealous?
> JOHN: We're not a couple.
> IRENE: Yes, you are....
> JOHN: Who ... who the hell knows about Sherlock Holmes, but—for the record—if anyone out there still cares, I'm not actually gay.
> IRENE: Well, I *am*. Look at us both [*Sherlock* "Scandal"].

Irene implies that sexual identity becomes especially complicated when Sherlock is concerned. John is straight, yet the homosocial bond between the two men is strong enough to elicit jealousy in John when Irene enters Sherlock's life. Irene is homosexual, yet desires Sherlock. The evidence above indicates that Sherlock, who overhears this conversation, is a *bi*-romantic asexual, as he is strongly, if not sexually, attracted to them both.

Conclusion: "The story of two men and their frankly ridiculous adventures"[14]

"He's Sherlock. How will we ever knows what goes on in that funny old head?"
—*Sherlock* "Scandal"

Every discussion of Sherlock's relationships comes back to John because John is Sherlock's central relationship. Even The Woman, in declaring her affections for Sherlock, acknowledges John's importance. Though she is dangerous to Sherlock, almost beating him, she does not shake him as much as the Hound manages to do for a moment in the next episode when Sherlock fears he cannot trust his perception anymore—she does not make his pulse race or alter his senses. Sherlock's speech to her as he reveals that he has unlocked her code also reveals something about himself in that moment: he's thinking about John and what John thinks of him. The speech is for both Irene's and John's benefit: "I imagine John Watson thinks love's a mystery to me, but the chemistry is incredibly simple, and very destructive" (*Sherlock* "Scandal").

In the rare moments when Sherlock tries to work without John, he flounders. Even though Sherlock attempts to praise Molly by saying Moriarty was wrong to miss that she "was the person who mattered the most," when she attempts to fill John's role, she is rewarded by being called John's name (*Sherlock* "Hearse").

While John is unambiguously straight, his love for Sherlock is also unambiguous. He is his best friend. John becomes his partner in work, his "live-in PA," his confidant. At first, he is a go-between for Sherlock and his brother, but we soon realize that John is closer and more loyal to Sherlock than Mycroft has been or ever shall be.

Sherlock's feelings for John may be more complex. Although Sherlock tells John he's not interested in a relationship on their first day together, he later reveals that he's not above considering their time together a date:

> HOLMES: I need to get some air—we're going out tonight.
> WATSON: Actually, I've got a date.
> HOLMES: What?
> WATSON: It's where two people who like each other go out and have fun?
> HOLMES: That's what I was suggesting [*Sherlock* "Banker"].

His relationship with John, necessarily asexual due to John's heterosexuality, could be exactly what Sherlock wants and needs in a partner. Perhaps that is why he never corrects anyone who assumes they are together.

When, at the end of the second season, Moriarty threatens Sherlock's "friends," Sherlock responds with a concerned, "John!?" Here, Sherlock ignores the "s" on the word. His friend*s* are in danger, but it is John who matters. It is John whom he calls at the end, to say goodbye to, to give a false confession to, in the hopes that it will provide some form of posthumous protection. And, at the graveyard, it is John he is watching (*Sherlock* "Reichenbach"). Each theory about how Sherlock escaped the roof needs John as a witness—each scenario is in fact constructed for John, as John's grief—real and raw—is what will sell the story (*Sherlock* "Hearse"). When Sherlock is shot, Moriarty encourages him to die, mockingly, listing the people who will be sad. It is John's name that snaps our hero's eyes open—that brings him the will to live. After the shooting, it is John he is protecting by not identifying the shooter. When he shoots someone later, it is to protect one of John's pressure points, Mary. As Magnussen says, "Look how you care about John Watson—your damsel in distress" (*Sherlock* "Vow").

We know for sure that this relationship is homosocial, not mutually homosexual. Whether in Sherlock's heart it is merely homosocial or homoromantic/bi-romantic is still a relative mystery, though, after an analysis of the clues, it seems elementary that Sherlock is one of the many variations of asexuals.

The series depends on Sherlock being able to read the clues around him—on being able to amaze us with his skills of deduction. The series also depends on us not always being able to read Sherlock. Our detective—like his great enemies—is hard to read. He has to be—to make us more impressed with his abilities. All we know is that the friendship he has with John defines them both. So much so that Sherlock even uses John to define himself: "How would you describe me, John? Resourceful? Dynamic? *Enigmatic?*" (*Sherlock* "Banker," emphasis mine).

Not that there's anything wrong with that.

Notes

1. While Sedgwick's argument analyzed the Victorian era, it is routinely applied to our own, as Ron Becker's statement later in the paper illustrates.
2. *Modern Family* is an example—while the show is praised for bringing a gay couple into mainstream living rooms, cultural critics note that the couple's plot lines are not ever about sex, while sex is explored frequently in the plotlines of the heterosexual couples on the show.
3. It should be noted that while I work on both British and American popular culture, I am usually watching from an American TV set, which means that the reactions I see in the news to what is on television tend to be American. However, the apparent newsworthiness of the first gay

kiss on *The Archers* in 2004 illustrates that reactions might not be so very different across the pond.

    4. Even when he's getting married, Mrs. Hudson is not convinced that he has not been in a homosexual relationship with Sherlock, as evidenced by her outburst: "So soon after Sherlock?!" ("Hearse").

    5. In fact, the series has a nod to a type of fan-fiction called slash fiction, which features homosexual relationships, usually between leading males, in one of The Empty Hearse Club's members' theory of how Sherlock escaped death—ending in a kiss between Sherlock and Moriarty ("Vow").

    6. According to the OED. It should be noted that the earliest recorded uses referred to the relative asexuality of nuns and women in comparison to secular people and men, respectively.

    7. At least, in the beginning of the series. It is possible he had sex with Janine when posing as her boyfriend. If that is the case, though, then sex was part of a character he played rather than the product of desire.

    8. He also understands enough about people to manipulate Molly when he needs her help in the lab and to fake a relationship with Janine.

    9. There is almost nothing in scientific literature and even less in literary scholarship on asexuality.

    10. Sherlock exploits this disadvantage with Janine, believing that her loving him and thus trusting him is "[human] error" ("Vow").

    11. We might wonder: would some of the mayhem have been avoided if Sherlock had given Jim a call? ("Game").

    12. Interestingly, although Sherlock says Magnussen is "the most dangerous man," they are not paralleled as much as Sherlock is with his other foes. They both have mind palaces, both attempt to find weaknesses to exploit, and are both arrogant, but they do not have the affinity seen with Sherlock's other villains ("Vow").

    13. At first, it might seem that Magnussen also shares sexual "perversions," as he licks the face of a victim, but his other ways of establishing dominance—territorial pissing, washing his hands in Sherlock's drinking water, face/eye flicking, and so on—are not sexualized.

    14. "The Sign of Three."

Works Cited

Becker, Ron. *Gay TV and Straight America*. New Brunswick: Rutgers University Press, 2006. Print.
"The Blind Banker." *Sherlock: Season 1*. Dir. Euros Lyn. BBC, 2010. DVD.
DeLuzio Chasin, CJ. "Theoretical Issues in the Study of Asexuality." *Archives of Sexual Behavior* 40 (2011): 713–723. Print.
"The Empty Hearse." *Sherlock: Season 2*. Dir. Jeremy Lovering. BBC, 2014. DVD.
"The Great Game." *Sherlock: Season 1*. Dir. Paul McGuigan. BBC, 2010. DVD.
Henry, Matthew A. *The Simpsons, Satire, and American Culture*. New York: Palgrave Macmillan, 2012. Print.
"The Hounds of Baskerville." *Sherlock: Season 2*. Dir. Paul McGuigan. BBC, 2012. DVD.
"His Last Vow." *Sherlock: Season 3*. Dir. Nick Hurran. BBC, 2014. DVD.
Lavigne, Carlen. "The Noble Bachelor and the Crooked Man: Subtext and Sexuality in the BBC's *Sherlock*." *Sherlock Holmes for the 21st Century: Essays on New Adaptations*. Ed. Lynnette Porter. Jefferson, NC: McFarland, 2012. 13–23. Print.
Lurie, Rod, dir. *The Contender*. DreamWorks, 2000. Film.
OED. "asexual, adj." OED Online. September 2013. Oxford University Press. 2 December 2013 http://www.oed.com/view/Entry/11430.
_____. "asexuality, n." OED Online. September 2013. Oxford University Press. 2 December 2013 http://www.oed.com/view/Entry/11431.
"The Outing." *Seinfeld*. NBC. 11 February 1993. Television.

Real Time with Bill Maher. HBO. 19 July 2013. Television.
"The Reichenbach Fall." *Sherlock: Season 2*. Dir. Toby Haynes. BBC, 2012. DVD.
"A Scandal in Belgravia." *Sherlock: Season 2*. Dir. Paul McGuigan. BBC, 2012. DVD.
Sedgwick, Eve Kosofsky. *Between Men: English Literature and Male Homosocial Desire*. New York: Columbia University Press, 1985. Print.
"Sherlock Uncovered." *Sherlock: Season 2*. Special Feature. BBC, 2012. DVD. Disc 2.
"The Sign of Three." *Sherlock: Season 3*. Dir. Colm McCarthy. BBC, 2014. DVD.
"A Study in Pink." *Sherlock: Season 1*. Dir. Paul McGuigan. BBC, 2010. DVD.

The Veneration of Violation in *Sherlock*

Zea Miller

> HOLMES: Who would sponsor a serial killer?
> TAXI DRIVER: Who would be a fan of Sherlock Holmes?
> —*Sherlock* "A Study in Pink"

For the past few years, there has been an interesting trend in popular culture coalescing around various products and website posts professing *a belief in* Sherlock Holmes. It is not the iconic Sherlock Holmes of yesteryear, some quaint or shadowed yet recognizable image, but always the likeness of the actor Benedict Cumberbatch, who plays the titular character on the BBC's *Sherlock* television series. The trend is most often seen in the form of image memes, posters, and other trinkets plastered with the message, "I believe in Sherlock."[1] Yet, what does such a belief mean? If beliefs are things absent facts, then as to the series and its characters, generally, what nonfactual is there (left) to believe in? Specifically, after you watch Sherlock Holmes kill a man (*Sherlock* "His Last Vow") or torture another as he lay dying, mortally shot by the physician-soldier John Watson (*Sherlock* "A Study in Pink"), what is there to believe in?[2] The series has plainly established that its version of Sherlock Holmes resolves mysteries. There is no need for faith, then, because there is no chance he might stop, midway, and simply quit a case. What, then, of faith in how he treats people, especially women? Do fans believe he will be unkind to Ms. Hudson? Do they believe that he will be cruel to Molly Hooper in order to carry the day? Of all things to believe in, it should be that the protagonists will prevail, but at what cost and to whom?

To the extent that Sherlock Holmes and John Watson are iconic characters who are predisposed not only to be heroes but also to be successful in their pursuits, the ideal audience inescapably forgives or likely forgets what should be the intolerable means and methods the detectives employ to their advantage.³ The success of the BBC television series *Sherlock* is a testimonial to the narrative's sheer masculinist agenda: the roles of women are degrading and their treatment equally so, which no screen time for Irene Adler's tokenism can offset. While structural scholarship on detective narratives might address how such success is entirely dependent upon smooth if formulaic social interaction, it cannot be the case for this series, for the movements of the antisocial Sherlock Holmes, coupled with the relationship-challenged John Watson, forcibly expose the degree to which they operate within a pervasive, patently masculine logocentricity.⁴ So much so that the questions we must ask will tilt away from interrogating the altogether timeless social index in which the iconic detectives operate to the particular one in which this series has been translated.⁵

Set in present-day London, the narrative unobtrusively operates in a society with political and social disapprobation of chauvinism. Yet, if this is true, then what are the forces that protect the masculinist operation of these detectives in a society that should otherwise deny it? How poorly may Holmes and Watson now behave toward or with women and still be venerated by both fans and the narrative's aggrieved characters? What assumptions of impolitic gender roles might the characters recognizably parlay into shtick and stock indexicality without compromising the narrative? How disarmed must the ideal audience of this television series be to forgive and forget egregious male trespass against, censure of, or silencing of the exertion of women's agency? Advancing these questions, this chapter will examine the ways in which the central male characters of the series have interacted with women in their adventures, the ultimate result of which will call into question the very hero worship, or at the least reflexive admiration, the series cultivates.

The Veneration of Sherlockness

From recent television series like the BBC's *Sherlock* and CBS's *Elementary* to the broadly distributed feature films fittingly titled *Sherlock Holmes*, and from critical books to derivative merchandise, it is inescapably plain that the Sherlock Holmes narrative has achieved a fashionable currency in popular culture and has, as would be anticipated, inspired its critics.⁶ The narrative has positively resonated with its international multitudes of fans. When fans venerate the hero, they celebrate the triumphs of the hero, and therefore also approve of the hero's course through the narrative.⁷ Popular detective narratives are constructed to eliminate neutrality: the audience inevitably sides with the detective and his or her projects. Since the BBC television series *Sherlock* transpires within this predefined genre, it is clear to the audience that the mystery will be solved and the genius of the detective validated. What's more, the audience will enjoy the vicarious experience.

The problem is that the enjoyment comes at a cost we often do not recognize, in which audience admiration for a malformed system of justice is coextensive with other structural malformations. Through our enjoyment of the *Sherlock* narratives, we validate the masculinist agenda advanced by the heroes: truth revealed by men who forcibly, if not willfully, obtain access to spaces controlled by women. Moreover, our validation is a product of the veneration the system was built to inspire. Sherlock Holmes and John Watson in *Sherlock* are "men on a mission," while the women in their world exist simply as details. Yet, the plot operates within and through the constriction of a genre. The issue of veneration is not trivial. The genre demands that we approve the means to ends that cause and support the ongoing veneration. The genre, by asking us to admire people who we would not venerate if we personally encountered their actions, inflicts its will upon what would have been ours.

There is a thought experiment that I like to present to my students when discussing the structural aspects of genre: rather than concept mapping or compiling a list of what makes a genre work,[8] we explore what would make one fail, and then adjust such attributes by severity or degree so as to uncover where the breaking points are and what lies on either side.[9] What we find is that no matter the genre, whatever the imposed narratological stresses, there are myriad points whereby the superstructures buttressing generic forms destabilize or collapse altogether. The variations imposed need not be extraordinary to illustrate the case.[10] Take, for example, a focus on detective fiction. Certainly, if an amiable detective were to murder the subject of a mystery every week, then the act would give rise to serious doubt about the coherent stability of the genre,[11] but so, too, would any detective who capriciously decided midway to quit every investigation. After all, who would enjoy watching or reading such a narrative?

The very break from genre conventions is not enough to destabilize a genre presentation; rather, the break must also imperil the ideal audience's desires for the piece. To that end, what would it take for those who do enjoy the BBC's *Sherlock* to stop enjoying it? How far could the variables be pushed before they break? If such variables were already pushed beyond repair, and still the ideal audience enjoys the series, then what does it say about such variables or the audience? What would make the BBC's *Sherlock*, a detective narrative based on the world of Conan Doyle's Sherlock Holmes, fail? Plenty of things, certainly, and while they need not be extraordinary, they also need not be extranarrative. We can just as easily turn to how both the series and characters within it treat female characters as we can to the centralized extralegality that advances the plot. As to the latter, the extralegal quality is endemic to the genre and requires broader exploration than this chapter might realize.[12] As to the former, we simply have to return to the episodes and question how far the characters could have bent until they broke.

Whether or not the latest iterations of the characters within Sherlock Holmes's world can be broken beyond recognition is certainly a matter of perspective. On the one hand, traditionalists would suggest that Conan Doyle's texts defined the realm of possibility. For them, appeals to the stereotypical would carry the day. Their (re)works are set contemporaneously with Conan Doyle's. On the other hand, modernists believe that there can always be room for reinterpretation, or variation, and still others who think that it is acceptable for major deviation from Conan Doyle's characterizations and their works can be set in either the present or the future. It is this camp that must be careful not to terribly distort characters, for one cannot appeal to both a standard and a non-standard: Sherlock Holmes anew cannot simultaneously embody "Sherlockness" while throwing it away. This then is the boundary all camps would recognize: does the icon break? In other words, is the new character Sherlock Homes still recognizable as Sherlock Holmes?[13]

I suggest that the way television and movies realize (that is, to make real) Sherlock Holmes is to appeal to a framework of qualities that I would label Sherlockness. The reincarnatory properties of recurring characters, like those of Sherlock Holmes, can appear self-evident, because generations of fans adore and venerate similar popular British exports, such as Doctor Who and James Bond, who appeal to comparable frameworks for subjective continuity and acceptance. That the qualities of Sherlock Holmes we see in the BBC's *Sherlock* can be read as valid suggests the ease with which an audience comes to recognize the symbolic as a performative quality through time and culture:

> A proper name, when one meets it for the first time, is existentially connected with some percept of other equivalent individual knowledge of the individual it names. It is then, and then only, a genuine index. The next time one meets with it, one regards it as an Icon of that Index. The habitual acquaintance with it having been acquired, it becomes a Symbol whose Interpretant represents it as an Icon of an Index of the individual named [Peirce 2.329].

Thus, an audience who has, through life in a patently western popular culture, become very familiar with Sherlock Holmes perceives a certain symbology composed of essential characterizations through iconographic representation against a lifetime index, replete with historic antecedents, of what it must mean to be Sherlock Holmes. All it takes, then, for a televisual or cinematic audience to believe the portrayal of Sherlock Holmes is a title sequence and a reference alongside stock behaviors, stock appearances, and confirmation bias.[14]

To the extent that the current, ideal audience of the BBC television series *Sherlock* is willing to accept Sherlock Holmes as an antisocial character who is also a self-professed sociopath (*Sherlock* "A Study in Pink"), how far does that tolerance go? This is no rhetorical question. If the ideal audience accepts a sociopathic Holmes unblinkingly, then how likely would it be that such an audience would not expect and eventually dismiss the inevitable project of a sociopath? What fair trade allows the solving of cases to outweigh intolerable behavior? None.[15] In the course of each episode, the audience eventually celebrates the triumphant resolution of the mystery, but to celebrate is also to approve of the means to the ends. Thus, audience complicity in rape culture is to condone taking advantage of female characters. Veneration can never be neutral.

Violation

> *Trigger Warning: Please note that there will be moments in this discussion that both address sexual violation and explore such through examples both real and imagined from the television series.*

I first stumbled upon the notion of rape culture from a blog post about the well-known World War II kiss between a sailor and a nurse.[16] An important lesson from the blog was that what we might see as iconic, prolific, widespread, or even adored can be undermined by an oblique or lateral thought in due course: perhaps what was, was not what was caught on film. It is no stretch to imagine how this very idea can be applied elsewhere and certainly now to *Sherlock*. Clearly, fans love the show (as do I, I must admit). But what are we not seeing? Where are the moments of venerated violation in *Sherlock*?

Discussion must begin with the triumph of Irene Adler, a character of considerable importance to this volume about gender. Adler is introduced in the first episode of the second series, titled "A Scandal in Belgravia," as a formidable woman: a complex, intelligent, dominatrix power broker. In this episode, Sherlock Holmes has been commissioned by an equerry at Buckingham

Palace to secure Adler's cellphone, for there are compromising photos of a royal woman with Ms. Adler stored on it. Later, Sherlock Holmes lies to Adler's assistant, a woman, in order to gain access to her home (to be fair, she is aware of the deception). Adler walks naked into the drawing room where Holmes has been waiting. After a bit of discussion, and with abandoned sexual innuendo, Holmes opens Adler's strongbox, which is rigged to fire a gun upon opening, and thus he intentionally murders (with Adler's complicity) one of the three CIA agents who are also on a mission to retrieve her phone. Soon after, during a pivotal scene, Adler plunges a syringe into Holmes's shoulder, thereby injecting him with a substance that will eventually cause him to lose consciousness. Before he falls lifeless, Adler severely slaps him while demanding that Sherlock Holmes return the stolen cellphone:

>ADLER: Give it to me, now. Give it to me.
>HOLMES: No.
>ADLER: Give it to me.
>HOLMES: No.
>ADLER: Oh, for goodness' sake! Drop it.
>>*At this point, Adler assaults him with a riding crop.*
>>I said drop it.
>>*Holmes drops the phone.*
>>Ah, thank you, dear. Now tell that sweet little posh thing the pictures are safe with me. They're not for blackmail, just for insurance. Besides, I might want to see her again.
>>*Adler now pins him down with the riding crop to prevent him from rising.*
>>Oh, no, no, no, no, no, no. It's been a pleasure. Don't spoil it. This is how I want you to remember me. The woman who beat you [*Sherlock* "A Scandal in Belgravia"].

Let us situate this in clearer terms. As to her cellphone, Adler is the aggrieved party. As to the extralegality of stealing her phone, the disposition of the transgression is both suspect and obvious. Therefore, Adler can make a claim to her property and Holmes can claim its contents, which provides tension in the scene. Adler, as the aggrieved party, attempts to restore equilibrium[17] by demanding the return of the property. When this simple negotiation fails, the situation transitions from a larceny claim to criminal assault. The first party, Adler, drugs Holmes. She initiates a demand that the second party, Holmes, rejects. The command is repeated and so is the denial. Thus, consent is continuously denied to the abusive party by the abused party, whereupon the abusive party continues the abuse until consent can no longer be given. When the abused party attempts to escape, the abusive party suppresses the attempt. Finally, the abusive party instructs the abused party to note the situation in memory as the time when they were abused. This scene is a rape culture narrative.[18] What's more, the villainous trope of emphasizing defeat is venerated as a power play by a strong woman. This is no matter of a woman performing a "masculine" characteristic for power, but a villainous one that should be decried as a genderless wrong. After all, this was not Adler facing Holmes on equal terms and footing; this was no battle of wit and intelligence. Adler played dirty.

This scene was not about the cellphone; if it were, then the plot would be about the restoration or disequilibrium issuing from a transactional matter of acquisition, loss or lack, and fallout, and very likely by gunpoint or guile. The narrative structure could, in such a case, be violent or lead to it, but it would center on the transactional power of property, not violation as power or authoritarian expression of power through violation.[19] This was a narrative of violation, which is certainly a form of violence, and it undermines any favorable power reading of Adler.[20]

To be sure, few things betray gender prejudices in context[21] better than direct, dissimilar, or opposing replacements.[22] Toward that end, and notwithstanding its revulsion, let us imagine—or, by the trigger warning above, not—the roles in the foregoing incident reversed. In this alternate history, Holmes takes a syringe and thrusts it into Adler's shoulder with sinister intent, thereupon injecting her with a substance that will cause her to pass out. When she does not collapse quickly enough, he slaps her and then assaults her with a sexualized riding crop. Meanwhile, he demands she *give it to him* while she repeatedly says *no*. When she tries to rise, he pins her down with the riding crop and says, "This is how I want you to remember me. The man who *beat* you." Would it be venerated? A critic might suggest that, in the actual scene, Adler was only ardently trying to recover her property and livelihood, her dispossessed labor capital if you will, but to that critic another could say Holmes was simply recovering property from a quasi-enemy of the state to support his livelihood. By force or fists, violence or violation, the means and the ends are divorced. The method of recovery drove the scene, not the motive.[23]

The veneration of violation is fostered by the space where Adler can be, and indeed is, triumphant in a non-cerebral, unfair match. To drug is not to outwit, though episodes "A Study in Pink" and "A Scandal in Belgravia" suggest otherwise, in that the win is not a mental feat, but a product of cheating. Adler's triumph over Holmes is not by intellect but by gendered force. How? The concept of emasculation is possible only within a masculinist field of operations. "Losing to a woman" who "hits below the belt" and "plays like a girl" makes force gendered in a system that is already gendered, while turning Adler into a dominatrix pseudo-rapist does not change it but reveals it, and not as different but as real.

Beyond Adler, rape culture is as far reaching in the narrative as extralegality, one often paralleling and sustaining the other. When, for the sake of the case, Holmes breaks into people's homes warrantless, and without police taking the lead (thus behaving as an extralegal detective), we cannot ignore the gender implications of violation. When Holmes needs to, so to speak, "grease the wheels," during an investigation, we similarly must situate it within contemporary gender politics. For example, how likely would it be for any professional lab technician to put her career in jeopardy simply because a man noticed and commented on her hair? In the *Sherlock* television series, Molly Hooper is willing to give Holmes unfettered access to her lab and morgue, and whenever her resolve strengthens against it, Holmes then breaks it down with sophomoric flattery. Every time Holmes requires assistance from a professional woman, he lies, and what is worse, he does it to gain access to their private, controlled spaces. That he never needs to flirt with men to gain access to spaces is enough to illustrate the point.

To the extent that female characters feature in the BBC series *Sherlock*, they are stereotyped and aggrieved. This need not be the case, because there is no structural necessity to injure female characters while finding the truth or object required for conclusion. What do we anticipate about any unaired episode of *Sherlock*? Project unseen, we might assume that a person or series of events will cause Sherlock Holmes to pursue an explanation so as to reveal a mystery or pursue an object in dispute. This is a Propp[24] reduction of character: the detective is but a character "subordinate to the action" (Barthes 105). What is required, then, for the conclusion of the narrative will never be that the detective qua detective must operate within a masculinist field of operations. There is an order, a grammar if you will, to the construction of these plots, and at no point does stereotyping women or hurting them advance a plot any differently than not. Opting to do so, then, while knowing it to be unnecessary, reveals the problem clearly.

Ms. Hudson is the quintessential aggrieved woman: despite protests that she is "a landlady" and "not a housekeeper" ("A Study in Pink"), she nevertheless facilitates a home for two adult men and does so not only without thanks but also with cold dismissals. In the fourth episode, "A Scandal in Belgravia," Ms. Hudson is cleaning the flat and brings breakfast. She is taken hostage, but Holmes saves her. We are to admire this, but it certainly raises the biggest question the ideal audience has yet to answer: how poorly can the sociopathic Sherlock Holmes from the BBC's *Sherlock* continue to treat Ms. Hudson before we would we fail to celebrate the triumphant reveal at the end of the episode?

Ms. Molly Hooper, a lab technician at St. Bartholomew's morgue, is severely ill-treated throughout the series. In the very first episode, her entire career is sidestepped for Sherlock Holmes's ambitions, in that (a) she allows Holmes to use her lab illegally, including access to it and an ensuing beating of a corpse; (b) she is *instructed* to relay non-work-related information to him; and (c), when she asks him if he would care for some coffee, on a date, he treats her like a waitress and gives an order. In the second episode, Holmes sways her through blatantly overt interpersonal manipulation:

> HOLMES: I need to examine some bodies.
> HOOPER: Some?
> HOLMES: Eddie Van Coon and Brian Lukis.
> HOOPER: They're on my list.
> HOLMES: Could you wheel them out again for me?
> HOOPER: Well, the paperwork's already gone through.
> HOLMES: You've changed your hair.
> HOOPER: What?
> HOLMES: The style. It's usually parted in the middle.
> HOOPER: Yes. Well.
> HOLMES: It's good. It suits you better this way. *Holmes grins.*
> *Hooper smiles, pleased she was noticed, and turns around.*
> *Holmes frowns as if inconvenienced by the nicety and exposes its insincerity* [*Sherlock* "The Blind Banker"].

Thus, we see Holmes manipulating Hooper again and again for his own purposes. We are to find this action resourceful. It is simply a rape narrative: a transaction proposed to someone disinclined whereupon their force set against the transaction is overcome. When consent is manipulated, what are fans to think?

In the first episode of the series (a character-revealing stage), we are introduced to Sergeant Donovan, who acts at times as the voice of cautious reason in the show. She protests the hero's extralegal arrival at a crime scene. Her colleague, Anderson, rightly expresses concern over the potential for the crime scene to be contaminated by Holmes. So, instead of alleviating their misgivings, Holmes sexually harasses them. Holmes's intellectual superiority dismisses them as antagonists to his agenda, saying to Anderson (after detecting that both Donovan and Anderson are wearing the same deodorant), "I'm sure Sally came round for a nice little chat and just happened to stay over. And I assume she scrubbed your floors, going by the state of her knees" ("A Study in Pink"). We are to find such a verbal display impressive.

There are two episodes worth reviewing for our purposes here. In the second episode, "The Blind Banker," Dr. Watson falls asleep on the job—typically a terminal infraction—but Dr. Sarah Sawyer, who has hired him, covers for him and assumes the entire burden of patient care herself. Instead of then firing him, she goes on a date with him! Van Coon's secretary is used as an unwitting smuggling mule, temporary storage for a stolen artifact that in the end allows her boss to take care of her financially. Sherlock Holmes lies to Van Coon's neighbor to gain illegal access to Van Coon's apartment by way of her private space. We are to find this ploy clever, but is it not yet another example of a man lying to a woman to violate her space through false pretense? Sherlock Holmes also breaks into Soo Yin Yao's flat for answers. There is more here than disregard for the law. The audience wants Holmes to succeed. After violating Yao's private space, Holmes is attacked and the audience then roots for him to survive, conflating hope with permission by wishing Dr. Watson to break in to help. The third episode was probably the worst episode in which to be a female character. A terrified woman, who has the character name of Crying Woman, no less, has been strapped to explosives and is freed as a damsel in distress. Holmes manipulates Mrs. Monkford while she grieves. Connie Prince dies from a Botox-injected beauty fantasy. A character named Blind Lady explodes for trying to do the right thing. A female astronomer is killed. And in the end, we find out that men manipulated a female museum curator.

I have compiled a spreadsheet to trace characters by episode, gender, recurring or non, killed or not, aggrieved or not, if so by whom, and related details. The data indicate the following percentages, within gendered totals of the last quality removed, for series 1–3:

Female & Non-Recurring & Killed: 15 percent
Male & Non-Recurring & Killed: 14 percent
Female & Non-Recurring & Aggrieved: 43 percent
Male & Non-Recurring & Aggrieved: 30 percent

Non-recurring male characters have a 14 percent chance amongst other non-recurring male characters of being killed or aggrieved. Compare this with female characters, of whom the non-recurring have a 15 percent chance amongst other non-recurring female characters of being killed and a 43 percent chance of being aggrieved. Non-recurring female characters are thus more likely to be aggrieved by Sherlock Holmes and/or John Watson by simply being in an episode than are non-recurring male characters.

By the greatest imaginable leeway granted to the writers and directors of the series, these percentages alone call attention to a tendency of violation. The BBC's *Sherlock* seems bent on violating, aggrieving, and killing off women. Worse than merely the outright, disproportionate mistreatment, the plotting is just intricately sinister enough for an audience not to notice it. Who will remember the aggrieved woman amid schizo-plot twists galore? The audience? The next time an episode is recounted, notice the plotting: how far does it progress before it is no longer about the victim, and how often are people shocked at how poorly women are treated?

Conclusion

To the extent that a particular television series can sustain a popular level of currency and thereby obtain purchase in various, ongoing general and academic conversations, we are obligated to examine whatever mechanism gives rise to such widespread admiration and scrutiny. Is Sherlock Holmes iconic enough to warrant the interest? Perhaps, but this particular iteration is too well received to simply tie to a now stock cultural icon. Sherlock Holmes the quitter would be hilarious to too few of us, and too jarring to the rest. Likewise, the solitarily confined Sherlock Holmes, episode after episode, is not going to inspire television executives to green-light such a series. In this way, personality and autonomy play at least an equal role in securing audience reception. If this is so, then why do masculinist assumptions readily flow through the manifold narratological structures of a series set in our modern world? Dare we answer? If we know that the veneration of violation is unnecessary, then its inclusion should be no more strident than genre-breaking moments. Its unobtrusiveness, then, suggests the problem.

I am certainly not the first to wonder about audience admiration for violence. From coliseums to Las Vegas boxing rings, and from novels to silver screen heroes, there is an "edge of your seat," "must turn the page," "can't look away" sensibility, an anxiety that appeals to our curiosity. Is it any coincidence that, short of voyeurism, extralegal detective narratives often resort to violence and are the ultimate expression of rampant human curiosity? That there are appeals to violence and violation is not the issue. A genre that builds parallel structures with our reality will faithfully (though sometimes excessively) reproduce violence and violation. That the reproduction is venerated is the issue, and not simply as a matter of ethics or taste but of scope: what is the limit to venerating the violence? If we agree that violence and violation can be venerated or not, then there must be intersecting planes on a spectrum, resulting in a sense that the violence and violation are either sufficiently venerable or insufficiently venerable. If showcasing rape and murder were not enough, then how far would be enough for a sociopath to imperil audience admiration?

Notes

1. The message is tangled with the unresolved conclusion of the second season and the reverberations therefrom, to be sure, but its currency in our real world can be easily read as fans believing in (even if only for fun), and thus venerating, this particular Sherlock Holmes.
2. This is a purposeful allusion to theistic belief in the face of "The Problem of Evil" and thereby questioning "belief" in Sherlock Holmes despite the overwhelming evidence of violence. For more on the classic philosophical problem, please see Tooley's entry on "The Problem of Evil" in the *Stanford Encyclopedia of Philosophy*.
3. Taking into consideration diverse media and variations, Sherlock Holmes and John Watson narratives are certainly thought to be both entertaining and have extensive cultural currency. They are, after all, popular culture icons. Nevertheless, such narratives must build parallel structures to our own world so as to populate it with such Foucauldian "anatomies" and "technologies of power" (Foucault) (the police, the prosecutorial system, the carceral system, and so on) that fuel the plot. While the structures remain similar, the audience's understanding shifts: what might be fine in their world is not in ours, and *vice versa*. The extralegal detective who breaks into homes, for example, might be entertaining when part of a narrative but would certainly be intolerable in reality.
4. Howsoever delayed, detective narratives must ultimately arrive at the reveal. The extent to which this reveal is dependent upon human interaction varies, but the interrogative mood remains: some characters are simply informants who drive the plot forward. The interrogative process, as a social field in a power domain, requires deftness for the favored transaction of information. Thus, for characters who are not socially adept, as ours are, the only way in which they might bypass the socially interrogative is by violating the social altogether. Such violation need not necessarily be masculine, but the way in which this series privileges the violation as masculine is through men forcibly obtaining access to women's spaces while, at the same time, normalizing it.
5. Within our current popular culture, from books to television series to movies, by their very recurring presence throughout different media over time, Sherlock Holmes and John Watson are undoubtedly iconic, in that there are characteristics and tropes leveraged to unobtrusively convince the audience of their legitimacy. As to how their social index might be timeless, we need only look at the reimagining of their presence and social patterns at times other than the original writings. Television series today, such as the CBS series *Elementary* and the BBC series *Sherlock*, illustrate the point perfectly. Even *Star Trek: The Next Generation* leveraged Sherlock Holmes narrative elements (including a "USS Sherlock Holmes, NCC-221B"), and if Data (an android character) could convince an audience of Sherlockness, then surely there is an iconography with currency in play (*Memory Alpha*).
6. That this book has an audience only reinforces the point. It is not alone. Research on detective fiction has thrived on these works, occasioning a handful of other texts that critically analyze and evaluate all, thanks in part to their popularity but also because they appeared in a relative

cluster (BBC's *Sherlock*: 2009; *Sherlock Holmes*: 2009; *Sherlock Holmes: A Game of Shadows*: 2011; CBS's *Elementary*: 2012 [*IMDb*]). The films grossed worldwide over a billion U.S. dollars, with *Sherlock Holmes* at $524,028,679 and *Sherlock Holmes: A Game of Shadows* at $545,448,418 (*Box Office Mojo*), while the television series continue, and derivative content thrives on social media websites.

7. The moment of triumph for the detective genre is the reveal, that moment when the genius uncovers all and/or causes the mystery to evaporate. For those who venerate the hero, the consequences are, problematically, both damned and touted. One cannot simultaneously suggest that the methods were right, in the end, if they were also and always wrong.

8. When thinking about what makes a genre work, it is fruitful to consider, better yet, what gives rise to the impression of work. This presupposes that there could be an unqualified semblance of work set against a structural limit, incongruence, or malformation preventing a genre (or presuppositions thereof) from working altogether rationally. In other words, what do the narratological beams construct in ways that we find conform to (broken or real) ideals? Here, we can imagine a narrative in which a child is afraid of a tree tapping against a window during a thunderstorm. Yet, if that child went downstairs and caused the immediate demise of the tree (through methods we can imagine were unsupervised), then the horror aspect we anticipated through setting, title, and description evaporates. It is the same with extralegal detective fiction operating in a world thematically organized by justice through a legal, Foucauldian anatomy of power.

9. Admittedly, this approach was inspired by Sartre's *Being and Nothingness*, in which he quotes from Spinoza *"omnis determinatio est negatio,"* or, "all determinations are negations," and suggests that "non-being is not the opposite of being; it is its contradiction" (Sartre 47). Thus, in this way, genrelessness is not determined by genre features, but by the presence of genre breaks.

10. However, I should mention that extremes do help when beginning such a project, especially when providing examples to students to inspire discussion. For instance, the model 1980s teenage comedy would shatter under most circumstances of direct, rampant, interpersonal violence. While the example might be unlikely, likelihood cannot, tautologously, be a litmus test for excluding all that is not likely. Rationality, to be sure, can carve a boundary, and therefore can be useful for certain suspect examples, but not all plots are rational.

11. Such an event would upend the necessary pivot towards structural justice, which we see near the end of the *Sherlock* episode "A Study in Pink" when John Watson (a doctor, we are assured) fires a fatal gunshot into the villain, an event eventually turned comedic about how poorly the villain had driven a taxicab (*Sherlock* "A Study in Pink").

12. From warrantless searches and invasions of privacy to murder and torture, *Sherlock* does not attempt to hide the brazen extralegality of triumphant detectives at the expense of the displaced police.

13. That is, apart from confirmation bias, and setting aside the title sequence and dialogue, is the character Sherlock? How might we tell?

14. Though, to be fair, notwithstanding multimedia presentations of Sherlock Holmes, the audience need not experience Sherlock Holmes as a portrayal to recognize him, in that (a) I have a LEGO figure of Sherlock Holmes on my desk that no one suspects to be a legitimate policeman or indistinct private investigator and (b) there are many costume shops where people purchase outfits, unperformed in plastic, because they believe it transformative enough, even so.

15. The argument by analogy supports such a flat denial: we would find it appalling for a physician to cure a condition through means that would cause harm to others; we would likewise find it unethical for the cop to fabricate false evidence so as to secure the conviction of a known criminal. It is no different for a detective, extralegal or otherwise. There are, of course, utilitarian, consequentialist objections to the deontological ethical framework of this footnote, though the legal frameworks that order our society deny their arguments any purchase.

16. For more, see http://www.cratesandribbons.com/2012/09/30/the-kissing-sailor-or-the-selective-blindness-of-rape-culture-vj-day-times-square/.

17. Conceptual appeals to (dis)equilibrium here are taken from Todorov's *Poetics of Prose* (1977).

18. While I do not wish to begin a debate on how authentically one films or represents rape culture, the cinematography in this scene was quite telling: wobbly camera, blurriness, disorientation, power, and more industry-standard techniques that serve to prove the point.

19. Although the manifold connections between violation, violence, and power, "for it is as power that violence is being asserted," are well established (especially in feminist discourses), it is important to note the extent of these interactions as a function of authority, in that "violence often comes dressed in the garb of authority, power, right or legitimacy, even when it in effect announces their absence" (Dodd 46).

20. As the audience would discover later in the episode, once Adler's power (seated in the phone) dissipates by castration, she is set adrift, powerless to the extent that Holmes rescues her from men who would assassinate her.

21. Indeed, Page suggests in *Literary and Linguistic Approaches to Feminist Narratology* that "one of the central tenets of feminist narratology" is that operations of gender and narrative in feminist narratology can be understood through "contextualization" (2).

22. Pinup advertisements, for instance, radically reveal their blatant sexism by men replicating the poses to sell the same product. Absurdity is powerful, and it cuts both ways. This is not to sidestep the conversation on how the binarism of gender is, to be sure, problematic and destructive, but it is in this case useful to appeal to representations. For more on gender, binarism, and danger, please see Hélène Cixous and Catherine Clément's "Sorties: Out and Out: Attacks/Ways Out/Forays" in *The Newly Born Woman* (1975).

23. By labeling it essentially rape, the discussion can bypass the proper disposition of property (and the lengths to which it would be appropriate to ensure same) to that of power and forces, for as Ellis suggests in *Philosophy of Nature* "in order to describe the essential properties of anything, it is necessary to abstract from any external forces that may be acting upon it to say how it would be or behave in the absence of such forces" (101), such that in this case if the desire for property evaporates and the actions of parties are sustained as a function of how to struggle, then the disposition of property as a motive is irrelevant to the consequence.

24. See Propp's *Morphology of the Folktale* (1928), the use of which here is through Barthes' analysis in *Image–Music–Text* (1977).

Works Cited

Barthes, Roland. *Image–Music–Text*. New York: Hill and Wang, 1977. Print.
"The Blind Banker." *Sherlock*. BBC. London. 2010. Television.
Box Office Mojo. 2013. Web.
    1: http://www.boxofficemojo.com/movies/?id=sherlockholmes.htm.
    2: http://www.boxofficemojo.com/movies/?id=sherlockholmes2.htm.
Cixous, Hélène, and Catherine Clément. "Sorties: Out and Out: Attacks/Ways Out/Forays." *The Newly Born Woman*. Minneapolis: University of Minnesota Press, 1975. Print.
Dodd, James. *Violence and Phenomenology*. New York: Routledge, 2009. Print.
Ellis, Brian. *Philosophy of Nature: A Guide to the New Essentialism*. Durham: Acumen, 2002. Print.
Foucault, Michel. *Discipline and Punish: The Birth of the Prison*. New York: Vintage, 1977. Print.
"The Great Game." *Sherlock*. BBC. London. 2010. Television.
"His Last Vow." *Sherlock*. BBC. London. 2013. Television.
"The Hounds of Baskerville." *Sherlock*. BBC. London. 2012. Television.
Internet Movie Database (IMDb). 2013. Web.
    1: "Sherlock Holmes." 2009. http://www.imdb.com/title/tt0988045/.
    2: "Sherlock Holmes: A Game of Shadows." 2011. http://www.imdb.com/title/tt1515091/.
Memory Alpha. 2013. Web.
    1: "USS Sherlock Holmes." http://en.memory-alpha.org/wiki/USS_Sherlock_Holmes.
    2: "Sherlock Holmes." http://en.memory-alpha.org/wiki/Sherlock_Holmes.
Page, Ruth E. *Literary and Linguistic Approaches to Feminist Narratology*. New York: Palgrave Macmillan, 2006. Print.
Peirce, C. S. *Collected Papers of Charles Sanders Peirce*. Ed. Arthur W. Burks. Cambridge: Harvard University Press, 1958. Print.
"The Reichenbach Fall." *Sherlock*. BBC. London. 2012. Television.

Sartre, Jean-Paul. *Being and Nothingness: A Phenomenological Essay on Ontology*. Trans. and intro. Hazel E. Barnes. New York: Washington Square Press, 1956. Print.
"A Scandal in Belgravia." *Sherlock*. BBC. London. 2012. Television.
"A Study in Pink." *Sherlock*. BBC. London. 2010. Television.
Todorov, Tzvetan. *The Poetics of Prose*. Ithaca: Cornell University Press, 1977. Print.
Tooley, Michael. "The Problem of Evil." *The Stanford Encyclopedia of Philosophy*. Ed. Edward N. Zalta. 2013. Web.

"Now, Watson, the fair sex is your department":
The BBC's Sherlock and Interpersonal Relationships

BY KATHRYN E. LANE

The BBC's *Sherlock* premiered in 2010 to rave reviews and an almost cult-like following by the middle of the first episode. Considering that Sherlock Holmes is a decidedly Victorian construct one may wonder why the fascination with the character and his cases would be so common today, over a hundred and twenty-six years after the publication of *A Study in Scarlet* (1887), the start of the Holmes canon. Christopher Morley comments in his "In Memoriam Sherlock Holmes" from *The Complete Sherlock Holmes* volume I, published in 1930: "Perhaps no fiction character ever created has become so charmingly real to his readers. It is not that we take our blessed Sherlock too seriously; if we really want the painful oddities of criminology let us go to Bataille or Roughead. But Holmes is pure anesthesia" (7). Morley further comments, "we are epicures. We must begin in Baker Street; and best of all, if possible, let it be a stormy winter morning when Holmes routs Watson out of bed in haste" (8). Morley continues, "[and] we are off. Gregson and Lestrade will get the credit, but we have the fun" (8). As Morley reminds us these are not simply mysteries, but adventures. And, because we have Watson letting us in on the "secrets" of the cases, we feel a part of the adventure. Morley sees Holmes as escapism. However, I don't think the answer is that simple. If it were, Holmes wouldn't have survived the march of time. If anything, Holmes gives the reader—and in the case of BBC's *Sherlock*, the viewer—things to ponder. Whether we want to debate how the infamous detective could really tell that a footprint was planted or whether he made the "right" decision in not further pursuing a criminal, Holmes has always prompted thought and much debate.

However, is our fascination today that surprising when we consider how little has really changed since the Victorian period? Our fascination continues because we're not all that different than our Victorian counterparts. We are still struggling to figure out who we are; we are still facing new technology that unsettles us; and we have seen what Jaffe claimed could well happen in the Victorian period—"a gentleman might someday have to beg" (qtd. in Kestner 19). We're still looking for a hero and Holmes—fallible, confusing, arrogant, condescending, Bohemian—is that hero.

In his book *Sherlock's Men: Masculinity, Conan Doyle, and Cultural History* (1997), Joseph A. Kestner writes, "Doyle sustains the idea of the hero by engaging readers in perennial acts of reconstruction" (24). The BBC's *Sherlock* draws specific attention to this act of reconstruction repeatedly. First the characters aren't the Holmes and Watson that we've met in the Doyle canon—instead they're Sherlock and John, names that arguably allow viewers to connect with them more than if they went by the same titles as their Victorian counterparts. As Louisa Ellen Stein and Kristina Busse write in their "Introduction: The Literary, Televisual and Digital Adventures of the Beloved Detective" (2012):

> This increased emphasis on character accessibility is also manifest in the series' move from last to first name, from Watson and Holmes to John and Sherlock, perhaps a more crucial shift for the character of Holmes than for John Watson, who was already rendered accessible. Here the whole series is presented as "Sherlock," announcing the more human presentation of the character [12].

As Stein and Busse posit, Dr. Watson has always been accessible to the reader, and hence the viewer, because he's served as our narrator. He's the one that tells us what we know Holmes would never take the time to explain. However, in the BBC's series, we become more of a voyeur of the legendary partnership through camera angles, character's infrequent eye contact with the camera, and the series' focus on following Sherlock. For example, we see Sherlock being physically assaulted in an apartment during "The Blind Banker" (2010) while John is yelling at him about being stuck outside the apartment, unaware of the fight going on inside. This is just one instance of the viewer seeing the details of the case along with John, versus having John serve as a narrator and intermediary as is most common in adaptations of the Sherlock Holmes canon.

The second act of reconstruction of the traditional Sherlock Holmes is done through technology and all the "evils" it can bring with it. Sherlock is a man comfortable with technology—although he'd rather someone else do the texting for him. Stein and Busse comment, "When the BBC premiered *Sherlock*, it re-envisioned a character who had been adapted and re-adapted in multiple media forms for over a century" (10). The modern Sherlock has a website in which he catalogues the 243 types of cigarette ash versus the 'treatise' his Victorian predecessor published. Furthermore, Sherlock is very aware of the technological advances available—whether tracking a phone remotely via an internet application or searching the weather conditions on his smart phone to determine a victim's whereabouts. "The series recasts the famous detective as a millennial thinker, showcasing his youthful technological expertise as he easily navigates flows of digital information that others would find confounding," state Stein and Busse (10). For the viewer, we are again placed in the voyeur position as we see visual representations of technology overlaying the action on screen. When a text message is received, it appears on screen amidst the action of the scene. When Holmes chooses search terms, we see where his mind is going—albeit briefly. As Stein and Busse theorize, "In a sense, the series posits that a Sherlock of today could not embody the necessary cultural brilliance without extreme digital literacy" (11). The Sherlock Holmes that we may have loved following through gaslit streets and hansom cabs, has evolved as our society has. "As creators Steven Moffat and Mark Gattis have emphasized, this re-envisioning of Sherlock as a fully modern figure is in a key sense not a re-envisioning at all; but rather an updating of a character who was crucially modern within his original Victorian context" (Stein and Busse 11). Whether we want to term Sherlock's techno-savvy as reconstructing or updating of our classic detective, the reality is that technology and its hold on our modern world are things that Sherlock cannot escape.

With a reconstructed hero who is digitally-literate, it's not surprising then that the main emphases of season two are technology and publicity. The first episode of the second season opens with Sherlock unhappy about the public interest in him. In fact, he tells John directly: "I'm a private detective. The last thing I need is a public image" (*Sherlock* "A Scandal in Belgravia," 2012). He's annoyed by John's blog and all the publicity it has brought their way. Additionally, he'd rather not do public appearances when a case has finished. However, as a man who makes his living as "a consulting detective" and runs his own website, we know he must be aware of the value of publicity. We, as the viewer, realize that Sherlock has never really wanted true anonymity but we can understand his reticence to be hounded by the press. Our understanding comes from the common desire for fame alongside the awareness that fame may be more than we could handle. We live in a society in which young people commit suicide because of cyber-bullying; therefore, we understand the negative impact technology can have on our lives.

Furthermore, in the final episode of season two, "The Reichenbach Fall" (2012), we see fully how technology can distort public opinion as Sherlock becomes the 'villain' because Jim Moriarty can rewrite the script due to his superior technological skills. Jim erases his own identity and creates a non-threatening alter ego known as Richard Brook who he posits is an actor hired by Sherlock to play the master villain of Moriarty. Because the viewer has been beside either Sherlock or John the entire time, we see the lie—complete with a new digital footprint—for what it is. However, in a world in which identity theft is one of the most predominant crimes, we can understand how easily a computer can change a person's life. Moriarty's plan is genius because by using the press and erasing his own identity, he makes Sherlock appear to be the 'true' villain. He's changed the view of Sherlock in the press, he's erased evidence, and, most importantly, he's planted doubt in the minds of the public. Sherlock—our frustrating, beloved hero—is ultimately faced with an impossible decision and a noble sacrifice: kill himself or be responsible for the death of three people that he considers "friends"—John Watson, Mrs. Hudson, and Detective Inspector Lestrade ("The Reichenbach Fall"). Sherlock—forever the hero—makes the noble sacrifice and the scene closes with three assassins packing away their tools, the kills not taken. We then move forward in time to John sitting in his therapist's office, the rain pounding away. John has put the viewer's worst fear into words at the start of the episode when he states, "My best friend ... Sherlock Holmes ... is dead" and we are left wondering what has become of our hero and if our adventure has ended ("The Reichenbach Fall"). Because we've been positioned alongside either John or Sherlock throughout the series, we too feel bereft at the loss of Sherlock. I contend that this is where the third act of reconstruction comes into play. The viewer has become a part of the text—and each new viewer rewrites it just a bit, putting a part of themselves into the text.

This re-visioning of Sherlock is another layer of the reimagining happening on screen in the BBC adaptation. This ultimately means that each viewer will know a different Sherlock Holmes than their neighbor down the street or another viewer on another continent. If each version of Sherlock is overlaid with a bit of each viewer customizing him—his thoughts, his feelings, his insights—figuring him out should be easy. Yet, Sherlock remains a mystery that fans avidly debate. Lyndsey Faye in her "Prologue" to *Sherlock and Transmedia Fandom: Essays on the BBC Series* (2012) contends that fans' fascination is due to the fact that we "want to know more than the detective himself would willingly allow" (6). We are fascinated by Sherlock Holmes—always have been—and the BBC adaptation gives a new insight into Sherlock and his relationships through the modern interpretation happening on screen. Perhaps, the biggest 'secret' of the series isn't whether or not Sherlock is a fake—as Moriarty posits in "The Reichenbach Fall"—but instead if he is he gay or straight. Determining the answer to this 'secret' appears to be our final act of reconstruction; however, is it an answer we really want?

The continued reconstruction of our hero is interrupted repeatedly by references to Sherlock's (and hence, John's) sexual orientation. This element of discord appears in the first episode, "A Study in Pink" (2010). The question of the character's sexual orientation arose as a misunderstanding and became a punch line that has lasted throughout the series. However, the sexual orientation of these characters—despite their responses—is something that other characters 'read' incorrectly repeatedly in the series. These mis-readings serve for a chuckle as John can't understand why everyone keeps mis-reading their partnership. However, as the series progresses, we see him become alternately annoyed and then accepting of the mis-readings that impact his life. Sherlock remains oblivious to the mis-readings. I believe that the series' writers are calling attention to this element—this secret—of the legendary partnership intentionally. In today's society in which almost nothing is private, the full scope of the relationship between Sherlock Holmes and John Watson is; and whether friendship or a romantic liaison, this secret keeps the viewer fascinated. Everyone loves a secret and the level of the relationship between Sherlock and John in the BBC adaptation is 'the secret' we all want to know but don't.

In fact in the first episode of season two, "A Scandal in Belgravia," John asks Mrs. Hudson: "has he ever had any kind of ... girlfriend, boyfriend, a relationship, ever?" Her answer of "I don't know" seems baffling and prompts John to ask, "How can we not know" with a stress on the "we" emphasizing that John and Mrs. Hudson are the people with whom Sherlock most frequently interacts in his day-to-day life. If anyone would know if he's currently or ever has been romantically involved with someone, it would be them. However, as Mrs. Hudson points out, "He's Sherlock. How will we ever know what goes on in that funny old head?" Her disclaimer that "he's Sherlock" clearly states that she's accepted that she can't figure him out, further emphasizing that he doesn't function the way everyone else does. Sherlock is firmly established as the most obtuse puzzle in the room. No one will ever figure him out. And, yet, I believe that is why we're fascinated: because he's a puzzle that we can project onto and accept that we're going to be wrong. Much like in life, we may or may not be proven correct and we'll have to adjust our thinking once more facts are available. He's the mystery we're trying to figure out just slightly before the detective reveals all in the denouement.

An example of a fan who has attempted to decode Sherlock is online blogger and transcriptionist, Ariane DeVere. Ms. Devere has transcribed all of the *Sherlock* episodes and made them available on her site. DeVere's transcriptions are obviously a work of love as she spends well over 10 hours per episode transcript. She has focused on accuracy in her transcription of the character's spoken lines; however, it is in Ms. DeVere's stage direction that we see her reading of the non-verbal communication between the characters. In one particularly fraught scene between Sherlock and John, Ms. DeVere describes the eye contact as "eyesex" between the two characters in "The Great Game" (2010) transcript:

> JOHN: I'm not gonna stand here so you can humiliate me while I try and disseminate ...
>
> SHERLOCK (interrupting): An outside eye, a second opinion. It's very useful to me.
>
> JOHN: Yeah, right(!)
>
> SHERLOCK: Really.
>
> (John turns back to him and the two of them have intense eyesex for several seconds. Eventually John nods unhappily because eyesex is all he's going to get for the time being.)

This is (presumably) not how the eye contact was described in the series' script but Ms. DeVere's transcription allows for her interpretation of the interaction. I wouldn't go so far as to say "projection" but instead that Ms. DeVere's reading of the relationship between Sherlock and John as (at least) homoerotic then colors her reading of the non-verbal communication between the characters. There are many fans that agree with Ms. DeVere's reading and it is often in line with the way other characters in the series read the men's relationship. However, in the commentary to the first season's first episode, "A Study in Pink," the series' writers and producers discuss the original Holmes's sexuality and its impact on the depiction of the detective in Sherlock. To Steven Moffat and Mark Gatiss, Sherlock's sexuality is a non-issue because that is how Conan Doyle wrote it:

> STEVEN: Now, this is one of the supposedly controversial things—actually a subject we never discussed at all, which is Sherlock's sexuality, because although people talk about it being ambiguous or mysterious, the truth is that the books are completely clear: he's not interested at all. He's interested in what his brain is doing, not the other end of his body.
>
> MARK: "All the rest is transport."
>
> STEVEN: But the fact is people say "Golly, he shows no interest in women, therefore he must be gay." He shows no interest in men either. That's just not what he does.

As this commentary illustrates, the series' writers aren't writing in "eye sex" to the stage directions; so why then do we assume? First, because we've been conditioned to believe that you are either hetero or homosexual; one or the other. Very few people consider "asexual." Interestingly, the actor Benedict Cumberbatch who portrays the titular character has commented that he's been approached on the street and thanked for bringing awareness to asexuals. Whether one agrees with such a classification or not, it would appear that the actor at least is aware of his character's perceived asexuality.

I believe that the series' writers and the actor playing Sherlock specifically play on this asexuality to replace the disguises so famously used by Holmes in the original Conan Doyle stories. In a world in which so much is public, Sherlock is keeping one secret that no one knows. It becomes part of his persona and therefore is mutable. In the commentary for "The Great Game," Cumberbatch states, "I think this was one of the most satisfying things to get my teeth into as Holmes because we're not doing putty noses and silly wigs and sunglasses as disguises, so the idea that he can mercurially change characteristics in order to seduce people into confessing, or just getting what he wants or controlling the situation even, is really very good fun to play." The modern interpretation won't include elaborate disguise so the ability to gain information and possibly mislead another character must come from somewhere. I contend that is what Sherlock's secret does for him—allows him to be a blank page rewritten as needed per situation. However, this further example of reconstruction doesn't keep Sherlock from sharing in some of Holmes's views and difficulties with women.

Considering that Holmes has found women frustrating from the start of his career in *A Study in Scarlet* (1887), it's not surprising then when he tells Watson, "the fair sex is your department" in "The Adventure of the Second Stain" (1904) in the original Conan Doyle canon. His statement to Watson at this point is well-founded as Watson has been married, widowed, and remarried by this point in their history together. Women were a puzzle that Holmes thought he understood but their emotions made them unpredictable. When women appear in the Conan Doyle canon as clients, he's solicitous but he doesn't trust their observations.

"A Scandal in Bohemia" (1891) is the first story in which we see Holmes bested and it's no mere coincidence that this besting is done by a woman—both beautiful and brilliant. One could argue that Holmes here is representative of the male's attempt to understand Woman, what some would claim to be a "universal" struggle. After all, Holmes only refers to Adler as "the Woman," and yet the description of Adler is reminiscent in many ways of the

Victorian "New Woman" who was rapidly shaking up the societal norms of Conan Doyle's time.

Conan Doyle's description of Adler in the original short story states, "She has a soul of steel. She has the face of the most beautiful of women, and the mind of the most resolute of men" (193). Beautiful, no doubt, but brilliant and resolute as well—a challenging opponent for our detective. "A Scandal in Bohemia" includes several disguises worn by Holmes and Ms. Adler; a fire for a diversion, the secret revealed but not utilized, and a chase that ends with an "empty nest" (204). Watson's commentary closes the story with the following: "And that was how ... the best plans of Mr. Sherlock Holmes were beaten by a woman's wit. He used to make merry over the cleverness of women, but I have not heard him do it of late. And when he speaks of Irene Adler, or when he refers to her photograph, it is always under the honourable title of *the* woman" (205).

Just as our hero has been reconstructed in his modernity, so has the iconic "Woman" of the Conan Doyle canon. In the *Sherlock* episode "A Scandal in Belgravia," Mycroft Holmes hands Sherlock a photo and states, "Irene Adler, professionally known as 'The Woman.'" Sherlock has no idea who she is or the scandals with which she's been connected which prompts his attention. However, as Irene's occupation of dominatrix is revealed, Mycroft assumes Sherlock will be put off by Irene's sexual nature. Sherlock is his usual unflappable self and leaves Buckingham Palace asking only for a box of matches or a lighter. Irene Adler doesn't worry him as he assumes she will act as expected. Anyone familiar with Conan Doyle's original short story will suspect Sherlock's plan of action—don a disguise; fake an injury; ask for help; once inside, create a diversion that will give away the hiding place—all of which is successful. However, what is surprising in the BBC adaptation is "The Woman" herself. From the instant she appears on screen, Irene doesn't act as expected. When she appears in her sitting room to greet her unfortunate and unexpected "guest," Irene is completely nude shocking Sherlock and the viewer. She sees through Sherlock's deception immediately as evidenced by her asking him, "Oh, it's always hard to remember an alias when you've had a fright, isn't it?" In this instant, Irene has the upper-hand and she takes it as far as she can by straddling Sherlock and "defrocking" him of his attempt at a disguise—a minister's collar.

Furthermore, Irene's nudity has not only served to stun the two men in her sitting room but she has also stripped Sherlock of clues by removing all the telltale signs which he reads so cleverly. It's apparent in the episode that Sherlock is trying to read Irene but her lack of clothing leaves him blank. This prompts

Irene to question, "D'you know the big problem with a disguise, Mr. Holmes?" ("A Scandal in Belgravia"). She is not only calling Holmes on his disguise and his falsehood in entering her abode but as the next line reveals, "However hard you try, it's always a self-portrait." She is letting him know that she truly sees him and sees more than he wants to reveal. Because Irene can't have the upper hand and Sherlock feel comfortable, he has to establish his superior intelligence and that's done by discussion of the mysterious death "of the hiker with the bashed in head." Irene is quick to tell both John and Sherlock "I like detective stories—and detectives. Brainy's the new sexy." Her statement that brainy is the new sexy is aimed at Sherlock and he turns it on her quickly—and simultaneously calls her on her 'shock factor' dressing, stating "...you cater to the whims of the pathetic and take your clothes off to make an impression. Stop boring me and think. It's the new sexy." The interplay between the character of Irene and Sherlock allows us a glimpse into a part of the detective that we know he would never willingly disclose. Although it at first appears that the interaction between Sherlock and Irene is flirting, both characters use the rhetoric of games to refer to their interactions throughout the episode.

The storyline continues as one would expect but with numerous 'blips' that speak to Irene's character. When a group of armed CIA henchmen enter the sitting room, pointing guns, and demanding entry to the safe that contains the phone holding the blackmail material, Sherlock opens it once John's life is threatened. However, an eye-dip from Irene has alerted Sherlock that the safe is booby-trapped and this disturbance allows he, John, and Irene to subdue the armed henchmen. As the safe has now been opened, Sherlock takes the phone and refuses to return it to Irene. Irene, of course, has already claimed that the phone is "her life" and she cannot allow it out of her possession ("A Scandal in Belgravia"). This leads to her following Sherlock upstairs, drugging him, and eventually beating him with a riding crop to regain possession of her highly-sought-after technology. As she prepares to depart, she tells Sherlock, "This is how I want you to remember me. The woman who beat you. Good night, Mr. Sherlock Holmes." We realize the play on "beat" here as she has literally taken a whip to Sherlock but more importantly—and what will keep Sherlock in the game—is that she's outmaneuvered him. At this moment, Irene is the victor having regained her phone and physically incapacitated Sherlock.

When Sherlock regains consciousness, his first conscious thought is of Irene as seen from the following dialogue:

SHERLOCK: Where is she?
JOHN: Where's who?

SHERLOCK: The woman. That woman.
JOHN: What woman?
SHERLOCK: The woman. The woman woman!
JOHN: What, Irene Adler? She got away. No one saw her ["A Scandal in Belgravia"].

The viewer realizes several things in this scene. For those familiar with the original Conan Doyle story, we realize this is where the original story ends; however, there's more to come as this happens in the first half of the episode leading to the impression that Irene and Sherlock's interaction will continue because the rewriting taking place on screen will continue. Next is that Sherlock is referring to Irene as "the woman," "that woman" which could imply she's wiped all other women from his mind for the moment. Furthermore, even though John may not realize it, Irene has continued the game with Sherlock by returning his coat, programming his phone to emit an orgasmic recording when she texts him, and leaving a red kiss-mark on his left check. Sherlock realizes the game will continue when he grasps that his coat has been returned to him. The next morning's text messages (and ensuing moans) assure him (and hence the viewer) that the parry between the two of them isn't over.

The relationship that develops between the two appears distant as it's primarily text messages until Irene trusts Sherlock with her phone. On Christmas, she leaves him her phone in a package on his mantelpiece—signaling to him that she will soon be dead. It's no surprise then when Sherlock identifies a body at the morgue at St. Bartholomew's Hospital with "that's her"—implying Irene Adler. Of course, it isn't her face that he recognizes in the morgue to make the positive identification. It's her body which implies that he's been aware of her body the entire time. (Perhaps not as asexual as everyone thinks, hmm?) This method of identification is unusual causing the character of Doctor Molly Hooper to question Mycroft, "Who is she? How did Sherlock recognize her from ... not her face?" ("A Scandal in Belgravia").

Mycroft asks Sherlock how he knew Irene was dead and again Sherlock assumes that she will act in a predictable fashion when he answers, "She had an item in her possession, one she said her life depended on. She chose to give it up" (*Sherlock* "A Scandal in Belgravia"). Sherlock has been drawing conclusions here but his conclusion that Irene is dead is incorrect as the viewer learns later in the same episode. Her death lasts all of one week—Christmas Eve to New Years' Eve—before she needs to recover her phone.

Irene first reveals her continued health to John who is enraged to see her. He begs and then demands that she tell Sherlock she is alive. This leads to the realization that Irene has been "flirting" with Sherlock the entire time via text message:

> IRENE (Reading text messages from her phone.): "Good morning"; "I like your funny hat"; "I'm sad tonight. Let's have dinner" ... "You looked sexy on 'Crime-Watch.' Let's have dinner"; "I'm not hungry, let's have dinner."
> JOHN: You ... flirted with Sherlock Holmes?
> IRENE: At him. He never replies.
> JOHN: No, Sherlock always replies—to everything. He's Mr. Punchline. He will outlive God trying to have the last word.
> IRENE: Does that make me special?
> JOHN: ... I don't know. Maybe [*Sherlock* "A Scandal in Belgravia"].

One could read Sherlock's lack of response to Irene's text messages to mean that he isn't mentally engaged but as he's been morose since identifying Irene's body in the morgue, we, as the viewer, know that isn't the case. Once Sherlock realizes that Irene is alive, he sends his one and only text message to her: "Happy New Year/SH." He's now actively participating in the dialogue between them but he still doesn't trust her. In the next scene of the episode, Sherlock is back in Molly's lab x-raying Irene's phone. He realizes that there are "four additional units wired inside the casing; I suspect containing acid or a small amount of explosive" which will make the phone useless in terms of recovering the material on it. However, it's in this scene with Molly that we hear Sherlock refer to his relationship with Irene as a game. He states, "She sent this to my address, and she loves to play games." By leaving him the phone without the passcode, she's left him a puzzle to solve ensuring his attention is always partially on her phone and hence, her.

However, the "game" between the two isn't over until Sherlock has solved the puzzle ("A Scandal in Belgravia"). After faking her death and her 'resurrection,' Irene goes to 221B Baker Street and asks for Sherlock's help. In so doing, she clearly shows her trust for Sherlock when she states, "I knew you'd keep my secret." Sherlock's reply of "You couldn't" is proven false when she replies, "But you did, didn't you?" Irene's reading of Sherlock is that he will remain the "chaste romantic figure" that Tom Bragg labels him in his discussion of the original Conan Doyle story (17). She's been reading him just as he reads others. However, it appears that it's only Irene that Sherlock can't read. As the episode draws to its denouement, Irene's betrayal of Sherlock is revealed.

She has given him another puzzle to solve which he does in just a few seconds. Once she has the solution, she texts Jim Moriarty—the villain of the series—who uses the information to destroy a plan of Mycroft's. Sherlock doesn't know that he has just unwittingly betrayed his brother or his country but he realizes in a few hours after being faced with an enraged Mycroft on a plane of dead bodies. Mycroft states, "That's all it takes: one lonely naïve man desperate to show off, and a woman clever enough to make him feel special" ("A Scandal in Belgravia"). Sherlock assumes his brother is talking about the Ministry of Defense man who Irene has mentioned having "tied up" earlier in the episode. Mycroft's response, "I'm not talking about the M.O.D. man, Sherlock; I'm talking about you" leaves Sherlock confused and ultimately humbled—an unlikely moment for our hero.

Later we see the game rhetoric re-appear when Mycroft is trying to browbeat the information out of Irene. She stands resolute when she answers, "Telling you would be playing fair. I'm not playing anymore" ("A Scandal in Belgravia"). However, for Sherlock, the game hasn't ended because the puzzle of the phone's passcode remains. Irene reads his interruption into her conversation with Mycroft as Sherlock's ego but he realizes that Irene has been playing all of them in a game and that he is actually the key. Sherlock says to Irene, "you got carried away. The game was too elaborate. You were enjoying yourself too much." It's obvious he's figured out the puzzle of how to unlock Irene's phone as he begins typing in letters and tells her, "I've always assumed that love is a dangerous disadvantage ... thank you for the final proof." Irene's response is to assure him that "Everything I said; it's not real. I was just playing the game." Sherlock's response of "I know" makes the viewer question how much of the game he's been aware of the whole time and how much of it he's realized in the last few minutes. However, his final response to Irene of "And this is just losing" reinforces that Sherlock is the victor. The scene closes with Sherlock righting the wrong he's done to Mycroft by turning over Irene's phone and leaving Mycroft's office/home. It would appear that our hero has won the game but we cannot help but question if it's really over yet?

The next scene of the episode takes place sometime later. Mycroft has come to deliver the news to Sherlock, via John, that Irene has been taken in by an American witness protection "scheme" and will "survive—and thrive—but he will never see her again." John's question of "Why would he care? He despised her in the end. Won't even mention her by name—just 'The Woman'" solidifies the realization that Sherlock can—and does—feel deep emotion ("A Scandal in Belgravia"). However, Mycroft reads Sherlock's reaction differently than John. He questions, "Is that loathing, or a salute? One of a kind; the one woman who matters." John's answer of "He's not like that. He doesn't feel things that way.... I don't think" leaves the viewer with the same doubts that we suspect are now niggling in John's mind. What Mycroft tells John—and they decide not to tell Sherlock—is that Irene has been beheaded by a terrorist cell in Karachi. When told that Irene is in America and will never bother him again, Sherlock takes it in stride. But, he demands her phone from the government evidence bag. John leaves thinking that Irene is finally gone and that the phone has become a memento. Only Sherlock knows that he saved her life in Karachi and that their game can continue. If, when, where, or how their game will continue remains to be seen in upcoming seasons.

In direct contrast to Irene Adler in the original Holmes stories and the BBC "reimagining" is the character of Mrs. Hudson, the landlady. In the original Conan Doyle stories, Mrs. Hudson is a peripheral character at best. She's relevant because she brings in tea, has provided a "home" for Holmes and therefore, through him, us the viewer; and she's willing to crawl about on her knees in "The Adventure of the Empty House" (1903) to help Holmes fake his "resurrection" and foil his would-be assassin. She's a tool—and as many scholars notice—one of such irrelevance to Conan Doyle that she's called Mrs. Turner in "A Scandal in Bohemia" but Mrs. Hudson throughout the remainder of the Holmes canon. Mrs. Hudson is important because of what she provides, not because of some innate trait. Consider Watson's summation of Mrs. Hudson in "The Adventure of the Dying Detective" (1913):

> Mrs. Hudson, the landlady of Sherlock Holmes, was a long-suffering woman. Not only was her first-floor flat invaded at all hours by throngs of singular and often undesirable characters but her remarkable lodger showed an eccentricity and irregularity in his life which must have sorely tried her patience. His incredible untidiness, his addiction to music at strange hours, his occasional revolver practice within doors, his weird and often malodorous scientific experiments, and the atmosphere of violence and danger which hung around him made him the very worst tenant in London. On the other hand, his payments were princely. I have no doubt that the house might have been purchased at the price which Holmes paid for his rooms during the years that I was with him. The landlady stood in the deepest awe of him and never dared to interfere with him, however outrageous his proceedings might seem. She was fond of him, too, for he had a remarkable gentleness and courtesy in his dealings with women [434].

From this description it appears that Mrs. Hudson is probably the most understanding landlady in history—albeit well-paid. However, in the BBC's interpretation, Mrs. Hudson is not only a well-rounded character but important enough that we see Holmes become violent when she's threatened. In the modern reimagining, this is no simple landlady.

We meet Mrs. Hudson in the first episode of the first season of *Sherlock*, entitled "A Study in Pink" (2010), as the two potential flat mates—Sherlock Holmes and Dr. John Watson—meet at Baker Street to see their new abode. John comments on the potential price of renting in the neighborhood which prompts Sherlock to explain that Mrs. Hudson is giving him "a special deal. Owes me a favour. A few years back, her husband got himself sentenced to death in Florida. I was able to help out." John's assumption that Sherlock cleared the man, "Sorry, you stopped her husband being executed" is quickly refuted when he replies, "Oh no. I ensured it" tells us something about Mrs. Hudson; but, at that moment, we're not sure what. One would think that the wife of a condemned killer would be a hardened woman but the woman who opens the door to 221B and welcomes her new boarders is very matronly and welcomes Sherlock with a hug. We realize quickly that there is more to the story of Mrs. Hudson's husband and how she's come to know Sherlock—whether she was a witness or a client at one point—we're left wondering. However, the warm relationship between Sherlock and Mrs. Hudson is evident from the very beginning. She may not fully understand Sherlock and may be horrified by what she finds in her refrigerator but she is accepting of his eccentricities.

In the series' first episode it is Mrs. Hudson who first bring brings up the puzzle of Sherlock's sexuality. She is the first person to misconstrue the relationship between the two men, asking, "What do you think, then, Doctor Watson? There's another bedroom upstairs if you'll be needing two bedrooms" ("A Study in Pink"). The implication here is that the two men would share a bedroom—obviously inferring an intimate relationship—however; John is quick to answer, "Of course, we'll be needing two." Interestingly, Mrs. Hudson's response to John's refusal is acceptance and a sly reference to her "alter ego" of Conan Doyle's first story—*A Study in Scarlet*—when Mrs. Hudson was named Mrs. Turner—with her reply, "Oh, don't worry; there's all sorts round here. Mrs. Turner next door's got married ones."

When Sherlock dashes off to look at a crime scene, his parting words to his landlady are "Mrs. Hudson, I'll be late. Might need some food." She replies with "I'm your landlady, dear, not your housekeeper." Her response is quick and attempts to clarify her position in the household. It's ignored by Sherlock and shortly after by John as well who requests biscuits to go with his "cuppa." She replies again with "Not your housekeeper!" (*Sherlock* "A Study in Pink"). This statement of "landlady, not your housekeeper" becomes something of a mantra for Mrs. Hudson throughout the series. Her repeated clarification is what makes the following scene from "The Hounds of Baskerville" (2012) so funny:

SHERLOCK (standing up and facing her): I thought you weren't my housekeeper.
MRS. HUDSON: I'm not.
>(Making a frustrated noise, Sherlock stomps back over to the harpoon and picks it up again. Behind him, Mrs. Hudson looks down at John who does the universal mime for offering someone a drink. She looks at Sherlock again.)

MRS. HUDSON: How about a nice cuppa, and perhaps you could put away your harpoon.
SHERLOCK: I need something stronger than tea. Seven per cent stronger.

This interaction proves that Mrs. Hudson is attempting to 'mother' or care for her boarders, going far beyond the expectations of a landlady. Furthermore, the ways in which she's involved in her boarders' lives is obvious as she's constantly coming in to straighten up, bringing in groceries, leading visitors up the stairs, and even being present at their Christmas party.

It appears that both men are willing to ignore Mrs. Hudson's insistence on simply being their landlady and not their housekeeper which may lead the viewer to think Mrs. Hudson isn't important to the lives of Sherlock and John. However, as we see in "A Scandal in Belgravia," Mrs. Hudson is very important to both men. It appears that everyone in the world is searching for Irene Adler's phone which she has left with Sherlock. The CIA not being the type to give up, they've forced their way into 221B and taken Mrs. Hudson hostage to get the information they want. Sherlock deduces all this within seconds of entering the building and he's prepared when he finally faces off with Nielsen, the CIA agent who has injured Mrs. Hudson. Sherlock outsmarts and overpowers Nielsen and releases Mrs. Hudson from her restraints. He then exacts revenge upon Nielsen for hurting Mrs. Hudson—not the usual actions of a run-of-the-mill tenant, needless to say. In fact, he tosses Nielsen out a window for terrorizing Mrs. Hudson. Once Lestrade arrives at the scene he asks Sherlock, "And exactly how many times did he fall out of the window" to which our hero replies, "It's all a bit of a blur, Detective Inspector, I lost count." The implication here is that Sherlock tossed Nielsen out of the window more than once. Shortly afterward Sherlock is seen entering Mrs. Hudson's flat—221A Baker's Street—and the viewer learns that the CIA wasn't as off-base as we might have first suspected. Mrs. Hudson has hidden the so-sought-after camera phone on her person, keeping it safe for Sherlock. When John asks, "She's in shock, for God's sake, and all over some bloody stupid camera phone. Where is it anyway?" Sherlock's reply is "Safest place I know" at which point the phone materializes from Mrs. Hudson's cleavage. She explains, "You left it in the pocket of your second-best dressing gown, you clot. I managed to sneak it out while they thought I was having a cry." From this statement, it would appear that Mrs. Hudson has become more than a landlady but, in fact, serves as the "boys'" housekeeper. Sherlock's statement, "Mrs. Hudson leave Baker Street? England would fall" clearly shows how crucial he feels she is to the balance of his life.

However, in the final episode of season two of *Sherlock*—"The Reichenbach Fall"—when Mrs. Hudson has reportedly been shot, Sherlock doesn't rush to her side. He recognizes the distraction for what it is and intentionally puts distance between himself and her when he states, "She's my landlady." He justifies his non-action by stating, "alone protects me." John, however, sees the discrepancy in words and actions, pointing out, "Doesn't she mean anything to you? You once half killed a man because he laid a finger on her." His amazement is obvious and his anger at Sherlock culminates in him calling the other man "a machine." He refutes Sherlock's statement that "alone protects me" with his reply, "No. Friends protect people" but he does, in fact, leave Sherlock alone leaving him (and the viewer) to think that Sherlock may have successfully kept "his friends" safe from the nefarious plans of Moriarty. We learn quickly that this isn't the case as Mrs. Hudson is one of the "friends" set to die by Moriarty's plan to end Sherlock's life. However, it is our hero who lists the "friends" being targeted:

JIM: Your friends will die if you don't.
SHERLOCK: John.
JIM: Not just John. Everyone.
SHERLOCK: Mrs. Hudson.
JIM: Everyone.
SHERLOCK: Lestrade.
JIM: Three bullets; three gunmen; three victims. There's no stopping them now. (Pause) Unless my people see you jump.

This exchange is significant because it reveals through Sherlock's own listing who he considers "friends" ("The Reichenbach Fall"). John Watson is obvious as he and Sherlock are flat mates and work together. However, if Mrs. Hudson is "just" Holmes's landlady as he claims in the scene prior then she wouldn't be the second name that he calls when faced with a threat against his "friends" which is the initial threat. Sherlock's emotional attachment to Mrs. Hudson, which has been made obvious earlier in the same episode, is now illuminated when he lists her as his second "friend" ("The Reichenbach Fall"). This is more than a previous client or a landlady. Mrs. Hudson allows Sherlock to show his emotions in a non-threatening relationship. He's always claimed that women confuse him but Mrs. Hudson isn't a sexualized woman to Sherlock; she's his friend—a far more valuable, and enduring relationship.

An examination of the two significant female characters in the Conan Doyle canon—the "Woman" and Mrs. Hudson, the patient landlady—shows how the BBC's modern interpretation has changed the characters and how these characters have impacted the depiction of the iconic detective. The character of Mary Morstan in the original Conan Doyle canon becomes Mrs. Watson, ultimately causing the "separation" of the detective and his helpmate. However, Mrs. Watson doesn't figure in the BBC series any further than being the person who has consoled Dr. Watson during Holmes's absence of two years following the Reichenbach Falls.

In the Conan Doyle canon, Mary is a blank character waiting to be written. The modern BBC revisioning writes a Mary that is the antithesis of Victorian womanhood. She has short hair, she's often shown in slacks, she has a dark, dark past, and she's a former CIA assassin. This modern Mary is most assuredly not the "little woman" that Victorian readers would've pictured setting up a house with their beloved Dr. Watson. Yet, as we see in Season 3, Sherlock defends Mary once John is aware of her questionable past—and her having shot Sherlock earlier in the episode—by saying "you chose her" ("His Last Vow," 2014). Sherlock's theory is that John has become "addicted" to a life of high adrenaline and imminent danger; due to this "addiction," he's been drawn to Mary and her dark past, even though she has kept it a secret throughout their courtship. John is devastated to learn that Mary isn't who he imagined her to be and his loss of an "idyllic" life turns to anger. However, he overcomes his anger to forgive his wife her previous life, stating, "Your previous problems are your past, your future problems are my pleasure." Season three has established that Mary can, in fact, add something to the 'dynamic' duo because she has observation skills of her own as well as genuine emotion for both men. In fact, John and Sherlock will face off with Sherlock's new nemesis, Charles August Magnuson, to protect Mary from public exposure. Season three ends with Holmes being brought back from his exile of "4 minutes" and Mary and John as a cohesive unit. Unlike in past seasons, John's romantic life hasn't impeded his relationship with Sherlock but instead strengthened it. Future seasons will undoubtedly see a continued exploration of the "blank space" of Mary Watson and what a well-rounded female character adds to the iconic partnership.

Interestingly, it's a character that doesn't appear in the Conan Doyle canon at all that leaves the viewer with the most questions, though. The character of Dr. Molly Hooper appears in the BBC series but there is no female doctor or detective in the original stories. However, Molly serves as the coroner of St. Bart's and obviously has some connection to Scotland Yard which is evident from her established rapport with Lestrade and other Scotland Yard personnel. I contend that the BBC's modern Molly is a veiled reference to another Victorian-era detective—Lady Molly of Scotland Yard written by Baroness Emmuska Orczy. Without a character to 'revise' in the modern interpretation, it's not surprising that the relationship between Sherlock and Molly is nothing like his relationship with Irene or Mrs. Hudson. Sherlock's relationship with Molly is an area of ambiguity that is revealed bit by bit each season.

"The one person he thought didn't matter at all to me is the one person who matters the most," explains Sherlock in the season three trailer, entitled "Many Happy Returns" (2013). This statement is followed by a montage of familiar characters—Doctor Molly Hooper, Mrs. Hudson, Anderson—in a beard, Detective Inspector Gregg Lestrade, Mycroft Holmes, and finally Dr. John Watson. The trailer offers "exclusive insights" and the exclusive for "the one person who matters the most" shows a scene between the Brothers Holmes in discussion of John Watson and how he's moved on with his life. However, I contend that this scene is intentionally misleading. As we've established previously, John is the first person threatened by Moriarty in "The Reichenbach Fall" episode that ended season two; and as it's obvious that the "he" in the sentence is Moriarty, and since this is a reference to those threats we must read more carefully. In "The Reichenbach Fall," there are two scenes with Dr. Molly Hooper that offer clues to this statement. Both scenes take place in St. Bart's morgue where Molly serves as coroner. Early on in the episode, Sherlock uses Molly's lab to analyze evidence leading to a kidnapper. While he's working, Molly notices that Sherlock is watching John when John isn't aware and it prompts the following conversation:

MOLLY: You're a bit like my dad. He's dead.
SHERLOCK: Molly, please don't feel the need to make conversation. It's really not your area.
MOLLY: When he was … dying, he was always cheerful; he was lovely—except when he thought no-one could see him. I saw him once. He looked sad.
SHERLOCK: Molly.
MOLLY: You look sad … when you think he [(John)] can't see you. [(Pause)] Are you okay? And don't just say you are, because I know what that means, looking sad when you think no-one can see you.
SHERLOCK: You can see me.
MOLLY: I don't count.

Molly's statement that she "doesn't count" isn't surprising to regular viewers of the show as Molly has been depicted as obviously in love with a man who doesn't know she exists as more than a tool. Molly serves as another example of Sherlock's inability to read women.

This depiction of Molly as someone useful for tasks is seen throughout the series but is encapsulated well in a scene from "A Scandal in Belgravia" when Irene, John, and Sherlock are trying to figure out how to retrieve Irene's phone from a safety deposit box where it's supposedly been stashed for safe keeping. As the group is trying to think of how to pick up the phone without being seen, John's first thought is to use Molly. He states, "Well, we can't just go round and get it, can we? [(Pause in which he seems to be struck by inspiration.)] Molly Hooper. She could collect it, take it to Bart's; then one of your homeless network could bring it here, leave it in the café, and one of the boys downstairs could bring it up the back." One could well argue that John sees Molly as a tool on par with Sherlock's homeless network and the takeout boys in the café below. He never considers the danger that this might put her in. Of course, Sherlock already has the phone so Molly doesn't need to be pressed into service; however, this scene gives a clue into how he uses Molly. Considering this, it's not surprising then that Molly thinks—and states in the scene above—that she "doesn't count" to Sherlock. However, when faced with the true depth of Moriarty's plan and the implications of this plan to his life long-term, he goes to Molly for help as seen in the following scene in a darkened room at St. Bart's from "The Reichenbach Fall" episode:

> SHERLOCK: You're wrong, you know. [(Startled by his presence in the darkened room, Molly jumps and spins toward him.)] You do count. You've always counted and I've always trusted you. [(Pause)] But you were right, I'm not okay.
> MOLLY: Tell me what's wrong.
> SHERLOCK: Molly, I think I'm going to die.
> MOLLY: What do you need?
> SHERLOCK: If I wasn't everything that you think I am—everything that I think I am—would you still want to help me?
> MOLLY: What do you need?
> SHERLOCK: You.

This scene—albeit brief—is significant for two reasons. The first is that Sherlock admits to Molly that he feels his death is imminent; something he's worked to keep from John—his closest friend. Secondly, Molly's faith in him is rock solid. When faced with the possibility that some part of him is a falsehood, her faith in him is resolute. Molly proves her loyalty by offering to help despite what issues might arise. Many viewers read this scene to mean that Molly would help Sherlock fake his death, which may, in fact, be how he pulls it off. But, if it is how Sherlock survives the fall from the roof of St. Bart's, then it means his faith in Molly is absolute. Everyone he cares for—that Moriarty knows he values enough to threaten—believes Sherlock to be dead. The closing scene of this episode shows John and Mrs. Hudson still mourning his death by visiting his grave. And, yet, if Molly has helped fake Sherlock's death then how can we question his faith in her? She's obviously more than just a tangentially-connected colleague whose work space he wants to borrow when convenient. She is someone he trusts, even though we, as the viewer recognize, he's not a man who trusts easily.

Season three sees further development in the relationship between Sherlock and Molly. First, it's clearly established that she is somehow involved in helping him fake his death. Secondly, after a "falling out" with John about his faked death and two year absence, Molly is who Sherlock calls to fill in for John. Molly functioning as a John stand-in is made explicit throughout the episode's early "investigation" scenes because Sherlock keeps imagining John's critique of him and keeps responding with "John" ("The Empty Hearse," 2014). Sherlock appears to be unaware that he's holding a dialogue with John in his head but Molly and the viewer are very aware of the fact she is a stand-in. As the scene ends, Molly and Holmes are leaving the "crime scene" and Holmes states that Molly "is the one who mattered the most because without you, I couldn't have done it. You made it possible" referencing faking his death. His acknowledgement of Molly's significance to his plan working and her feelings for him is a huge step forward for our "high functioning sociopath."

In his two year absence, Molly has moved on romantically, becoming engaged to a young man named Tom; and it's her involvement with Tom that prompts Sherlock to acknowledge that she can't be his permanent partner. He realizes that Molly and he working together would be detrimental to her love life and therefore cannot continue. Molly goes back to her role of friend and colleague in the rest of the season. In "His Last Vow," we see that Molly's adoration of Sherlock has also changed when she slaps him three times after he fails a drug test. She is livid that he would destroy "his gift" and demands he say he's sorry ("His Last Vow"). Sherlock does apologize while also acknowledging how glad he is Molly is no longer wearing her engagement ring. She's now available and has her anger with him proves, she's willing to stand up to him. However, this isn't the only reason Molly is valuable to Sherlock. Later in the same episode, after being shot, Sherlock imagines Molly talking him through whether or not he can avoid bleeding out, the oncoming shock, and the possibility of death. Even though it may be Sherlock's knowledge coming through in this imagined version of Molly, it shows that Sherlock does value Molly's medical knowledge. However, as his attempt to use Molly to stand-in for John proves in "The Empty Hearse," he sees Molly as more than just a medical expert. He sees her as a friend. Who knows? Perhaps in this new character of Molly the series' writers may find a mate for Sherlock, something Conan Doyle would never have attempted. Viewers will have to tune in to see if Molly remains "the medical expert" or if her relationship with Sherlock develops into more.

The reconstruction of the famous detective and his friend will continue when season four airs in 2016, as will the fandom and the further re-visioning by fans. More layers will be added while more mysteries are solved. However, Sherlock will always remain partially an elusive mystery the viewer cannot solve lest we ruin the "adventure" upon which we've embarked. If he becomes easy to read—and easy to categorize—then he loses a bit of his power and he's less Sherlock Holmes. So, even though, we think we want to know, we don't really. We want the mystery and the adventure and Sherlock Holmes will remain that in each new interpretation.

Works Cited

Adams, Guy. *The Sherlock Files: The Official Companion to the Hit Television Series*. London: Ebury, 2012. Print.
"The Blind Banker." *Sherlock*. Writ. Stephen Thompson. Dir. Euros Lyn. British Broadcasting Corporation. BBC 1, London, 1 Aug. 2010. Television.
Bragg, Tom. "Becoming a 'Mere Appendix': The Rehabilitated Masculinity of Sherlock Holmes." *Victorian Newsletter* 116 (2009): 3+. *Literature Resource Center*. Web. 13 Sept. 2013.
Conan Doyle, Sir Arthur. "The Adventure of the Dying Detective." 1913. *The Complete Sherlock Holmes*. By Conan Doyle. Vol. II. New York: Barnes & Noble Classics, 2003. 434–445. Print.
_____. "The Adventure of the Empty House." 1903. *The Complete Sherlock Holmes*. By Conan Doyle. Vol. II. New York: Barnes & Noble Classics, 2003. 5–20. Print.
_____. "The Adventure of the Second Stain." 1904. *The Complete Sherlock Holmes*. By Conan Doyle. Vol. II. New York: Barnes & Noble Classics, 2003. 208–229. Print.
_____. "A Scandal in Bohemia." 1891. *The Complete Sherlock Holmes*. By Conan Doyle. Vol. I. New York: Barnes & Noble Classics, 2003. 187–205. Print.
_____. *A Study in Scarlet*. 1887. *The Complete Sherlock Holmes*. By Conan Doyle. Vol. I. New York: Barnes & Noble Classics, 2003. 3–96. Print.
DeVere, Arianne. "*Sherlock* transcripts." *LiveJournal*. N.p., n.d. Web. 17 Dec. 2013.
"The Empty Hearse." *Sherlock*. Writ. Mark Gatiss. Dir. Jeremy Lovering. British Broadcasting Corporation. BBC 1, London. 1 Jan. 2014. Television.
Faye, Lyndsay. "Prologue: Why *Sherlock*? Narrator Investment in the BBC Series." *Sherlock and Transmedia Fandom: Essays on the BBC Series*. Ed. Louisa Ellen Stein and Kristina Busse. Jefferson, NC: McFarland, 2012. 1–8. Print.
"The Great Game." *Sherlock*. Writ. Mark Gatiss. Dir. Paul McGuigan. British Broadcasting Corporation. BBC 1, London, 8 Aug. 2010. Television.

"His Last Vow." *Sherlock*. Writ. Steven Moffat. Dir. Nick Hurran. British Broadcasting Corporation. BBC 1, London. 12 Jan. 2014. Television.

"The Hounds of Baskerville." *Sherlock*. Writ. Mark Gatiss. Dir. Paul McGuigan. British Broadcasting Corporation. BBC 1, London, 8 Jan. 2012. Television.

Kestner, Joseph A. "Theorizing Holmes/Theorizing Masculinity." *Sherlock's Men: Masculinity, Conan Doyle, and Cultural History*. Aldershot: Ashgate, 1997. 1–39. Print.

"Many Happy Returns." *Sherlock*. Writ. Mark Gatiss and Steven Moffat. British Broadcasting Corporation. BBC 1, 24 Dec. 2013. Television.

Morley, Christopher. "In Memoriam Sherlock Holmes." 1930. *The Complete Sherlock Holmes*. By Sir Arthur Conan Doyle. New York: Barnes and Noble Classics, 2003. Vol. I. 7–10. Print.

"The Reichenbach Fall." *Sherlock*. Writ. Stephen Thompson. Dir. Toby Haynes. British Broadcasting Corporation. BBC 1, London, 15 Jan. 2012. Television.

"A Scandal in Belgravia." *Sherlock*. Writ. Steven Moffat. Dir. Paul McGuigan. British Broadcasting Corporation. BBC 1, 1 Jan. 2012. Television.

"The Sign of Three." *Sherlock*. Writ. Stephen Thompson, Mark Gatiss, and Steven Moffat. British Broadcasting Corporation. BBC 1, London. 8 Jan. 2014. Television.

Stein, Louisa Ellen, and Kristina Busse. "Introduction: The Literary, Televisual and Digital Adventures of the Beloved Detective." *Sherlock and Transmedia Fandom: Essays on the BBC Series*. Ed. Louisa Ellen Stein and Kristina Busse. Jefferson, NC: McFarland, 2012. 9–24. Print.

"A Study in Pink." *Sherlock*. Writ. Steven Moffat. Dir. Paul McGuigan. British Broadcasting Corporation. BBC 1, London, 25 July 2010. Television.

About the Contributors

Ayaan **Agane** is an adjunct professor of English at Framingham State University and an editor. Her areas of specialization include gender and sexuality, and her critical work focuses on intersections between what is considered deviant sexuality and transnationalism, specifically how border crossing (of cultural materials or persons) informs sexual paradigms.

Maria **Alberto** is an M.A. candidate in the English program at Cleveland State University. Her research interests concern the manifestation and function of intersections among literary and cultural traditions, especially in the way that digital media, audience participation and critical theory have revolutionized the production and transmission of classical narrative(s). Her scholarly work reflects a similar intersection among cultural studies, narratology, intertextuality and critical theory.

Lucy **Baker** is a PhD candidate at Griffith University where she teaches in the Humanities department. Her work is interdisciplinary, using sociology, feminist theory, literary studies and ethnography to research the ways fans interact with gender and media within their own creative works. Her research interests are gender, textual analysis, literature and media.

Nadine **Farghaly** is a PhD student at the University of Salzburg. Her research interests mainly focus on gender representations within popular culture. She is the editor of a collection on *Resident Evil* (McFarland, 2014) and co-editor of another on *The Big Bang Theory* (McFarland, 2015).

Greg **Freeman** is a singer, songwriter, author and digital publisher. Though American roots music history—particularly that of blues and gospel—is his primary area of specialty, he also enjoys studying and writing about the visual arts, as well as sculpting, painting and photographing works of his own. His scholarly nonfiction has appeared in encyclopedias, including the *African American National Biography*.

Lindsay **Katzir** is a PhD candidate at Louisiana State University specializing in nineteenth-century British literature, with an emphasis on Jewish studies. Her research interests include literary representations of Jewishness, Anglo-Jewish writings, Jewish women's theological prose and Yiddish literature. She also works on nineteenth-century gothic literature, sensational and detective fiction, adaptation theory and postcolonial studies.

Kathryn E. **Lane** is an assistant professor of English at Northwestern Oklahoma State University, specializing in Romantic and Victorian literature. Her research interests include "silenced" female authors of the Victorian period, feminist theory, popular culture and the teaching of writing.

Katharine **McCain** is an M.A. candidate in the English program at Georgetown University. Her research interests include modern popular culture and fan studies, with an emphasis on transformative works. Specifically, her recent work has focused on defining contemporary fanfiction and its place within a literary and academic context.

Zea **Miller** is a project manager at the Center for Cognition and Neuroethics at the University of Michigan–Flint and a PhD candidate in theory and cultural studies at Purdue University, where he explores the interplay of structure and meaning in cultural artifacts so as to uncover systemic models and rationally interrogate their coherence. His research interests include structuralism, semantics, semiotics and genre, particularly in detective fiction and science fiction.

Hannah **Mueller** is a PhD candidate at Cornell University, where she teaches writing courses on science fiction and participatory culture. Her research interests include popular culture, online culture, film, television, literature as media, fan studies and feminist and queer studies.

Rhonda Lynette Harris **Taylor** is a professor emeritus of library and information studies, University of Oklahoma. She taught graduate courses in popular culture and libraries, library information setting management, multicultural librarianship and the organization of information.

Benedick **Turner** is an associate professor of English at St. Joseph's College, New York, where he teaches classes in ancient, medieval, early modern and Victorian literature. He is the author of a recent article on gender and work in Tennyson's "Gareth and Lynette." His scholarship focuses on Arthurian literature, Sherlock Holmes literature and television, poetry, and gender.

Joseph S. **Walker** studies contemporary American literature and film. His recently published work includes essays on the television shows *Arrested Development*, *Community*, *The Sopranos*, and *Mystery Science Theater 3000*, the film *True Grit*, and the novels of Charles Portis and Kinky Friedman. He is also an active member of the Mystery Writers of America and his short stories have appeared in *Alfred Hitchcock's Mystery Magazine*, *The First Line*, and other anthologies and journals.

Karma **Waltonen** teaches various writing and literature courses at the University of California, Davis. She is the editor of *Margaret Atwood Studies* and co-author of *The Simpsons in the Classroom: Embiggening the Learning Experience with the Wisdom of Springfield* (McFarland, 2010). More recent publications include articles on time travel in *Star Trek* and on the ethics of religious cults in *Doctor Who*.

Elizabeth **Welch** is an award-winning filmmaker and scholar. Her passion is inspiring others through her films and her academic focus is in media representations. She has worked on documentaries revolving around rape culture, fandoms, and LGBT representations in the media.

Index

Adams, James Eli 22, 38*n*3
adaptation 99, 106, 107, 108, 114, 115, 116
Adler, Irene 22–28, 30–33, 37–38, 38*n*5–6, 98, 99, 100, 101, 102, 103, 104, 105, 106, 107, 108, 110, 111, 113, 114, 115, 116, 117, 147, 179–180, 182, 186–187, 229–37, 239, 241; *see also* Woman
"Adventure of the Dying Detective" 235
"Adventure of the Empty House" 23, 27, 235
"Adventure of the Second Stain" 229
The Adventures of Sherlock Holmes 108, 142
adventuring 98, 100, 101, 104, 107, 108, 113
"The Angel in the House" 163, 165, 168, 169; and Archibald, Diana C. 163, 164
Archibald, Diana C. 163, 164
asexual 192–193, 197–206, 229, 232

Baker St. 233, 236
BBC 8, 13, 17, 98, 99, 106, 107, 116
BBC Sherlock 192–205
beauty 86–88, 90
Bechdel Test 186
Becker, Ron 193–194
The Beekeeper's Apprentice 181
Beeton's Christmas Annual 7
Bell, Dr. Joseph 7
"The Blind Banker" 112, 164, 196, 204–205, 224
body 71, 72, 74, 75, 76, 78, 79, 80, 82
Bradley, C. Alan 86
Bragg, Tom 124, 233
Brett, Jeremy 8, 19
Brokeback Mountain (film) 13
bromance 140–141, 135, 174–175, 177–180, 182–183, 185–188, 191
Brook, Richard 226; *see also* Moriarty, Jim
Brooke, Jonatha 163; and Patmore, Coventry 163; and Woolf, Virginia 163, 165

Bruce, Nigel 9
Buckingham Palace 91–92
Burke, David 8, 10
Busse, Kristina 224–225
Butler, Judith 38*n*3
Butlin, James 37

Calabash Pipe 119–120
The Casebook Of Sherlock Holmes 8, 179, 190; "The Disappearance of Lady Frances *Carfax* (episode) 10
CBS 8, 15
celibacy 100, 105, 106, 113, 116
Central Intelligence Agency (CIA) 237
Conan Doyle, Sir Arthur 98–117, 134, 161, 168, 228, 229, 230, 232, 239
The Contender 195–6
Conway, Tom 9
costume 86–87, 90, 93
Countess of Morcar 89
cross-dressing 99, 103, 104, 108, 114, 116
cult cinema 177
Cumberbatch, Benedict 13–14, 17, 115, 229

Davis, J. Madison 126
de Lauretis, Theresa 142
Deluzio Chasin, CJ 200
de Merville, Violet 100
Derschowitz, Jessica 15
detective fiction 98, 99, 102, 103, 108, 116
Devere, Ariana 228
disguise 23–24, 27–30, 32–34, 38*n*5, 38*n*8, 100, 101, 102, 103, 104, 106, 108, 110, 229, 230–231
Disney, Walt 181
Ditzian, Eric 13
Doherty, Robert 15, 121, 142
domesticity 161–162, 164–165, 167–170, 172
dominatrix 67, 74, 77

249

Donovan, Sally 111
Downey, Robert, Jr. 11, 13–14, 19, 175–178, 183–184, 190–191
drag 85
Dunn, Gaby 140–141

Elementary 8, 11, 15, 18, 37, 106, 121–132, 134–136, 139, 142–144
"The Empty Hearse" 36, 38n8, 109, 167, 194, 196, 204–206, 242, 243
enculturation 139

Family Tree (Bbc Series) 119–121
fans 147–148, 150
Faye, Lindsey 226
female Watson 122–23
femininity 98, 100, 102, 104, 107, 108, 111, 114, 162, 163–164, 170; and management 165, 168, 170; and morality 163, 165–167, 169–170; and sentiment 163, 165–166
feminism 98, 107, 114, 115, 117
feminist film 142
femme fatale 66, 68, 69, 70, 71, 72, 84
"The Final Problem" 12, 22–23, 29–30, 38n4
Freeman, Martin 11, 13–14
Fry, Stephen 182

A Game of Shadows 174–175, 181–184, 186–187, 188, 190–191
games 231–2, 233, 234
Garrick Theatre 16
Gatiss, Mark 107, 117, 225, 228
gender performance 99, 100, 102, 103, 107, 108, 115
gender roles 98, 99, 100, 102, 104, 111, 160, 161, 163–164, 167, 170–171; in Victorian homes 162, 163, 166
genre 152
Gillette, William 16
gold 91–92
Granada Television 8–10, 25–26, 108
"The Great Game" 164, 165, 194, 196–197, 201, 203, 206, 228, 229
The Great Mouse Detective 181

Halberstam, Judith 22, 25, 36, 38
Hall, Jasmin Yong 124
Hardwicke, Edward 8, 10
Harris, Jared 182
Harrison, Michael 25–26
"Harry" 91–92
Henry V 133

"His Last Vow" 36, 67, 79, 80, 81, 82, 84, 109, 112, 113, 115, 166–167, 196–197, 201, 205–206, 239, 242
Holmes, Mycroft 13, 27–28, 30, 36, 91–92, 94–95, 98, 108, 109, 111, 113, 115, 182, 187, 230, 232, 234, 240
Holmes, Sherlock: as action figure 13, 19; asexual relationship with Watson 10–11; bromance with Watson 12–13; devotion to Watson 9, 12; disinterest in opposite sex 11; marriage to Miss Faulkner 16; as metrosexual 8; modern-day significance 7; need for Watson 8; one-upmanship 9, 18; sexual tension 17; sexy image 11, 19; social inadequacies 14
Holmesians 176, 178
homoeroticism 123–24, 175, 177–180, 182–185, 187, 189–191
homosexuality 14, 192–206
homosocial bonds 140
homosociality 192–197, 204–206
Hooper, Dr. Molly 109, 232, 233, 239–243
The Hound of the Baskervilles 8, 236–237
"The Hounds of Baskerville" 165, 166, 167, 194–195, 199, 204
House of Windsor 14
How Sherlock Changed the World (documentary film) 7
Hudson, Mrs. 13, 109, 187, 226, 227, 235–239, 240, 242
Hunnicutt, Gayle 108

I Love You, Man 13
identity theft 226
"The Illustrious Client" 100
industrialization 136
instinct 88–89, 91, 94
intertextuality 148
Irving, Sir Henry 16
Islam 107, 108, 111

Jaffrey, Raza 16
John, Sir Elton 14

Kestner, Joseph A. 224
King, Laurie R. 123, 181
King of Bohemia 86–90, 93, 95
Krasner, James 124
Kromm, Sandra 8, 17

Law, Jude 11–14, 175–176, 178, 183, 188, 190–191

Lestrade, Gregory 226, 237, 238, 240
"The Lion's Mane" 105
Liu, Lucy 11, 15
logic 68, 76, 79
Lovibond, Ophelia 16
Lyceum Theatre 16

Macbeth 133
Magnuson, Charles August 115, 239
Maher, Bill 192
"Many Happy Returns" 240
masculinity 85, 87, 89–91, 95–96, 98, 99, 100, 102, 103, 104, 105, 107, 109, 110, 111, 114, 115, 116, 163–165, 170, 172; and authority 164–165, 170–17; manliness 22, 24–27, 36, 38*n*5–6; and work 164
"The Mazarin Stone" 104
McAdams, Rachel 177, 179, 186
McBain, Ed 128
media fandom 175, 178, 181, 184, 188–190
The Memoirs of Sherlock Holmes (television series) 8
men's clothing 89, 92–93
Meyer, Nicholas 9, 19
Miller, Jonny Lee 18, 129
mind 86–88, 90, 96
misogyny 184, 186–188
Moffat, Steven 98, 99, 107, 108, 110, 111, 113, 114, 115, 116, 117, 119, 161, 162, 225, 228
Morstan, Mary 109, 113, 115; *see also* Watson, Mary
Moriarty 12, 14, 21–23, 27–37, 38*n*4, 91–92, 95–96, 98, 111, 113, 174, 182; bisexuality 19
Moriarty, Jamie 147, 153–155; *see also* Adler, Irene
Moriarty, Jim 226, 233, 238, 240; *see also* Brook, Richard
Morley, Christopher 223
Morstan, Mary 179, 182–183, 186–187, 239; *see also* Watson, Mary
Much Ado About Nothing 133
Murray, Mina 111

nakedness 85–86, 92–93, 95–96
NBC's *Dracula* (2013) 111
neo–Victorian fiction 99, 117
Norton, Godfrey 100, 101, 114

opera 101
Othello 133

pastiche 176–177, 181, 189
Patmore, Coventry 163
photographs 85–89, 93, 95
Polasek, Ashley D. 120
Posner, Judge Richard 19
postfeminist femme fatale 66, 68, 69, 71, 72, 74, 76, 80, 81, 82
The Private Life of Sherlock Holmes 176, 191
procedural 128-
publicity (within episode) 225, 226
Pulver, Lara 98, 107, 108, 116

queerbaiting 174–175, 184–186
queerness 146, 149–150, 152, 154–155, 160–162, 167, 168, 171

race 148–150
Rathbone, Basil 9, 19
rationality, 100, 102, 105, 110, 115
reconstruction 224, 225, 226, 227, 230
"The Red-Headed League" 137
"The Reichenbach Fall" 33–37, 39, 195, 197, 201–203, 205, 207, 226–227, 238, 240–241
Reichenbach Falls 12, 23, 33–37, 174, 239
Reilly, Kelly 179
religion 85–86
The Return of Sherlock Holmes (television movie) 123
The Return of Sherlock Holmes (television series) 8
re-visioning 226, 232, 243
Riley, Brendan 127
Ritchie, Guy 7, 11–13, 15–16, 19, 37, 160, 169, 174–179, 181–185, 187–189, 191
Ruskin, John 163, 169

St. Bartholomew's Hospital 232, 240, 241, 242
San Diego ComicCon 175
Sarjeant, William A. S. 86
"A Scandal in Belgravia" 26–28, 30, 67, 73, 74, 75, 76, 77, 78, 84, 85–86, 91, 93–94, 96, 98, 99, 106, 107, 108, 109, 110, 111, 112, 113, 114, 115, 116, 167, 194–195, 197–198, 201–204, 227, 228, 229, 231, 232, 234, 236, 241
"A Scandal in Bohemia" 10, 23–25, 30–31, 37–38, 66, 67, 73, 74, 75, 76, 83, 85–86, 95, 98, 99, 100, 102, 103, 104, 105, 106, 107, 108, 110, 111, 113, 114, 116, 117, 229, 230, 235
Scotland Yard 14, 18

Scott, A.O. 12
Sebastian (BBC character) 112
"The Second Stain" 105
secrets 85, 88, 95–96
Sedgwick, Eve Kosofsky 192, 194, 205
Seinfeld 193
sexual orientation 227, 228
sexuality 68–77, 84, 149, 156
Sherlock (telelvision series) 8, 11, 13, 98–117, 181, 189–191; "A Study in Pink" (episode) 13–14, 18–19
Sherlock Holmes (character) 98–117
Sherlock Holmes (film) 7, 11, 16–17, 167–170, 174–175, 177–179, 181, 185–186, 188–191
Sherlock Holmes (1939–1946 film series) 9
Sherlock Holmes (play) 16
Sherlock Holmes: A Game of Shadows (Film) 7, 11, 19, 167, 169–172
Sherlock Holmes Returns (television movie) 123
Sherlock Holmes: The New Frontier 119
"Sherlock Uncovered" 202
Sherlockians 176, 178
shorthand 68, 72, 73, 78, 79, 80, 81, 82
"The Sign of Four" 67, 78, 80, 81, 84, 168
"The Sign of Three" 113, 165, 166, 196–197, 206
slash 175, 178, 181, 183–185, 187, 189–191
Smith, S.E. 141
Starr, Michael 15, 18
steampunk 177, 184, 189
Stein, Louisa Ellen 224, 225
Stout, Rex 86, 90, 122–23
Straight Panic 193–195
The Strand Magazine 7
"A Study in Pink" 13–14, 18–19, 21, 29–30, 112, 162, 164, 165, 193–195, 198–201
A Study in Scarlet 104, 134, 223, 229

technology 224–225, 231; text messages 225, 232, 233
10 Things I Hate About You 133
They Might Be Giants (film) 123
"The Three Garridebs" 106
transgender 87
Turner, Mrs. 235, 236
20th Century–Fox 9
221B Baker Street 162
type 66, 68–72, 74, 76, 78, 80, 82, 83

Universal Studios 9

"The Valley of Fear" 38n4
Victorian 22, 25, 38n5–6
Victorian England 134, 136
voyeurism 224, 225

Warner Brothers 106, 107, 108, 117
Watson, Dr. Joan 11, 15, 124–26; asexual relationship with Holmes 15; sexual tension 15
Watson, Dr. John 8, 98–117, 223, 224, 240; as action figure 13; asexual relationship with Holmes 10–11; bromance with Holmes 12–13; devotion to Holmes 9–10; inferiority to Holmes 10; sexy image 11–12
Watson, Mary 12, 239; *see also* Morstan, Mary
Westenra, Lucy 111
Whedon, Joss 133
Wilde, Oscar 14
Wilder, Billy 176, 188, 191
Woman 229–232, 234–237, 241; *see also* Adler, Irene
women 153–154
Woolf, Virginia 163, 165

www.ingramcontent.com/pod-product-compliance
Lightning Source LLC
Chambersburg PA
CBHW021402230426
43666CB00006B/614